# THE PRIVATE LIFE OF
# THE AMERICAN TEENAGER

# THE NORMAN/HARRIS REPORT

# The Private Life of the American Teenager

JANE NORMAN and MYRON W. HARRIS, Ph.D.

RAWSON, WADE PUBLISHERS, INC.
New York

**Library of Congress Cataloging in Publication Data**

Norman, Jane, 1935–
  The private life of the American teenager.

  Includes index.
  1. Youth—United States—Attitudes.  2. Youth—United States—
Interviews.  3. Social surveys—United States.
I. Harris, Myron W.  II. Title.
HQ796.N565        305.2′3′0973        80-51249
ISBN 0-89256-141-6                    AACR2

Published simultaneously in Canada by McClelland and Stewart, Ltd.
Composition by American–Stratford Graphic Services, Inc.
Brattleboro, Vermont
Manufactured by Fairfield Graphics, Fairfield, Pennsylvania


Designed by Jacques Chazaud

First Edition

to Matthew Masch, a strong and gentle
youth who left us in his passage
from boyhood to manhood


to Richard Norman, whose keen perceptions
and honest insights forced us to narrow
the distance between our adult observations
and the teenage realities

# ACKNOWLEDGMENTS

*Special thanks to:*

Julia Coopersmith (who knows how valuable she has been), Eleanor Rawson (who has guided us all the way), Sharon Morgan, Bob Quigley and Irv Siegelman of Xerox Education Publications, Peggy McGarry and Crossley Research, Andrew Seltzer, Bea Goldstein, Kit Aspen, Lisa Dyniewski, Scott Chou, and the tireless Lyn Pines, Carol Hyatt, Barbra Baum, Etta Friend, Jordon Schwartz, Dr. Richard Hanusey for his faith and encouragement from the beginning, Frank Beazley and Hilda O'Connell for their loving support—without whose help *The Private Life of the American Teenager* would never have been possible.


And to the thousands of teenagers who gave us their trust and revealed themselves to us so honestly.

# Contents

# THE PRIVATE LIFE OF
# THE AMERICAN TEENAGER

# The Survey

**W**e began this project with one thought in mind: to find out what it's like to be a teenager today. How do our young people feel about their parents, about themselves, about friendship, sex, dating, drug use? What are their greatest hopes, fears, and dreams? To find out, we went directly to the source and conducted the largest survey ever done on adolescents. Over 160,000 young people participated, and the data in *American Teenager* are based on their responses. Unless we know how our kids feel, how can we begin to cope with their problems or relate to them?

The questionnaire we devised covered almost every area of a teenager's life, and we first tested it in Philadelphia and New York high schools. The enthusiastic response reinforced our belief that we had touched sensitive and important issues.

However, in order to obtain the largest cross section of thirteen-to-eighteen-year-olds, it was necessary to gain the cooperation of school systems throughout the country. How could we convince them to allow their students to respond to our questionnaire? The thought was staggering. Fortunately, we had worked with Xerox Education Publications on a previous study that involved children ages eight to fourteen (a survey conducted as part of a network television program dramatizing preteen problems), and they agreed to participate in this new project as well.

Through publications that have a readership of many millions of school-age children, we were able to reach adolescents in the schools, with the cooperation of their teachers. A special questionnaire appeared in *Current Science, Current Events, Read, Know*

*Your World Extra,* and *You and Your World.* Teenagers throughout the country filled in the questionnaire in their individual classrooms. The respondents were asked not to write their names on the questionnaire, so that anonymity would allow them to answer as truthfully as possible. Each teacher tabulated his or her class's responses and sent the results to a central tabulating source.

In order to get a more complete breakdown by sex, age, geographical location, and demography, as well as another test environment other than home or school, an additional 857 teenagers were polled in an extensive 80-question survey prepared by us and conducted nationally by Crossley Surveys, Inc. At each interview site, primarily in shopping centers and malls throughout the country, teenagers who were willing to participate answered the questionnaire in private.

The two surveys provided the statistical information we needed. But we also wanted teenagers to elaborate on the questions; we wanted to hear their thoughts and experiences in their own words. This information could be gathered only by in-depth interviews, so we talked at length on a one-on-one basis with over 100 teenagers. Their comments are quoted extensively throughout the book. They talked candidly about their fears, dreams, hates, embarrassments, and relationships. Since we were neither personally nor emotionally involved, they had the opportunity to express themselves in confidence to us with the knowledge that they would not be censured or criticized. In essence, they could talk freely and be listened to.

We wanted them to tell us about their drug and drinking experiences: the peer pressure (or lack of it) involved; their reasons for drinking and using pot. We wondered if they tell their parents about their pot smoking, or if they would lie about it if their parents asked. Are there major differences in the background or activities of pot smokers and nonpot smokers? Are teenagers cheating in school because they feel they have to? Do they feel guilty about it? What bothers them most about the educational system, and what are their suggestions for improving it? What qualities in a teacher motivate them to want to learn? Do they believe in God? Will homosexual teenagers tell their parents about their homosexual feelings? Why are today's pregnant teenagers more likely to keep their babies or have an abortion than to marry the baby's father? Are there variations in responses and attitudes between single-parent teenagers and those with two parents; between teenagers with working mothers and those whose mothers do not work? These were the issues we wanted teenagers to address.

In their frank discussions, there are experiences that are sordid, reassuring, shocking, and heroic. We believe that you will come away, as we have, with a strong sense of respect for the struggles they go through as they grow to maturity. Check out what the majority of teenagers think; you are certain to find some of your own adolescents' views reflected.

"I like my father when he's not worrying what I think about him." (Adam, 14)

"All my sex education came from dating. You might call it on-the-spot training. My parents would be so embarrassed to talk to me about sex!" (Jim, 16)

"I had three girlfriends before my first boyfriend. I've known for a long time that I'm gay. By fourteen there was no question in my mind." (Thomas, 16)

"My parents think I smoke pot maybe once a month, but I'd never tell them how much I do it. They'd be shocked. I'm getting bored with it though. Now when I smoke, it's at night to relax, the way my parents would have a gin and tonic." (Leslie, 16)

"I personally don't want to have kids. I've seen what hell it is to raise them." (Bill, 18)

"I would definitely give my life for the United States. No way I'd let any assholes from outside come in and mess up this country." (Merle, 17)

"I'd never fight. My brother came back from Vietnam and who thanked him? There's no guarantee for me. If I get a leg blown off, is the government gonna take care of me?" (Charles, 18)

"My parents don't feel they owe me any kind of explanations, but they expect me to tell them everything that goes on in my life." (Marcie, 13)

"I always consider suicide a possibility." (Jack, 18)

"One time we were at the dinner table talking about a head shop, and my mother thought it was a place where you buy Head bathing suits or tennis clothes. She really is funny—and so naïve." (Doug, 15)

"Even if their mothers invite me, I never go to a white friend's house. If anything be missin', I know they'd blame me." (Arthur, 16)

"I guess my parents are fine for each other, but I wouldn't want to live like them. They don't talk, and I like to speak what's on my mind." (Belinda, 18)

Your teenagers may never have expressed any of these thoughts to you, not because they haven't had them, but because your kids (like most others) probably don't tell you everything that is going on in their lives. If you are living with adolescents, you know that their world is a very private one. Few of us are privy to our teenagers' feelings or their day-to-day actions outside the home. Therefore, as a parent, you worry whether your kids smoke pot, cheat in school, have sex, or dislike you as much as you sometimes think they do. If you rely on their dinner conversation, you'd never know what's going on. They may offer, "I got a B in an algebra quiz today," but rarely do you hear, "I'm stoned every day before school and how come you don't know it?" or, "Of course I'd live with Andy before I'd marry him. How else will I know whether it'll work out?" And although the number one fear among teenagers is losing their parents, has yours told you that lately?

When you discover that a great majority of young people feel embarrassed by their parents in some way, you are less likely to be defensive when your thirteen-year-old tells you that fussing over him in front of company or talking too loudly in a restaurant drives him crazy. When you realize that over 45% of girls thirteen to eighteen have had sexual intercourse at least once, you'll be better prepared to discuss your own sixteen-year-old daughter's worry that she won't be able to hold on to her boyfriend if she says no. When you know that 75% of our participants favor divorce rather than living with parents who fight constantly, it may ease the minds of those parents who are staying together for "the sake of the children."

Although you may not agree with your teenagers' views, just being aware of them makes communication easier. The participants in the study frequently commented that they hoped their parents would read the book and recognize some of the dialogue. We share their hope.

# 1

# Teenagers on Parents

---

- 83% say they can tell one or both parents how they think and feel at least sometimes
- 6 out of 10 think parents listen and care about their ideas and opinions, but 4 out of 10 think their parents don't care
- Getting a job heads the list of subjects on which teenagers want their parents' advice. Drugs are at the bottom of the list
- 51% think parents are not helpful when giving advice
- More than three times as many teenagers say mothers are easier to speak to and get along with than fathers
- 67% say parents usually respect their privacy
- More than 8 out of 10 feel happy that their mother is working outside the home
- 65% of all mothers of teenagers work either full-time or part-time

---

The familiar old enemy of so many parents—the "generation gap"—is not the real barrier between parents and teenagers. The term is an oversimplification that implies an unavoidable and incurable disease. Not so, according to our research! The real problem is one that occurs in every human relationship—failure to talk, listen, and try to understand another's point of view.

As our teenagers go through the turmoil of adolescence, they sometimes cope more easily than we parents do. They are anxious to make the transition to adulthood, to become independent and self-reliant, but we may not be ready or willing to let them go. While they are exercising their need to experiment, to test authority, to find out who they are and what they believe in, we are remembering them as sweet, docile five-year-olds. We forget that

5

they are experiencing very adult feelings, engaging in adult activities, reading Shakespeare and Kurt Vonnegut—while we tend to treat them as if they were still in the Dr. Seuss stage.

As they develop their own attitudes and values, we are forced to realize that we no longer have the influence we once had. We may become frustrated by our inability to cope with their newly displayed independence. We may not like many of their new ideas. We may not believe there's any common ground on which we can meet. We may sometimes doubt that they even want to talk to us. Yet, when we asked our respondents about communication with their parents, they were considerably more positive than we might have expected.

## Teenagers Want to Communicate

| | |
|---|---|
| Can you tell either one or both parents how you think and feel about most things? | |
| Yes, usually, sometimes | 83% |
| No | 17% |

More than 8 out of 10 can talk to their parents, at least sometimes. Even more surprising, most adolescents really do want to share more of their lives and their feelings with us.

In their struggle to establish their own identities, our kids are constantly trying out new ways of thinking. In April, your daughter may announce that she's deeply in love; by May, she'll never want to see her "beloved" again. On Monday, your fifteen-year-old son may be ready to take off for India to become a Buddhist monk; by Friday, his religious fervor has waned.

Our kids want to use us as sounding boards for these new ideas and emotions. They don't necessarily want our approval or agreement, but they do want our ear. They are in the process of learning how to think for themselves, and although the process itself can be frustrating for parents, the end product—a mature, self-reliant adult—is surely worth a little agony.

Chris is a sixteen-year-old who has been encouraged to make many independent decisions about his life. He describes how his parents' listening has fostered his willingness to be open with them. "Whenever my father is off his boat, it's great. We really talk. My mother is always around and you can talk to her about anything, too. They're both really thoughtful and never put you down. They're not the type to say, 'Don't do this, don't do that.' Ever since we were really young, seven years old, it was up to us. They'd counsel us, talk to us, hear our ideas, and for the most part let us do what we thought was best." And Amy, eighteen, remembers one particular incident in which her mother did not belittle or try to change a belief Amy held, even though she disapproved of Amy's philosophy. "My parents were always good about listening to what I thought. I'll never forget when I was around fifteen, I told my mother I didn't believe in God. That must have hurt her deeply because she's a very religious person. But instead of condemning me, she asked me why and we talked about it for an hour. At the time I even think I believed what I told her. I thought I was a living, breathing existentialist. She told me she was unhappy that God didn't figure into my life, but she never put me down. Since that time I've changed my views slightly, but I really admired her for not getting excited and blowing up. Maybe she knew I'd come around."

The key to real communication with young people is the readiness to listen and care about what they say even when we don't agree. Let's face it. Listening is easy when teenagers parrot our beliefs. The hard part is accepting their right to argue, disagree, and speak out against our tightly held views. If we really want open communication with our teenagers, we cannot belittle any of their opinions. They are testing not only *our* reactions but *theirs,* too. And our responses determine, to a large degree, the kind of relationship we'll have.

**Parents' Reactions Set the Tone for Further Communication**

We asked:

---

| | |
|---|---|
| What do your parents think of your ideas and opinions? | |
| Parents listen and really care | 61% |
| Parents listen to your ideas and opinions but they don't really care | 20% ⎫ |
| They put down your ideas and opinons | 13% ⎬ 39% |
| They don't listen to your ideas and opinions at all | 6% ⎭ |

---

Six out of 10 adolescents report that their parents really do listen and care, but 4 out of 10 say their views are either ignored or bypassed. Overall, the girls are slightly more positive; 63% applaud their parents' responses as compared with 57% of the boys. And the thirteen-to-fifteen-year-old girls express the most positive feelings on this issue, probably because they are most likely to agree with their parents. Throughout our survey, we note that younger girls consistently conform more closely to adult standards than do the boys or the older teenagers, and therefore are less likely to be in conflict with their parents.

Over and over, our teenagers express the wish that their parents would listen to their explanations before passing judgment or laying down the law.

### The No-Compromise Attitude

When parents refuse to consider any point of view other than their own, their teenagers tend to shut them out completely or confine conversation to unimportant issues. Ann, fifteen, tells us, "My parents can never compromise. It's always what they want to do. They say, 'When you're eighteen and out of school, you can do what you want to do. But as long as you're under my roof, you'll do what I want you to do.' No discussion. I'm not allowed to ask any questions or say what I think. It actually makes me feel like I'm unwanted. Like shit. Like what am I here for?" And another fifteen-year-old objects to the fact that his father can never admit that he's wrong. "He's too efficient and it's impossible to argue with him. After thirty seconds I give up. Even if it's something I've studied, he always has a better way to do things and he's not afraid to shove them in your face. I think things are more open with my mother, and when I talk to her she listens. My father doesn't make any effort to really get into a deep conversation. We talk, but not about anything that matters."

### Give Us Credit for Knowing Something

Teenagers also say that parents are often reluctant to acknowledge their competence, good judgment, or their good intentions. Douglas, a New Englander who is sixteen, explains: "Last year when the whole family went on a ski trip, the darned skis kept falling off the rack. It was a simple matter of fixing something that I knew how to do very well. I'd done it a hundred times when I took some friends in our car. But do you think my father would listen to me? It was so frustrating. Finally, after trying to do it, and finding he couldn't, he condescended to let me try. And of course there was nothing to it. He never gives me credit for knowing anything."

When our views are repeatedly ignored or denigrated, we begin to question their value, and our kids react the same way. Nothing bursts the positive self-image bubble more quickly than phrases such as, "That's a stupid idea," or, "That's a good idea, but . . ." Our teenagers don't expect our approval for everything they do, but how can they develop faith in their own ideas if we continually overrule their decisions? It is very important for us to use every opportunity available to encourage our adolescents' sense of worth. Paula, eighteen, spells it out: "I really like my parents. We're very sure what we feel about each other. They care what I think even when they don't agree with me." And for seventeen-year-old Cal, the freedom to speak out is the basis for his firm relationship with his parents. "Your feelings and ideas are very important and shouldn't be hidden. Anything that makes kids think should be in the open. Kids should feel free to say any damn thing they want. They worry that their parents will say, 'Hey, that's not a good idea. Don't do that. Where did you hear that?' I've never had that kind of crap laid on me. It's grounds for a relationship to fall apart. So many kids hate their parents simply because the parents don't trust them and don't let them talk. The worst part is they don't know anything about their kids. Then the kids say, 'Ah, to hell with my parents!' "

Differences in taste should not be grounds for an argument, but they are in Robert's family:

"My father never gives me a chance to explain to him the kind of music I like. If he'd sit down and listen to it with me I think he might like some of it. He doesn't give it a chance. All he does is scream and say, 'Turn it off!' So I turn *it* and *him* off." (Robert, 16)

## The Turnoffs

### Judging, Lecturing, and Criticizing

Sharon, seventeen years old, comments: "I get so hassled when I try to talk to them that I don't bother. I handle things better myself." And Randy, thirteen, admits that he closes off immediately in response to what he hears: "My father gives me an hour lecture if I bring something up to him, so I don't bother." In contrast, Ros keeps doors open because her mother does.

"My mom is really neat. When you talk to her she doesn't correct your grammar all the time like my father does, and if you say a 'damn' or a 'hell' she doesn't go crazy. She's not always telling me what to do and I don't feel she's always on my case. I think I like her better than my dad. I guess you're supposed to like your parents equally, but my mom is just more likable." (Ros, 15)

### Not Listening

With the best intentions, busy parents sometimes offer a preoccupied "Yes, yes, I'm listening" response to their talkative kids. Guard against such reactions. Our kids are not going to confide in us unless they believe we are really interested. And they are quite adept at picking up phony expressions of interest.

"My parents either ignore me or pretend to listen, but don't. You talk and talk and ask, 'Did you hear me?' and they answer, 'Uh-huh.' They really don't know what you said. It's not because they don't care, but I guess because they're too involved doing something else." (Paula, 16)

"I try to explain things to my parents, like why I cut school one day, but they don't react very well. They only hear what they want to hear, especially my mother. That's the typical mother reaction; what she doesn't want to hear is blocked out." (Jack, 16)

### Reacting with Anger or Panic

Many parents deplore the fact that they know so little about their teenagers' lives. Yet when a child's honesty triggers parental rage, future confidences are not likely to be offered. Two teenagers give perfect examples of the "tell and overreact" syndrome.

"My father's not around much and my mother always complains that I close myself off from her. So one time I told her about a friend who ran away, and instead of just listening, she went crazy. So I just say, 'Forget it, lady,' and keep things to myself or talk to my friends." (Abby, 15)

"One time I went to my mom and asked her what I should do about my busted bike. Another kid had run into me. All she did was scream at me and tell me, 'Why can't you be more careful? You never take care of your things.' She made me mad. I really needed her help. I felt bad enough about the bike and didn't need her to rub it in." (Gerry, 14)

We tend to forget that our kids get just as upset as we do about unpleasant incidents. Gerry's mother might have handled the situation with more understanding by first identifying with Gerry's unhappiness, and then offering to get help in fixing the bike. Later she could have suggested he put the bike in a safe place to avoid future mishaps.

### The Third-Degree Turnoff

When a spontaneous confidence leads to a probing third degree, teenagers often wish they'd never opened their mouths. Parents tend to focus on the facts instead of responding to the feelings a teenager may be trying to communicate. Willa, eighteen, explains: "It's not so much that they don't understand, it's just that they never stop asking questions if I tell them something. It's like opening up Pandora's Box. They want to know who, what, where, why, and lots more than I have any intention of telling them. It's a real pain. And the more I confide in my mom, the more she wants to know and then I'm restricted because of what I told her."

Teenagers are more likely to trust and confide in us when they know they won't be grilled. Listening to their ideas does not diminish our position as authorities. Quite the contrary, in fact. When we remain objective and respect their honesty, they feel free to seek our advice. However, they are definite about the areas in which they want (or reject) such advice.

## What Parental Advice do Teenagers Value?

Check the problems on which you would like your parents' advice. Don't check the ones you would rather handle yourself.

| | |
|---|---|
| Getting a job | 45% |
| Choice of college | 39% |
| School problems | 39% |
| Troubles with brothers and sisters | 29% |
| Health and diet | 23% |
| Drinking | 20% |
| Sex | 17% |
| Trouble with other kids | 16% |
| Drugs | 16% |

So much for the popular notion that teenagers believe they can do perfectly well without us; that they never want our advice; that they think we are ignorant and unhelpful!

### When More Advice Is Wanted

Teenagers recognize parental experience and expertise when it comes to such issues as jobs, college, and school. They know that we have worked with employers, made applications to colleges, and dealt with the idiosyncrasies of teachers and other school authorities. They feel comfortable discussing these less private matters with us. Even when it comes to such family problems as troubles with brothers and sisters, some parental intervention is welcome if it is unbiased. But there are exceptions, primarily when a parent steps in and arbitrates without knowing the whole story. Diane, seventeen, explains: "There are a lot of fights, and every time there is a problem, everyone runs to my mother for her to decide. The decisions she makes are unfair, especially if she wasn't there in the first place. It's kind of hard with parents not being there for the whole fight, to listen to both sides and tell which is the truth. I don't think it's theirs to resolve all the time anyway. If you make the kids resolve their own problems, there is a closer relationship."

### When Less Advice Is Wanted

In the more personal and intimate areas of relationships with friends, sexual feelings, or drugs the message is clear: "Don't intrude unless we ask for advice." And although some kids would like to discuss the private side of their lives, most don't since they know they're likely to hear a proliferation of parental do's and don'ts. Betsy, fourteen, says, "If I ever talked to my mother about sex, she would think I was having it instead of just asking about it." And Hal, sixteen, explains: "I could never ask my parents' advice about drinking. They don't drink at all and they'd just tell me, 'Don't drink, or else!'" An eighteen-year-old relates how his mother's attitude prevented him from getting the valuable advice he needed:

"I did the dumbest thing. My girlfriend found out she was pregnant and I told her we could go to my parents for advice. (She knew her mother would flip out.) What I didn't expect was that my mother would, too. I won't go into the language she used, but she really surprised me. We ended up getting an abortion but the help came from outside; not my parents." (Jeffrey, 18)

If parents are ready to offer advice and information about sex, drugs, and drinking, the time to do so is when youngsters need it, want it, and are more receptive to it: when they are pre- or early adolescents. Even then, the number seeking advice is limited, but it becomes even smaller as they get older. As eighteen-year-old Trini comments: "Sex is something parents better tell their kids about when they're young or it'll be too late. All of a sudden at sixteen or seventeen, kids aren't going to sit for a birds-and-bees lecture. They'd laugh!"

When our kids do seek our advice, do they accept it? That depends on how it's presented.

## The Most Effective Way to Offer Advice

We asked:

---

**When you ask your parents for advice, what do they do?**

| | |
|---|---|
| Give you a straight answer, but allow you to make your own decision | 49% |
| Start asking so many questions that you're sorry you ever brought up the question | 22% |
| Give you advice, but get annoyed if you don't follow it | 18% |
| Beat around the bush so you really don't know what to think | 11% |

22% + 18% + 11% = 51%

---

### Offer Advice Without Demanding That It Be Followed

According to our teenagers, asking for advice can be risky. If it's not followed, parents may get angry. Our kids also fear, with some justification, that we will overadvise and overexplain. Ralph, an eighteen-year-old from Chicago, explains: "If I go to my parents for advice, they ask so many questions and then they get furious if I don't take their advice. I know my father wants me to go to Princeton because he went there, but I might want to go to another college. He has to let me decide for myself. Parents can only go so far with their advice; then your own brain and intuition has to take over."

In contrast, Gary, sixteen, believes that his mother handles his requests for advice very well. "I really appreciate my mom's advice because she doesn't push it on me. She tells me what she thinks and she says, 'Do what you think is best.' She doesn't get upset if I don't take her advice, but I usually do take it (probably because she doesn't make me)."

Of course parents do have to intervene and offer advice at times, even when it isn't sought, and most teenagers recognize that. But it helps to know that most unasked-for advice is sloughed off, disobeyed, or followed only under pressure. Our young people are quite perceptive in picking up how we handle their requests for help. Our responses determine whether our teenagers will continue to confide in us, or whether they will ignore us and seek help elsewhere. And if we don't give advice because we're afraid it may prove wrong, or if we gloss over a troubling situation or offer some cliché, our kids *will* go elsewhere for help. Cahn, sixteen, tells us, "I asked my mother what to do about a teacher who was really unfair and all she did was side with the teacher and say, 'You better just get your act together and stop messin' around.' "

Other teenagers, like Karen, persevere. She really wants her mother's advice, so she's learned how to disregard the verbiage and extract what is helpful. "I don't think most kids give parents a fair break. It's tough to be a parent and sometimes we have to help. I let my mom ramble on and on when she's giving me advice about something but once I get past the lecture, I usually can filter out a piece or two of good advice. Now I say to her, 'Get to the point,' and she's becoming better. I gotta tell you, though, it took patience on my part." (Karen, 17)

When kids do seek our advice, we have a rare opportunity to exercise a positive influence. But in order to be genuinely helpful we must separate our own fears and anxieties from those of our children. We have to learn to respond to *their* concerns instead of focusing on our concern *for them*.

## Parental Anxieties

When anxiety dominates our reasoning, when we deliver advice in order to prevent our kids from doing things that worry *us* but not *them*, they know it. As Sharon, seventeen, explains: "My mother drives me crazy with her advice about how to act with boys. She must have been treated rotten by boys when she was young, because she's so worried some boy will take advantage of me. I know how to handle myself."

If we are fortunate enough to be sought out for advice, let's offer our thoughts freely and give our kids enough leeway to make their own decisions. We are not required or even expected to have all the answers. They recognize that advice is only one part of a solution, and they are anxious and willing to work things out for themselves after they have heard and integrated our thoughts. Being honest about what we don't know may even encourage them to approach us more often.

When kids do want to talk, do they feel one parent is more accessible than the other?

## Which Parent Is Easier to Talk to?

| | Percentage of teen-agers surveyed |
|---|---|
| Mother | 50% |
| Father | 15% |
| Both | 24% |
| Neither | 11% |

### Mother—Favored by More Than 3 to 1

Teenagers of both sexes agree that it's much easier to communicate and get along with their mothers. This is not surprising since she is the parent to whom children have the strongest attachment. Usually, she's the one who takes the child to kindergarten; who brings an umbrella to school if it is raining; who chauffeurs the child to various activities; who patches hurt feelings and broken bones, and reassures her child of love when it seems as though the rest of the world doesn't care. And she's often the more approving, less authoritarian parent. So it is only natural that children confide in her first. Eddie, seventeen, recalls, "Before my mother died, I could really talk to her. She was special. I could talk and she could lay it right back to me. We had a couple of arguments, but that happens with everybody. But since my mother passed away, I don't have anyone to care about me."

"I feel that if I have something to tell my mother, I can tell her and she'll always accept me. She'll be on my side and will rarely put me down. She's a very loving and supporting person. Even in an argument she can see both sides. My father makes me uncomfortable. He brings up bad moments and uses them against me, so I don't talk to him much." (Alec, 16)

"I can talk to my mother about a lot more things just because she's female, but also because we can argue a lot back and forth so that there's a two-way thing going on. We cut each other up, but it's okay." (Margo, 17)

Margo's comment points out the special nature of the mother-daughter bond. As girls begin to see themselves as women, they realize the value of their mothers' experiences and want woman-to-woman dialogue.

### Mother-Daughter Communication

Girls hunger for the help they can receive from a mother who is comfortable with herself and her own sexuality. They want to know about their bodies, their sensual feelings, but many mothers are too embarrassed or anxious to discuss these issues. There are girls who begin menstruating before they've even been told what to expect or what to do. Often, women tell their daughters nothing more about sex than "Don't ever let a boy touch you until you're married." But mothers must realize that they have a perfect opportunity to teach their daughters about being women, while at the same time establishing the close ties that are unique to the mother-daughter relationship.

"It's more important to me to have a relationship with my mother. My father is moody and uncommunicative. My mom holds back too, but when I get her in the right mood we can talk about female things." (Alice, 18)

"The other night I got up enough nerve to tell my parents I wanted to talk to them more. My mother said she thought I had been communicating all along, but then I told her all the examples. Like when sex started I had to find out about it in school and from my sisters. My mother was really embarrassed. I would be comfortable talking about it with her if she didn't cringe every time I brought it up. She's a little old-fashioned and behind the times." (Sara, 17)

In contrast, Joanie, seventeen, greatly appreciates her mother's openness, which she feels contributes to their being close. "She's not embarrassed to talk about things and she's told me some of the mistakes she made when she was my age. She was pregnant at sixteen and sure as hell doesn't want that to happen to me. We don't agree on everything, but it's nice to have someone to talk to who's been there."

### Mother-Daughter Competitiveness

Of course, the mother-daughter relationship is not without conflict. Rivalry may become particularly intense as the daughter begins to mature. She is becoming attractive to young men at the same time that Mother may begin worrying about her loss of attractiveness. Mother fears that her daughter is enjoying freedoms and sexual activities that she missed in her own adolescence. Competitiveness occurs when the mother uses her charm and sophistication so effectively that her daughter's boyfriends are attracted to her. Whether this is done deliberately or unconsciously, the daughter senses a threat. One seventeen-year-old tells us, "I resent my mother coming on to some of my boyfriends. I swear some of them pay more attention to her than to me."

Competitiveness can also arise if Father treats his daughter like an adored princess. Mother wants the girl to be loved, but she may be troubled by feelings of jealousy, particularly if she had always wanted (but never received) the same kind of affection from her husband and/or her own father.

> Ellen knew she was her father's favorite. He paid more attention to her than to Ellen's mother, and her younger sister was all but ignored. As a result, Ellen and her mother never got along well and when the parents divorced and eleven-year-old Ellen stayed with Mother, the conflicts between them intensified. Both of them felt abandoned by Father, but Ellen continually defended him even though she, too, was hurt by his departure.
>
> Gradually, the mother came to realize that she had been angry and jealous of Ellen for a long time. She realized that she had felt neglected by her husband because he had been so overattentive to Ellen. Almost two years passed before mother and daughter were able to share their feelings of loss and disappointment and stop competing.

The mother-daughter conflict is often more apparent when the two are close in age. One young, single mother of an attractive fifteen-year-old comments that every time she has a date, her daughter makes an appearance. "She becomes really obnoxious, and last Saturday we had it out. I told her that I didn't intrude on her social life and I expected the same courtesy. We talked about the fact that we both need our independent social lives, and that there are times Mike and I would love to have her company, but other times we prefer to be alone. I do think we understand each other better now."

## Father—Don't Underestimate His Value

In many families, Father is the less accessible parent, not only because he is not around as much, but also because he's still perceived primarily as the disciplinarian. However, those adolescents who do find it easier to talk to Father (21% of the boys, 12% of the girls) mention his ability to handle situations less emotionally and with less anxiety. Others say their fathers are less concerned with trivialities than are mothers. John, thirteen, says, "My mom nags all day about little things like brushing my teeth and not forgetting my coat. I have more fun with my dad, but of course he's not around too much. We get along much better now than when I was little."

### Father-Son Communication

Other boys report that communication with Father improves as he begins to appreciate his son for what he is, not just for what he accomplishes.

"My father is one of the few older people who isn't just concerned with how I do academically, athletically, and so on. He's more interested in me being happy and doing what I want. He doesn't push things on me and now that I'm older we can talk a little better." (Michael, 16)

Many boys wish that their fathers were not so hung up on the kind of appropriate behavior that often prevents them from showing affection. They want more than a slap on the back or a handshake. One seventeen-year-old describes his effort to break down the barrier between him and his father. "It would be so much easier to get close to my mom, but I don't want to get close to her. I'd rather get close to my dad. I really want a close relationship with him. That's my goal and I'm working on it. He's not a very open person and doesn't display any kind of affection for Mom or us kids. But we're starting to talk a little more now, and I hope it works out."

Father's presence as a figure for identification is enormously valuable. He has encountered many of the same problems as his son, but he has to relate to the boy as a human being, not just as an authority figure. Unless Father makes an effort to communicate with his sons (or daughters) when they are very young, it is almost impossible for him to initiate a close relationship when they are teenagers. Robin, seventeen, presents one side of this issue: "My dad never paid much attention to me when I was little so he really doesn't know me very well now. He tries to talk to me but it's awkward. He wouldn't understand things even if I told him." For Bruce, on the other hand, sixteen years of good talks have led to a close father-son bond: "I've always talked to my father about everything. He started coming to me late at night, like just before we went to bed. He'd come in and sit and just talk. So I guess it was him coming to me a long time ago when I was little that started us off talking and we've just continued ever since."

### Father-Daughter Communication—The Unrealities

Teenage girls also want the benefit of their fathers' experiences, and they enjoy spending time with a father who listens and understands. But the relationship can become strained if the father is overly protective and suspicious of his daughter, her boyfriends, and their activities. Lil's father has trouble accepting the fact that his sixteen-year-old daughter is developing into a sexually mature woman. "My father is a problem to talk to. He keeps wanting me to sit on his lap and he forgets I'm sixteen now. He still treats me like his little girl, but he'd be shocked if I told him what his 'little girl' was into."

Some teenage girls feel that their fathers are jealous, and that attitude often manifests itself in their overprotectiveness and inflexibility about rules.

"I'm my father's only girl and he's too overprotective. He's a typical Italian father and there's no reasoning with him. I'll tell him, 'Dad, I'm going on a date and I'll be home by twelve.' He says, 'You're not going out with any strange boy I don't know!' Then when he meets them he'll dream up some excuse why I can't see them. He's impossible!" (Joy, 18)

Fathers and daughters often find it difficult to discuss dating and other sexually related topics. Some fathers are simply too embarrassed to talk about sex, while others believe it's their duty to guard their daughters' virtue. As a result, these men miss a valuable opportunity to teach their daughters about male and female sexuality in a caring, supportive way.

Girls who are the "apple of their father's eye" have a different kind of problem, as eighteen-year-old Stacy points out. Because her father thinks she's perfect, he can't give her the help and support she needs. He set a standard that is impossible for her to live up to, and Stacy is well aware that his expectations are totally unrealistic. She says, "When I had to hand in my college portfolio, he said, 'Oh, that's wonderful. You'll be accepted in a minute.' Well, I didn't get accepted anywhere and it was my portfolio that was mainly the problem. If he had really looked at it critically he probably could have helped me. So I guess what I'm saying is that when I need help or someone to talk to, I go to my mother."

It's clear that our teenagers value honest dialogue with both parents, but if they can't get it from one, they will usually try the other. And they learn rather quickly which parent can fulfill their needs, assuming they are fortunate enough to have one parent who really listens and cares.

However, there are some kids who, for one reason or another, shut their parents out completely. Not every child is communicative, nor is every adult. Some teenagers prefer keeping things to themselves and they do not share confidences even with friends. This can be very frustrating for parents who want a close and loving relationship with their child and who make every effort to initiate and encourage dialogue. But in such a case, parents can do very little except wait. Dialogue may occur later, perhaps even years later. When formerly uncommunicative adolescents become adults they often establish new and more responsive relationships with parents.

## How Teenagers View Their Relationship with Parents

What words best describe your relationship with your parents?

| | Mother | Father |
|---|---|---|
| *Positive* | | |
| (Excellent, good, loving, friendly) | 55% | 45% |
| *Negative* | | |
| (Fair, poor, frightening, unhappy) | 39% | 61% |

Not surprisingly, the majority of our respondents have better relationships with their mothers. She is, after all, the parent who most teenagers say is easier to talk to and get along with. These statistics also indicate that despite our worst fears our teenagers do find value in their relationships with us. The shout, "I can't wait until I'm eighteen and can be on my own," may have validity in the search for independence, but it does not mean a total rejection of parents. What adolescents do reject are the parental attitudes and reactions that intrude on their individuality. They are quite specific about the positive aspects that strengthen a relationship and the negative aspects that weaken or destroy it.

## Positive Ingredients of a Good Relationship

### Trusting

"I know my parents trust me completely and I'd never do anything to betray that trust. A lot of my friends' parents don't trust them, and I feel sorry for them. I guess I'm lucky." (Mara, 17)

"There's just no trust. My parents think I smoke pot and God knows what else. I don't, but since they think I do, hell, I may as well. I'm getting accused of it anyway." (Toby, 15)

If we are going to raise a generation of trustworthy teenagers, we have to expect and provide mutual trust. Darcy, who is thirteen, believes that her mother's own problems as an adolescent hinder her from trusting her daughter. She explains: "I guess when my mother found out that my stepbrother tried to get involved with me sexually, that's when she started not to trust me. But that's when I needed more trust, not less. I found out she got pregnant and had my older sister when she was fifteen. I can understand that she doesn't want me making the same mistakes, but I'm not her. Because she doesn't trust me, I can't come to her as often as I would like to anymore."

Problems also occur when parents don't know whether they can trust the adolescent, and the burden of proving trustworthiness falls on the teenager. One eighteen-year-old is struggling with the consequences of a previously broken trust:

"If there was one thing I could change, it would be the communication between me and my mom. She doesn't trust me at all and it's hard to talk. I said to her, 'Mom, I wasn't too good last year but I'm being good this year.' She says that I haven't had enough time to prove myself. I don't know how long she wants. I'm not into drugs or drinking anymore (at least, not much), but I guess she'll never believe me. I have to admit I was pretty bad but I'm finished with all that now. It'll be hard for her to trust me again but I hope she'll come around." (Betsy, 18)

### Helping, but Not Overprotecting

Teenagers realize that in order to learn they have to make their own mistakes. They don't want to be coddled. They want the opportunity to be independent.

"My parents try to prevent a lot of things from happening. Like, 'What happened to me, I don't want to happen to you.' I think parents should realize that the only way to learn is by things happening to you. You have to experiment and find things out for yourself. If kids are protected too much, they're gonna have problems later on. If you're not exposed to problems when you're a teenager, you'll always be like an adult teenager who hasn't experienced teenagerism. This is supposed to be the big time when you learn everything and when things come into perspective. You just can't be told not to do things. My sister was, and though she won't say it, she's an old teenager and she's twenty-six." (Ted, 17)

"I was very overprotected when I was younger. My parents put me in a little world of my own. When I got into junior high and had to ride the subway in and out of the city, there were so many things I couldn't cope with. Like what do you call them—hostile people. For years I had trouble dealing with anyone who didn't like me. My parents always told me I was wonderful and later on it was a shock to find out I wasn't." (Brad, 16)

### Having Fun Together

Although teenagers don't want us around when they're with their friends, they do enjoy occasional family outings and activities (skiing, going to ball games, traveling). However, few teenagers find that parents can relax enough to enjoy being with them on an equal footing. And some parents don't believe that they should "socialize" with their kids at all. But shouldn't we savor those few occasions when our adolescents seek our company? Those moments are rare and pass all too quickly. There are plenty of other times to inform, offer criticism, guide, and act as the voice of "responsible" authority. We are foolish to allow opportunities for fun and relaxation to slip away. And our kids concur.

Rosie, eighteen, describes the lift she gets when she's with her father, and he, too, appreciates the relaxed moments they share together. "If I feel a little bit depressed, I can go to my dad and we can have lunch together. So he's almost like a boyfriend. You can go out and do things with my dad and have fun together." And Susan, who is thirteen, applauds her mother's willingness to participate in activities as well to watch her children perform in them. "I really like that my mother gets into a lot of the activities that we do. She goes to everything we're in, like plays and ball games. She's a good ball player herself; not many other mothers can catch and throw like she can. My friends can't believe it."

### Acceptance—Even When Teenagers Are Different or in Trouble

The mavericks and the outsiders need a special kind of parental support that is not always easy to give. Their behavior and activities are usually bewildering or frightening to those who love them, and their unorthodox ways strain parental patience. But that is precisely when they need us most.

"I told my mother I'm gay and she told me she can't do anything about it. She said it's my life and it's okay. She loves me whatever the way I am." (Sal, 15)

"My father would hit me when we had arguments but I never hit him back because that's disrespectful. He brought me up and I had to be quiet when I was young and nobody thought I'd be landed in jail. But I had to explore life for myself. The thing I like about my father is that he's always loving toward me. No matter what happens, he'd be right behind me. People don't know how much money my father spent to get me out of jail plenty of times. He spent $10,000 on me. I'm still his son." (Clinton, 18)

### Warmth and a Sense of Humor

"My mother is such a considerate person. She helps people out whenever they need it. Right now she took in my brother's girlfriend so she'll have a place to stay. She's really a good person. She shows a lot of love." (Ken, 18)

"My mother is kind of like my grandmother. Both of them know what they want and they get it! But they're warm like my father. He's not afraid to show any kind of emotion. And he's really funny. He and my mom both have good senses of humor." (Suzy, 18)

## Negatives That Get in the Way of a Good Relationship

### Nagging and Repeating: The "do it, do it now" Approach

"My mother tells me the same thing over and over again. Why do parents do that? I hear her the first time and the more she tells me to do something, the more I don't want to. She really drives me nuts. She'll say, 'What are you doing tonight?' I'll tell her I'm going to the movies. Then she'll say, 'You going out?' I have to answer, 'Yes, Mom.' Then she'll repeat, 'To the movies?' It gets to the point where I don't answer her anymore." (Beth, 16)

"My mother always gets on my back. Even at breakfast. I just come down tired and I'm eating my breakfast and she throws a list at me and says, 'Here's the things you have to do today.' If my little sister is making noise, it's always, 'Stan, keep her quiet.' Everything is my problem, anything that goes wrong. She never lets me breathe.

"Now my father, he just forgets everything. He's so involved in his business. I'll tell him that I'm going to a concert and when the day of the concert comes, he's forgotten all about it. Last time he said 'You're not going. You have to babysit.' I said, 'Hey, I told you two weeks ago about the concert.' And he just says, 'I guess I forgot.' It's so frustrating." (Stan, 15)

### Always Being Too Busy

Stan's complaint about his father is a common one. And we hear it about mothers, as well. Clara, fifteen, tells us, "My stepfather is open and I feel that he loves me. With my mother I don't feel that. My mother's the type to give love in material things. 'I'm out here bustin' my ass to keep a roof over your head. These things you're supposed to appreciate! I may not spend any time with you, but here I am giving you food, clothing.' The material things don't mean anything to me, but I like to receive love mentally. Giving me $25 doesn't show that you love me. Doing things with me, spending time with me, that shows you care. My mother doesn't give that. Whenever I ask my mother for five minutes of her time, she's always too busy. She's studying or has other things to do. My mother's not a physical person. She doesn't know how to sit down and hug her child because she never experienced it. Her mother never did that with her. Therefore, to her it's something strange."

### Not Giving Explanations—The "because I say so" Routine

"My parents don't feel they owe me any kind of explanation. That's the thing that bothers me most about them. Their answer is always, 'Do what I say because I'm your mother. Because I'm older.' That may be true, but they should tell me why I can't do something. They just take the easy way out." (Rachel, 15)

It only requires a few more seconds to say, "Tomorrow is a school day and I think you should use the time tonight to study or relax at home," rather than, "No, you can't go out tonight and that's all there is to it." Your teenager still may not like your decision, but at least he or she will understand the reasons for it. Even a very young child deserves to know why parents forbid a certain action or why they take a particular stand on an issue. Children of all ages are far more cooperative when they know parents do not give arbitrary orders, but have very definite reasons for applying restrictions.

### Delivering the "we were young once" Lecture

Teenagers resent comparisons between *our* adolescence and *theirs*. In their eyes, such comparisons simply aren't valid. Frances, sixteen, explains: "The main thing about parents is that they say, 'We were young once,' but there's no way to compare when they were our age. It's so different. Clothes, dancing, music, cigarettes, drugs. They had some of our same problems but we have new ones they don't know anything about."

Another sixteen-year-old feels that the "I was young once, too" approach robs her of her individuality. "You want to know what bugs me about my mother? She's molding me into her. At least, she tries. I'm not her. I don't want to be her. I'm me. She puts words in my mouth and even makes me look like her. She keeps saying, 'I know what teenagers are like because I used to be one, too.' "

### Addictions

Although teenagers may be sympathetic toward an alcoholic parent, drinking or any other type of addiction puts a definite strain on the relationship. Kids resent parents who lose control and act inappropriately when drinking, or who fail to function as role models. Tom expains:

"My mother's drinking drives me up a wall. She drinks mainly at night. Brandy and beer. She's lonely and she does it because she's bored. She was fine when she was working in the school district. She had friends and she was going out and didn't have time to drink. When she drinks she gets passive or drunk. She's fallen down the stairs twice. My sister and I water down the booze but the problem is my grandmother drinks brandy, and we can't get liquor out of the house. She wants it, and she owns the house. Half the reason my mother drinks, I'm sure, is because it's there. My grandmother is an alcoholic, too." (Tom, 18)

Our adolescents don't expect us to be perfect, but they do want to be able to depend on us and look up to us. And when their faith in us is damaged it's very difficult to repair. They don't want to be forced to take responsibility for us when they're just beginning to learn how to take care of themselves.

### Dishonesty and Hypocrisy

Teenagers are perceptive enough to tell the difference between honesty and artifice, and they are unanimous in their condemnation of the latter. David, sixteen, says, "My mother is sort of fake. She has two sets of personalities and I hate that. One goes along with what happens outside the house and one with what happens inside. When she's out with other people, it's all smiles and everything. She can be very angry, walk out, drive to school and then the next minute she's greeting people laughing and smiling. For me, it's odd to see that."

Sixteen-year-old Ivan concurs. "When my friends or I tell my mom things she laughs even when it's not that funny. Or if I tell her something about school, she reacts too much about it in a fake way. She pretends to be more interested than she really is."

Dishonesty in the form of lying or concealing is even more upsetting to our kids than pretense and "putting on an act." That undermines the very core of security that "family" represents. Home and family should be a refuge where honesty and dependability are taken for granted. We don't like to be lied to, and our kids feel just as strongly about evasions or white lies, particularly when parents try to cover up family secrets and problems.

## Family Secrets

"God! You really hit the point! There are tons of secrets in our family. They don't tell me one thing. Not one thing! I always have to find out from my cousin. When I ask my mother she says, 'Oh, it slipped our mind.' Or, 'We didn't think you'd want to know anyway.' I'd just like my family to level with me." (Sue Ann, 16)

Our kids generally know when something is wrong. If we resort to pretense and say, "Everything is fine, you're just imagining," we rob them of faith in their own sensitivity because they have to choose between their own good judgment and their trust in our honesty. Either the child will assume he's going crazy because he is seeing things that aren't really there, or he will be forced to admit that his parents have lied. Neither choice is very appealing.

## How Much to Tell?

Many parents are afraid to reveal a family problem because they are too upset to talk about it or even face it. A deeply sensitive mother, who was trying to ignore her husband's increasing withdrawal, was forced to confront the issue when her daughter asked if something was wrong between her and Daddy. Fortunately, the mother admitted that there was a problem, and a year later, when divorce was imminent, the child was neither surprised nor deceived.

Another mother was so upset at a stillbirth that she said nothing about it to her four-year-old son, even though throughout her pregnancy she had carefully prepared him for the arrival of a brother or sister. For years the child believed that his mother had caused the disappearance of the lost child and his distress resulted in hyperactive behavior. When his mother finally brought up the subject and answered his questions, his hyperactivity cleared up.

Obviously, the age and emotional maturity of a child will help determine what can be revealed and discussed in the way of family crises. But children need time to prepare themselves for tragedies, family split-ups, and turmoil.

## They Want to Know

Children are part of the family and they want the opportunity to share, help, and mourn with the rest of the family. They don't want to be on the outside, feeling alienated. For example, they think it is foolish for parents to give an inflated picture of the family's financial situation. How can they economize and help if they don't know financial problems exist? They also believe that death and illness have to be dealt with openly.

"You can't treat kids like they will break. When my grandmother was dying, I was about ten and everybody was all hush-hush. They walked around the house with long faces and they thought I didn't know. Finally one day when I was in my grandmother's room, I sat on her bed and said, 'Moms, you gonna die?' and I thought everyone in the family would! She looked at me and said, 'Barry, I think so.' We talked a little and I walked out. To this day, I'll never understand why my parents didn't just tell me." (Barry, 17)

"When my mom dates people and they call her up, she doesn't tell us about it. Sometimes my brothers tell each other secrets and I'm left out. But when we had to go on food stamps, my mother told me about that and she didn't tell my brothers. I was older and maybe she thought I'd be able to help her and I wouldn't be asking for money all the time." (Doris, 13)

If a family member disappears for a while, the experience can be even more traumatic for a child if she or he doesn't know why.

"There was a secret about my cousin who had been in a mental institution for three or four years. I knew she had run away from home, but I didn't know she was in an institution. She had tried to commit suicide. I just found out about it. I've seen her since then and I think if I had known about her problem, I might have been able to help her. I wish my parents had said something. That really bothers me." (Brenda, 18)

"My sister is eleven years older than I am and she went on a drug trip. I didn't find out until she told me herself when I was fourteen. I kept asking, 'When is Jennie coming back?' and they wouldn't explain it to me. I was only seven or eight and my parents were afraid it would make an impression on me, I guess. Still, I wish they had told me." (Frank, 17)

Teenagers who are let in on family secrets are usually able to handle the information. One seventeen-year-old, whose parents never kept things from him when he was little, describes the pleasure he receives from their trust: "Anything that the family was involved in, we would all sit down and discuss it. When my older brother, Lou, messed around three times with his girlfriend, they finally had to get married before the baby came. I knew about that right away. I don't think there are any secrets I don't know about and I think that's right."

When we evade an issue, we may be attributing greater importance to the situation than is warranted. If a friend or relative is ill, a child might assume the sick person is about to die. If parents panic when questioned about money, the child might interpret that reaction as a sign that the family is nearly destitute. If we keep our kids in the dark, we are doing them a disservice by underestimating their ability to understand and their willingness to help.

Two crucial issues merit special attention: embarrassment and privacy. Our attitudes and behavior in regard to these issues have an enormous impact on the quality of the parent-child relationship. If we embarrass our children and invade their privacy, there is very little chance for a positive relationship to flourish.

## Embarrassment

Our kids are very concerned about the opinion of others, especially peers, because they are still so insecure about their identities. And making light of their concern only intensifies their resentment.

Since we always seem to be embarrassing our teenagers, we asked our respondents how parents could spare them embarrassment. Here's what they say.

### Don't Reprimand Them in Front of Their Friends

This is the ultimate humiliation and one which caring parents will go to great lengths to avoid.

"My father hit me a lot when I was younger. It really scared me, but I thought everyone got hit with belts. But my mother hit me once in front of my brother's friends, and I hated that the most! One time I corrected her English in front of *her* friends and she got mad. When I asked her how come she could hit me in front of my brother's friends but I couldn't correct her in front of her friends, she said, 'I can do it because I'm your mother!' " (Joanne, 15)

"My dad's usually pretty good, even better than my mother, but last week I brought home a friend. Since I wasn't allowed out (I was being punished) my dad kicked my friend out and that was as embarrassing as hell. I was furious. He could have said something to me and I would have told Dave he had to leave. My father had told me I was grounded, but he never said I couldn't 'ground' somebody with me." (Charlie, 16)

### Don't Criticize or Praise in Front of Friends, Family or Strangers

"Oh, God, I hate it when they say stuff in front of their friends. Like how wonderful you are, or what you've done. It's so embarrassing!" (Mike, 15)

"When we go shopping and the people in the store start asking questions about school, my mother will come right out and tell them anything. Or if she's talking on the phone to my aunt, she'll say, 'Do you know what Sharon did today?' My father used to work in a hotel as a manager, and I'd meet these people who said, 'So you're Sharon. Your mom and dad told me all about you.' Lord knows what they said. They hardly knew these people and they'd tell them all these embarrassing things." (Sharon, 18)

### Don't Make Scenes in Public

"My parents and I went to a really fancy restaurant for their anniversary. When we got there the maître d', or whatever you call him, had no record of our reservation which my dad had made a month ago. My father was furious and really gave it to the man. People started to stare and I wanted to fall right through the floor. I guess my dad was right, but it was so embarrassing." (Dennis, 13)

"In public places my dad will yell at us or he'll put my mother down in front of guests. That's one of the most embarrassing things to do. And my mom, she started yelling at me in the middle of the hospital when I had a motorcycle accident last week. She yelled in the emergency room, 'You shouldn't be on a motorcycle at all.' It was embarrassing. They both always yell." (Keith, 17)

### Don't Treat Them Like Babies

"Do you believe in a restaurant my father still orders for me? I keep telling him I can order for myself, but he does it anyway. The waitress must think I'm two years old." (Anita, 13)

"I hate it when my mother calls around to all my friends if I'm a little late. It's embarrassing because she treats me like a three-year-old." (Gene, 14)

"My mother will take me by the hand, at age sixteen, and show me off to her friends when she has a party. She displays me like a pet dog. I hate that!" (Arnold, 16)

### Don't Pry into Friends' Lives

Teenagers guard their friendships tenaciously, and they resent parents who intrude or subject friends to a probing third degree. Missey, fifteen, explains: "I nearly died when my mother asked my friend whether her parents were still together or if they had split. It was none of her business and I know my friend was embarrassed. My dad pries, too. He always asks my friends what their fathers do for a living and it's so embarrassing. He's always checking up on my friends and I hate it."

### Don't Show Affection in Public

Dennis, thirteen, says it all. "Every time we go somewhere, my mother fixes my hair and adjusts my clothes. She pushes my hair out of my eyes and straightens my shirt. It's so stupid. And she even kisses me sometimes in front of my friends. God, it's embarrassing. I even hate it when she kisses me and there's nobody around."

### Don't Initiate Discussion About Private Matters

If our teenagers want to discuss intimate issues, they'll come to us. Jamie, seventeen, says, "My mother and father keep asking me all about the girls I go out with and want to know everything about my dates. If I want to tell them, I will. They don't have to keep asking. I know they're interested, but I just think it's personal." And Betsy, sixteen, expresses it even more strongly. "I wanted to kill my mother. I mean it; kill her. I was so embarrassed when she told my aunt that I finally got my period. It was none of her damn business!"

### Don't Act Inappropriately

Hank, sixteen, tells us, "My father gets drunk and sometimes when he comes home, I'm there with my friends. I always have to make excuses for him but I'm sure they know. It's really embarrassing and I'm sure my mother and sisters are embarrassed, too. One time he talked rotten to my mother in front of my friends. It was awful." Others, like sixteen-year-old Arlene, object when their parents behave like teenagers. "My father acts crazy sometimes. I had a birthday swim party and some of my friends (two guys) threw him in the pool. He acts kind of kiddish, like he's our age, and it gets embarrassing. And sometimes my mom will come down in the basement when we're listening to records and she'll start dancing and singing and makes a general fool out of herself. My friends start laughing but my mom doesn't realize they're laughing at her."

*Miscellaneous embarrassments* include: the rundown condition of the house; parents who show off who and what they know; parents who push their kids into unwanted relationships with peers of the opposite sex. And if you ask your teenager he or she is sure to mention other examples.

Many parents are reluctant to admit that their behavior can be embarrassing or that they may act foolishly at times. Others dislike being criticized by their children. However, if we ridicule or trivialize our kids' feelings of self-consciousness we are denying that their feelings count.

Our teenagers will readily express their embarrassment if we can listen without becoming defensive. But if we become antagonistic or show that we're hurt, they will often withdraw and keep their feelings of embarrassment as well as their resentment to themselves. John, fourteen, gives a perfect example when he says, "My mother always sings when my friends are in the car. God! Doesn't she know it's so embarrassing? Her voice isn't bad but all she knows is the old songs. I hate it when she does that, but I'd probably hurt her feelings if I told her."

Parents cannot always steer clear of embarrassing situations. At times, we have to act in ways that may embarrass our kids. But if we acknowledge their feelings, they're less likely to resent us. Jimmy tells the following story about his father's argument with an auto mechanic who failed to have the car ready when promised. "I know the guy was wrong," he told us. "He should have had the car ready, but I wish my father hadn't made such a big stink out of it. At least he told me later that he realized how embarrassing it was for me."

In most cases, however, solving this problem is as simple as recognizing and trying to avoid the actions that embarrass our teenagers.

## Privacy

The right to privacy is as important to teenagers as it is to adults. When we respect their privacy, we show that we believe in their right to possess an inviolable life space of their own.

Infants are totally dependent on their parents, but as they get older they want and need less parental involvement. By the time they reach adolescence, the balance between privacy and dependency becomes a matter of the greatest delicacy. Sometimes parents are willing to grant privacy only if teenagers prove that they are capable of handling their various chores and duties without parental supervision. For example, many parents refuse to respect the privacy of a child's room unless the room is cleaned.

Other parents feel that it's their duty to monitor phone calls. Their argument: "If you don't have anything to hide, why don't you want me to listen?" However, this is a misjudgment on two counts at least. It presumes that the teenager has no right to private communication with friends, and it implies that he or she is engaged in something improper or illicit.

When their right to privacy is violated, teenagers protect themselves in any way possible. They need to put some emotional and physical distance between themselves and other family members. Separating from parents is a vital part of a teenager's emotional growth. However, the process of achieving separation may seem inconsistent. The fifteen-year-old who insists on her right to have her door closed when her boyfriend visits may also feel neglected if Mother doesn't go into her room at another time to pick up dirty laundry. Although they're struggling to be independent, they still want to know that we are around and that we care.

Our survey shows that, for the most part, parents do respect their teenagers' right to privacy. Sixty-seven percent indicate that they have no problem with this issue.

---

Do you think your parents respect your privacy?

| | | |
|---|---|---|
| Yes | 44% | }67% |
| Usually | 23% | |
| Sometimes | 15% | }33% |
| Never | 18% | |

---

However, the 33% who say that parents rarely respect their privacy are very vocal about the type of invasions they resent. Consider what they have to say; it may help ease tension in your own home.

### Don't Walk into Their Rooms Without Knocking

"My father knocks and walks in at the same time. He takes it for granted that as long as he knocks, it's okay to enter. He'd kill me if I did that to him." (Kevin, 13)

"I don't feel my mother gives me much privacy. Sometimes I'm in my room and I just don't want to be near her and she says, 'Why don't you leave the door open?' She even checks on me in the middle of the night! I have a lock on my door because if I didn't my parents would be coming in and out all the time." (Adele, 14)

### Don't Listen to Phone Conversations, Read Diaries, or Open Personal Mail

"Sometimes my mom looks at my mail. I'll tell you how I know. I got this one letter from a boy. He asked me out in the letter and I thought it was for a Friday night, and my mom goes, 'No, it's Saturday night.' And I said, 'What! How do you know?' Was her face red! I would have been more angry if the letter had been real personal, but none of my letters are that juicy yet." (Cindy, 16)

"My parents always say, 'Why do you have to go in the closet to talk on the phone?' And I tell them, 'Because you always try to listen.' Sometimes they'll even pick up the phone and talk while I'm on. I hate that. I was really upset with my mother last week and I was talking to one of my friends about her. I said, 'This woman is the biggest nag and she's getting on my nerves!' She heard it all 'cause she was listening outside the door and I got into a ton of trouble. She shouldn't have listened." (Jo, 15)

"I had a key in my diary and my mother broke it open. Whenever I get a letter, they open it up and read it. When I come home from school I find my room disorganized and I know they've been through my things. When I was fourteen and my mother read my diary, she found a lot of things in it that she didn't like. She read a lot of things about my anger toward her and my stepfather, but I told her that it was private, and not for her to read." (Maria, 18)

### Don't Expect Them to Tell Us Everything

None of us wants to feel that we must reveal every aspect of our daily lives, yet many adults assume that their "parent status" gives them the right to pry. Our kids disagree. Carolyn, fifteen, explains: "My mother more or less expects me to tell her everything that goes on in my life. Like if I were to have sex with my boyfriend. Things like that. She expects that I should tell her because she's my mother. But when I do tell her, she doesn't react as an adult should. She has a fit and goes crazy. I'm very open with my mother. It's not like I hide things from her, but there are just certain things I don't feel I have to tell her." And our teenagers resent discussing matters that may be interesting to us, but are particularly distasteful to them.

"I don't like talking about school because I'm not what you would call your A student. My father and mother both work and they always want to know what's going on, like how I'm doing in my classes, and it drives me crazy. Lately, I've been doing really badly in history so they insist upon talking about history constantly. I feel it's an invasion of my privacy because I don't want to talk about history. I want to talk about, "Oh, I just met a new guy at school today,' and things like that. School is just not a part of my life that I like, and I'd rather not discuss it.

"Another thing, if I come in late, they want to know why, when, where. If I don't say anything to them, then I can't drive the car or I can't do a million other things. I think they're good about my material privacy, but not my personal privacy." (Rebecca, 18)

### Don't Throw Out or Give Away Things Without Asking

Objects such as faded and torn jeans, T-shirts, outdated magazines, and broken records may seem worthless to us, but to our kids these items are important. Many of us probably have objects in our desk drawers that date back fifteen years, and we would resent anyone disposing of these priceless bits of junk. If our teenagers can arrange to keep their "treasures" in a special out-of-the-way spot, why not allow them to hold on to pieces of their past?

Marilyn, thirteen, hates her mother's habit of throwing out things she wanted to keep: "My mother is always throwing my things out without checking to see if I still want them. I had a note from my girlfriend lying on my bed, and when I asked my mother if she had seen it she said, 'Oh, I thought it was just an old piece of paper so I tossed it out.' I was so mad!"

### Don't Go Through Desk and Dresser Drawers, Reading, Straightening, and Looking for Forbidden Objects

Teenagers view this as one of the most serious invasions of their privacy. In contrast, many parents believe they have the right to invade possessions in order to look for and confiscate drugs, diaphragms, or sex magazines. There is a great deal of controversy concerning the advisability or effectiveness of this kind of surreptitious search. Some experts approve of *any* action that brings suspected drug or alcohol abuse out into the open, while other professionals believe that no issue is critical enough to supersede the right to privacy. Those who hold the latter view feel that the search technique only generates resentment and distrust between parent and child, and will cause the drinking and drug habit to go underground, but not cease. Parents, as well as experts, remain divided on this issue. However, our experience is that most parents would search if they thought their children were lying about drug or alcohol use.

Adolescents are particularly resentful when they uncover evidence of a surreptitious search.

"Usually my parents respect my privacy very well. But I had one occasion where my dad invaded my privacy accidentally. Then he waited for a couple of months and came back and invaded it again, only this time on purpose—just to see what had gone on in the time he was gone. The only thing that made me angry was that he went back a second time. The first time he was looking for a book he had written, which he keeps in my dresser. He just happened to find all this stuff; personal letters, some gay magazines. Then he went back again. He confronted me. I had no idea he had been there, and this was over a period of about four months. He came down and talked to me about it and he was very understanding about the gay material, but it was upsetting that he had gone back to check a second time. I saw that as an invasion of my privacy." (David, 16)

Although many teenagers will tell parents that they need more privacy, if such a request doesn't work, most will resort to the safest solution—hiding and/or locking up their private belongings. Helen, seventeen, explains: "My parents are half good and half bad with my privacy. I have a room that nobody can go into unless they knock, which is great because that means I can hide all my little things. If they did find out about them, I would make the biggest scene you've ever seen. Last year my mother used to search my purse. She doesn't do it anymore because I told her it was none of her business, but I hide everything now, anyway."

In a survey we did in conjunction with the Xerox Education Publications in November 1977, we discovered that out of 637,479 young people ages 8 to 14, 41% would discuss the privacy issue with parents. But 26% would use the "hide-and-lock" technique. Not surprisingly, as children become older, hide-and-lock becomes even more prevalent. The remaining participants in the survey either retaliated by invading other family members' privacy, or yelled and made a scene when the invasions occurred.

We parents tend to worry when our adolescents start locking their doors. We wonder what they're hiding and why they're locking us out. But we have to realize that they're not really locking us out; they're locking themselves in. They need the chance to be alone.

### Not Controlling Invasions of Privacy by Brothers and Sisters

Teenagers get very upset when brothers and sisters borrow clothing, records, tools, and other possessions without asking. And all too often parents gloss over the situation, as thirteen-year-old Debbie confirms. "The other day I was looking for my Zeppelin album and I found out that my sister took it. She just took it; she didn't even ask. I wouldn't mind if she borrowed it, but the least she could do is ask me first. I don't have much privacy 'cause my room is small and I share it with my sister. She goes into all my things and my parents never say anything. I can't stand it."

When siblings violate each other's privacy, parents can help by affirming and enforcing each family member's right to privacy.

## When Privacy Is Respected

"I have a lot of privacy. My mom and dad are really good about it. I know a lot of my friends' don't, but my parents have always respected mine. They wouldn't think of opening my mail or listening in on telephone conversations. One day I left my diary on my bed and I knew my mom wouldn't read it. Thank God!" (Lois, 17)

"When I was fourteen, I'll never forget how great my mother was. I was so flat-chested and all my friends had started to develop and I was so embarrassed. So I used to stuff Kleenex in my bra and I must have looked ridiculous. But she never said anything to me, and to this day I adore her for not embarrassing me or invading my personal privacy. It would have been so easy for her to have laughed or said, 'What do you think you're doing?' but she never did. She was very sensitive to my problem and we still are able to talk and we're quite close." (Adele, 18)

However, one young man feels that his parents went to the other extreme. James, sixteen, tells us, "I feel my parents respect my privacy too much. That's the trouble with communication. If I don't want to talk about something she won't even touch the subject, and it just may be that I really do want to talk about it but I don't know where to start. Every once in a while, I wish they'd probe. When I come home late they're almost too good. They don't ask me where I've been. And every once in a while, I'd like the chance to rebel and secretly let them know that I'm not their goodie-goodie son."

Parents must strike a balance between intrusiveness and indifference. Only then can we assure our kids that we understand their need to have feelings, space, friends, and interests of their own. Privacy is always important, but it is particularly crucial during the adolescent years. When teenagers feel that they "belong" to their parents, they can't develop confidence in their own capabilities.

## Working Mothers

Since Mother is the parent with whom most teenagers feel they can communicate, we wondered whether her relationship with her teenagers is affected if she works. Do kids resent her time away from home? Are they pleased that she is employed? Or doesn't it make any difference?

In recent years, many critics have blamed working mothers for all the problems their children encounter. Our study is confined to the adolescent years, but within that age group our findings are striking:

—Within the entire range of behavior that we asked our teenagers to report on, from marijuana smoking to attitudes toward school and parents, there is almost no difference between those with working mothers and those whose mothers do not work
—Sixty-five percent of all mothers of teenagers work either full-time or part-time
—In one-parent families, 77% of the mothers work outside the home. In two-parent families, 62% of the mothers work
—There is no difference between whites and nonwhites in the percentage of families that have a working mother
—There is slightly more sexual activity among those whose mothers work (7% difference)

## More Than 8 Out of 10 Favor (or Do Not Oppose) Their Mothers' Working

If your mother works outside the home, how do you feel about it?

| | |
|---|---|
| Happy | 70% of responses ⎫ 84% |
| Unconcerned | 14% of responses ⎭ |
| Unhappy | 16% of responses |

Of the 16% who report unhappiness, half:

—Wish she were home more (cited more often by the younger group)
—Feel unhappy because they have more responsibilities (an answer given by more girls than boys)

However, the predominant theme is that the advantages far outweigh the disadvantages.

## Advantages of Having a Working Mother

Working mothers who worry about the adverse effects on their teenagers will find little support for such fears. Seventy percent of the teenagers whose mothers work are pleased that she does.

### Working Gets Her Out of the House and They Have More Freedom

Teenagers say there are fewer arguments when Mother is not home worrying about what they are doing. They appreciate the privacy and lack of tension, and see no reason for their mothers to feel guilty. Cindy, fifteen, attests: "Mom was home with me so much, watching over me when Dad left, that last year when she went to work it was great. It was really a relief! She loves her job and when she gets home we can talk. I can lead more of my own life and she has hers. We're much closer now even though she's away more." And Jason, sixteen, believes that mothers' and teenagers' lives need to be separate at times, in order to preserve the nonsmothering aspect of the relationship. "I'm glad my mother's not home too much. I get to go out a lot more often. If she were home all the time, I'd totally freak out because she'd have me staying in the house. When she's away I can let my anxieties out and be myself. It's better she works and leads her life and I lead mine. I like to keep them a little separated."

Adolescents also appreciate the trust their working mothers exhibit. Karen is proud of the fact that her mother will stand up for her daughter's ability to be responsible when she is on her own.

"The other day I heard one of my mother's friends say to her, 'Don't you worry that Karen will bring boys into the house when you're away working? Aren't you afraid that she'll get into trouble?' My mom said, 'Marion' (that's the woman's name), 'you sure must not trust your kids for you to say that. I trust Karen, and Lord knows if she wants to do somethin' wrong she'll do it whether I'm home or not. She'd find another place to do it, but I trust her.'" (Karen, 17)

### She Brings in More Money

There is no doubt that Mother's employment provides the family with additional financial security. Lori, sixteen, says, "I like it better when she works. I get a feeling that we have something. When she doesn't work, I feel, 'What are we going to do?' I feel more secure when she has a job and I think she does, too; tired and upset about different things, but more secure." And Stacy, fourteen, agrees, "My mom has a part-time job and she loves it. It gives her some spending money and my dad likes it too."

### Working Makes Her Happy

Most impressive are the ways in which they support Mother's work because they believe it is good for her. Working broadens her life, makes her more interesting, saves her from the confines of the house, and makes her happier. They also feel that working enables her to better understand her husband's work problems. As one eighteen-year-old comments: "They can both talk about what they went through at work. If a wife doesn't work, how would she know what her husband is up against?" And many speak of the pride they have in their mothers' accomplishments.

"I told my mother to try and get some work to keep herself busy. I told her, 'Look, Ma, you could even go to school and try to learn something. Then you could get a job.' So she went and took the test and got her diploma. I was real proud of her." (Herb, 15)

"My mom loves her work; she's a head dietician. She's good, too. She'd go bananas if she had to stay home all day. I know she's a lot more interesting than a lot of my friends' mothers are. I don't see how any woman could sit in the house all day with kids. It would be a real bummer!" (Bob, 16)

Teenagers can be very perceptive about their fathers' attitudes toward working wives. They recognize that when a husband respects his wife's ambitions and abilities, his encouragement strengthens the marriage. One seventeen-year-old girl appreciates that she has an understanding father. She says, "Up to a certain point, a mother has to please everyone in the family. But sometimes she has to do things to please herself! That's what my mom told us when she went to work. My dad was very encouraging to her and even helped her find a job. She told me how lucky she feels to have a husband who backs her up, and she said she can never feel any resentment toward him because he made her stay home. I don't know how long she'll work (she may even quit in a year or two), but at least she had a chance."

In general, our kids are an adaptable and supportive group. They want their mothers to be happy. And the freedom they gain often generates a sense of responsibility which, in turn, leads to greater independence. Working mothers can indeed take heart in these results, knowing that their work does not threaten the relationship with their adolescents.

# 2

# Teenagers on Sex;
# Living Together;
# Marriage;
# Homosexuality

- Nearly 6 out of 10 16–18-year-olds have had sexual intercourse
- Nearly 1 out of 3 13–15-year-olds have had sexual intercourse
- The average age for first sexual experience is between 15 and 17
- Nearly 6 out of 10 sexually active teenagers do *not* use birth-control methods, or use them only some of the time
- Nearly *three-quarters* of today's teenagers have *never* discussed birth control with their parents
- Almost *all* teenagers want more information about intercourse, birth control, and venereal disease (in that order)
- Only 13% of teenage girls would marry the father of the baby if they became pregnant. Nearly 3 out of 10 would get an abortion, and the rest would keep the baby or give it up for adoption
- 90% of teenagers surveyed believe in marriage, and 74% say they would live with someone before or instead of marriage
- Twice as many girls as boys fear that marriage would interfere with their freedom and career plans

Since the early 1960s, society has been in the process of reevaluating its sexual mores, standards, and expectations. The resulting changes in sexual values and practices may seem outrageous to some adults, but to our teenagers the so-called sexual revolution is a fact of life. They grew up at its height—in a time of open nudity in magazines and movies; of legalized abortions; of unmarried couples living together; of birth-control pills; of X-rated movies.

They see their divorced parents date and bring lovers home for the night. Some kids have seen their parents swap partners, and some have lived with a number of sets of parents as a result of this mate exchange.

Sex is constantly being examined clinically on the radio, television, and in countless books and magazines. Masturbation, clitoral stimulation, and multiple orgasms are no longer terms used only by sex therapists.

What effect has all this had on our teenagers' sexual behavior and attitudes?

Teens are sexually active at a younger age, some having intercourse as early as eleven years old. They are getting pregnant and having abortions as never before. Many, however, are electing to keep their babies and remain unmarried. A large percentage of young people expect to live with someone before getting married. Some admit to being bisexual, and many more homosexual.

There will probably never be a return to the preteen white dresses with pink sashes. Both girls and boys are dressing as sex symbols in their skintight designer jeans, even in prepuberty. Madison Avenue has created enticingly erotic ads and commercials that sell sexuality as part of the total dress package. Soap operas, movies, and television programs do not hesitate to dramatize previously taboo subjects such as rape, abortion, and incest.

There is no doubt that our teenagers feel freer to discuss and act upon their sexual proclivities in these liberal times.

But despite these great changes, many of the values, practices, and problems of yesterday still exist. Twenty years ago teenagers were also getting pregnant. The difference was that they went away to have their babies in order to avoid shame and condemnation. Twenty years ago some parents also sexually molested their children, but no one talked about it.

Although sex is a favorite topic in the media and among peer groups, most parents and kids are still uncomfortable discussing the subject together. Teenagers still have many unanswered questions. They still want to know how to "do it" and how to keep from getting pregnant. They still worry about saying the wrong thing on a first date. They are still concerned about their skin, their hair, their bodies. They worry about being sexually inexperienced and unpopular. Girls still care about their reputations. Both sexes still suffer rejection if their love affairs are unrequited. They still want to get married (although not as young), and they still want children (although not too many).

Of course, there have been radical and even shocking changes, but some things will always remain the same.

## Sexuality and Intimacy

Sexual activity is both a means of procreation and a form of recreation. Particularly for teenagers, the first is something to be avoided and the second is something to be hoped for. But sexuality is more than a biological drive; it is also an integral part of the human experience called intimacy.

As our youngsters grow into adolescents and young adults, they experience changes in two critical dimensions of their lives. The sexual feelings that had previously been expressed through auto-erotic behavior become even more pressing and exciting. At the same time, relationships with friends of the opposite sex become much more passionate and caring. As a result, the sexual exploration of another person's body becomes a primary source of sexual satisfaction. And gradually the physical aspects of sex are intertwined with the emotional experience of being close and intimately connected with another human being. When these two needs work comfortably together, so that the greater desire for closeness leads to and increases sexual pleasures, teens experience the first stirrings of adult love. This is significantly different from the kind of love previously felt for parents, grandparents, brothers, and sisters. And as their needs for emotional intimacy and physical satisfaction intensify, the ways in which adolescents cope determine much about their lives.

## The Double Standard Still Exists

The sexual revolution notwithstanding, our teens are still influenced by traditional distinctions between allowable male and female sexual activity. It is expected that boys will be more sexually aggressive than girls. The well-established myth equating frequent sex with masculinity still carries weight, and encourages boys to seek out and brag about sexual adventures. But the same behavior by young women is still referred to as promiscuity. Society encourages girls to focus on the emotional rather than physical aspects of a relationship. This places an additional burden of guilt upon our girls. Many who would like to have a sexual relationship shy away simply because they have been taught that they must protect their reputations in order to maintain their own and society's respect.

Parents insist that their daughters be proper and decent young ladies. Fathers, in particular, want to protect daughters from boys whose motives they suspect. We parents tell our girls in innumerable subtle and direct ways to guard themselves carefully. While we may convey the same message to our sons, the discovery that our fifteen-year-old son is no longer a virgin is much less likely to upset us.

"I'd love to have sex but I'm so afraid the boy will think less of me. It's not fair because nobody thinks less of him if he has sex with me. I really want to do it and of course I would use birth control, but right now there just seem to be too many negatives." (Marcia, 17)

"They never let me have boyfriends. Can you believe that? An eighteen-year-old girl without boyfriends? If I were a boy they never would have said that. One time I was living with this relative and she was leaning on my back because at fifteen I started dating guys. Any time I went out with a guy and she found out, if she didn't like him, she'd sit there and tell me that I'm not gonna be anything but a whore. I'm never gonna be anything in my life and it wouldn't shock her if one day she was walking by the street and she saw me standing on the corner. She didn't want boys around me at all. She was always suspicious. It wasn't fair." (Corinne, 18)

In view of the staying power of the double standard, the following statistics are not surprising.

| Have you had sexual intercourse? | Yes responses | |
| --- | --- | --- |
| 13–15-year-olds | 31% | |
| 16–18-year-olds | 58% | |
| Boys 13–15 | 41% | Total 13–18- |
| Boys 16–18 | 70% | year-olds |
| Girls 13–15 | 21% | 44% |
| Girls 16–18 | 46% | |

The number of boys who are having sexual intercourse is larger than the number of girls in the same age group. In the younger group, just about twice as many boys as girls report having had intercourse. In the older group, 7 out of 10 boys have had an intimate relationship, while almost 5 out of 10 girls have had a sexual experience.

Since boys gain status from their sexual experiences while, in many cases, girls lose status, we decided to run a rough truthfulness check on our results by asking our respondents whether they thought their friends had had sexual intercourse.

| Do you think most of your friends have had sexual intercourse? | Yes responses | |
|---|---|---|
| 13–15-year-olds | 34% | |
| 16–18-year-olds | 61% | |
| Boys 13–15 | 39% | Total 13–18- |
| Boys 16–18 | 62% | year-olds |
| Girls 13–15 | 29% | 47% |
| Girls 16–18 | 60% | |

The results are quite similar to the previous table, which probably confirms the honesty of the teenagers' answers concerning their own experience. The sixteen-to-eighteen-year-old boys believe their friends are less active sexually than they claim themselves to be. Are they exaggerating their own sexual activities to prove their masculinity? Or do they really believe it? On the other hand, the girls in both age groups think their friends are *more* sexually experienced than they. Do they really believe this, or are they camouflaging their own activities in order to avoid appearing promiscuous? It's hard to know. In any case, our interviewees are only surmising about the sexual activities of their peers. Although some friends do discuss their intimacies, others do not.

"I think most kids have sex between fifteen and seventeen. Girls probably a little older. They have a lot of sexual play before then, but not action. Just petting and stuff. Sex starts with the first really heavy relationship; when you find someone you really like." (Lennie, 16)

"I know a lot of my friends have had sex, but there are many that aren't ready. I think in many groups if you *aren't* a virgin you are looked down on. In other groups, if you *are* a virgin you're looked down on. It depends on the group." (Trudy, 17)

There are indications that earlier experiences occur more frequently among inner city adolescents. However, some suburban boys express surprise about the sexual activity of younger girls. Tim, fourteen, explains: "I met a fourteen-year-old girl from a supposedly very nice family, who was the closest thing to a nymphomaniac I've ever seen. She was really into kinky sex. It was fun for a while, but got boring later on. And another girl, who was the girlfriend of one of my friends, has screwed half the male population. And another one of my friends turns girls on with ludes [Quaaludes] and has sex with them, and girls flock to him. God, I like a girl with some brains who I can talk to, love, feel close to."

Fifteen-year-old Matthew agrees that many of his friends have had sex, but feels that the number is not quite as large as adults, or other teenagers, suppose. He says, "Adults think that everybody fools around, but everybody doesn't fool around. The majority of my friends have had intercourse, but I know some kids who give you a big long story about it, but they probably just make it up."

And a seventeen-year-old comments: "I would say if you go to an all-boys' school, they talk about it more and may actually do it less, but because there are no girls around, the guys almost feel they constantly have to talk about it because the girls aren't there to be with. I go to a co-ed school now and it's no big deal." (Joe, 17)

## Girls and Sexual Experiences

Teenage girls are very much aware of the pressure to "pair" and they often find it disconcerting to have to be part of a twosome in order to be accepted. Jennifer, eighteen, explains: "There's always pressure for a girl to have a boyfriend. It's like a contest. Most girls feel inadequate without a guy. It's society that creates the image of pairing. Something's wrong with that. Girls should be treated as individuals, and not just as the other half of a couple."

Because of this kind of pressure, some teenage girls have sexual relations before they are ready for the experience. Although many girls do feel confident and comfortable with their sexuality, others are insecure and unable to deal with their conflicting sexual feelings.

### Girls Who Have Sex Without Wanting It

Some feel exploited by boyfriends who threaten to walk out unless they agree to have intercourse. And if they do agree, they often end up feeling used, especially if the relationship ends or if it continues on a purely sexual basis. Sherrie, seventeen, explains: "I had intercourse twice even though I didn't want to. I was madly in love with this guy and he and his friend picked me up one night in their car and we drove around. Suddenly, he just stopped the car and told me if I ever wanted to see him again, I'd have to have sex right now with him and his friend. I loved him so much and didn't want to lose him so I did it. God, I hated myself and him afterward. I don't see him anymore and I'll never have sex with anyone unless I want to. Sex isn't a toy. It should be something very special." And Alison, who is eighteen, tells us, "I feel that I've been used a lot in my life. I was ugly, and guys used to laugh at me or else they wanted me to hop into bed with them and then afterward they'd do what they want. They'd want to cut off the relationship—period! You know, they tell you they want to be just friends. Now I keep my distance from people."

"I had sex for the first time when I was seventeen. I felt very pressured. He was twenty and for me that was a big deal. The experience wasn't good. Mentally I was prepared for it. It wasn't the sleeping with him that bothered me; it was the before and after. Before, I felt pressured, and after, I felt like 'What did I just do?' Two weeks later he broke up with me. It didn't mean a whole lot to him. I guess you could say it was the whole experience, not just the sexual part that was no good." (Anita, 18)

For these girls and others like them, a negative self-image fosters the belief that sexual activity is the only way to be popular and hold on to boyfriends. And, unfortunately, by saying yes before they're ready, their self-esteem plummets even further.

## Sex by Free Choice

On the other hand, young women who feel good about themselves have developed self-respect and strength that protects them from vulnerability and enables them to take charge of their lives. They decide what they want to do, and they do not succumb to sexual pressure. Belinda, eighteen, says, "I feel that now I know myself pretty well. Whatever anybody else does is all right with me. Like with my homosexual friends. Their life is their business. And the same with me. I don't feel pressured by anybody. My boyfriend and I have been together for three years and he's ready to go away to college. Sometimes when we go out, he wants me to have intercourse with him. I just tell him if he respects me for the kind of person I am, then he won't pressure me about it. Some guys I've gone out with have gotten so bad that I wouldn't see them anymore."

Many of the girls want to be in love before having sex. And fear of pregnancy is always in the back of their minds. As sixteen-year-old Georgia comments: "I call the shots because I'm the one that could end up with a baby. Not him." A seventeen-year-old states her feelings clearly when she says, "There's nothing more pathetic than a girl who has sex because she feels she should; not because she wants to. Some girls I know do it because they're afraid to lose a boyfriend if they don't screw him. That's stupid. Sex for a girl should be just like sex for a boy. If you want to have intercourse, fine. If you don't want to, that's fine, too."

Forty-six percent of the older girls are having intercourse; some on a regular basis, others occasionally. Those who are comfortable with their sexuality and feel ready for intimacy approach it realistically and joyfully.

"I've only had intercourse once, but I did it because I wanted to. I'd never let someone talk me into something like that. I really wanted to because it was with a guy I still think (or hope) I'm going to marry. It was even more exciting than I thought it would be. I didn't plan on it. I don't plan on doing it often, but it was nice." (Connie, 17)

"I enjoy sex and I'm not ashamed to say so. I just plain love fucking and almost wish I'd discovered it sooner. I don't sleep around, but if I like a guy and want to have sex with him, I damn well let him know." (Catherine, 18)

"My boyfriend and I have intercourse occasionally, but only when we both really want to. We're both learning together. I don't know if we'll get married, but even if we don't, it's been a beautiful experience for both of us and we're mature enough to handle it. A few years ago we wouldn't have been. We either do it at my house when no one is home, or a friend of his has an apartment and we go there. It may sound sneaky, but we don't feel that way. I'd hate to be married to someone and then find out we're not sexually compatible. I'd have sex with any man I thought I might marry." (Robin, 18)

## Boys and Sexual Experience

One dominant male concern is lack of sexual experience. Boys sometimes doubt their masculinity if they feel they don't measure up to the media image of the virile, aggressive male. However, the majority report that they're comfortable and pleased about their sexual experiences. Some of our respondents have a variety of partners; others are involved in more serious, committed relationships. And a number of boys said that their first sexual partner was a few years older than they were. "The first girl I had sex with was five years older than me. We kind of went about it together," explains Mitch, sixteen. "It was nice, very nice. She was really a great person and it messed me up after she left. There was real feeling, involvement. It wasn't like a Saturday night thing. Not like picking someone up. It was a special feeling."

"I've had intercourse four times. I cared about the girl at the time, but feelings change. Both of our feelings. The girl was older. Afterward I think I understood her more. We both kind of wanted it and I don't think she was sorry. I'm not." (Glen, 15)

"I've had sex with a variety of girls. Most of them I hardly knew. I was fifteen the first time. We were both drunk and we started talking and I said, 'Let's go upstairs.' I initiated it. It wasn't as great as I thought it would be. After that you get better at it." (Matt, 17)

"I was with friends that were bragging and boasting and I realized I had nothing to brag about. This was the summer before ninth grade. So I made up my mind I was going to do something about it. I even made up my mind who it was going to be with; one of the girls generally thought of as 'easy.' I started spending time with her. She came from a very wealthy family. It turned into something really odd. I found out later that her father occasionally beat her, which was hard on her. We went three months, going together and breaking up. She'd say, 'David, I'm falling apart without you.' She'd do stuff like take razors to her arms. It was not such a hot situation. She was my first sexual experience. I came to care for her and there was the point when I enjoyed being the father image to her, saying, 'Do this, and we'll do that.' And then after a while it got to the point where I just had to stay away." (David, 16)

## Boys Want More Than Sex

Although some teenage boys are living the macho role of the "love 'em and leave 'em" sexually aggressive male, others seek genuine intimacy in their relationships. Roger, seventeen, believes, "You should care about a girl to have sex with her. It's not a casual thing for me. It's something intimate and loving. Not just a lay."

And an eighteen-year-old tells us, "I think sex is just a natural thing between two people of any age who care about each other. It can happen at fifteen or twenty-five. Kids might experiment, but when you really love someone, it has a different meaning. Some guys are just pushy, and that bugs me. I respect a girl's feelings. Also, a lot of guys talk about having sex all the time. But if you really like somebody, not just sexually but every other way, you don't discuss your relationship with your friends. Your relationship is personal."

Some have already experienced the heartaches of adolescent love. One seventeen-year-old explains: "Everybody thinks girls are the only ones who are used or get hurt. But there are plenty of guys who don't want to open themselves up to a relationship because they've been hurt too badly. Girls get you to like them and then they won't return the feelings. They'll make excuses why they don't want to see you. I would rather have a girl be totally upfront with me and say, 'I just don't like you because . . .' and list the reasons. Or tell you that they're just not physically attracted to you. That I can understand. That's being honest.

"I just won't give myself to a relationship until maybe I'm thirty when people don't play games anymore. I love this one girl so deeply and the trouble is I let her know I adore her. She means everything to me, more than my family or friends. I thought we had something wonderful. But I really think girls like what they can't have. If you treat them rotten they like you.

"I don't think two people ever really love each other at the same time. It's depressing. If I didn't think it got better as you get older, I wouldn't care about living."

Adolescent relationships can be as complicated and painful as adult relationships, and teenagers' pain is often greater because they lack an adult's experience and perspective. They will rarely share these unhappy moments with us, and it takes a sensitive parent to understand a teenager's sudden sullenness and lack of interest in everyday activities. We can offer to listen if they care to talk, but they usually suffer in silence until time, or another involvement, heals their emotional wounds.

## How Important Is Sex?

The vast majority of teens tell us that warmth and friendship with the opposite sex are far more meaningful than the act of sexual intercourse itself. They like to spend time with someone who is easy to be with and in whom they can confide. They enjoy sharing common interests, such as music and sports. They enjoy going to movies and dances, touching and kissing, talking and being together.

Is having sexual intercourse:

| | All | 13–15 | 16–18 | Boys Young | Older | Girls Young | Older |
|---|---|---|---|---|---|---|---|
| Less important than other matters, such as dates and friendships with the opposite sex, touching, kissing, etc. | 67% | 74% | 61% | 69% | 54% | 78% | 66% |
| Very important | 27% | 19% | 35% | 26% | 46% | 13% | 26% |
| Frightening or embarrassing | 6% | 7% | 4% | 5% | 0% | 9% | 8% |

The difference between the sexes and age groups is quite striking. Not surprisingly, sex becomes a more important part of teenagers' lives as they mature. However, the greatest number of teenagers (67%) believe intercourse is less important than other aspects of a relationship. This is particularly true among the young women. (Seventy-two percent feel this way.)

Even the macho, sexually aggressive male seems to be a dying species. Today, most boys do not feel the need to be teenage sexual supermen. Instead, like their female peers, they seek warmth and caring. Fun and companionship are their top priorities. Eddie, fourteen, says, "Right now sex is not that important. I'll be ready for it any time if I meet the right person. But now I'm going with a girl and we just go to the movies, maybe smoke a joint, and just have fun talking and being together."

"I never feel pressured. I like taking my time with a girl. I don't like having sex all the time. I don't think it's essential. I went with this girl for six months. She was a virgin. She gave me a chance to have sex, but I didn't want to. It's not like I need it to live or something like that." (Walter, 16)

"We just go out with a bunch of guys and girls. We don't necessarily pair up. Sometimes we play Frisbee or softball. We may fool around, like kissing, but we're not going to do anything that we may regret. My stepfather says to watch out for guys; that they only want one thing from you. That guys are here now, but not to stay. Not like your family. I know that's not true with my friends. We've been together for years now and we haven't done anything that they would take advantage of me for. I have a friend named Seth and I love him. We go places together; do things together. You need friends like that." (Jane, 15)

Most of our kids are not those wildly impulsive hop-into-bed teenagers that adults sometimes believe populate the state of adolescence. They enjoy the opposite sex as friends as well as lovers. And many of them realize that they are not yet ready for sexual intimacy. Some, like fourteen-year-old Louis, may disguise their apprehension about having intercourse. "Lots of guys in my class say they've had it already. But I believe that thinking too much about sex gets in the way of other things you have to do." There is nothing unusual about Louis's feelings. Seven percent of our younger teens say they are afraid or too embarrassed to have intercourse, and a larger percentage feel that they are just too young. And there are still many in both age groups who, for practical or moral reasons, believe that sexual relations should only be experienced after marriage or when two people can show sufficient maturity.

"I don't think teenagers should mess around with sex because if a girl gets pregnant, what are you gonna do? She'd have to quit school and then what? I think intercourse should be after you're married. I'm not sure teenagers can handle sex." (Tom, 14)

"I think there is too much emphasis on physical pleasure and too little on the pleasures of just living." (Barbara, 16)

"Teenagers approach sex so mechanically. It should be something that happens when two kids feel ready. It shouldn't be so much of a decision. If the couple is smart [birth control] and mature enough, then there should be no trouble." (Esther, 18)

But if there is to be no trouble, our teenagers must be well informed.

## Sex Education

### Teenagers Don't Know It All

Many parents think teenagers already know everything they want to know about sex. In fact, parents often feel their teenagers know too much. However, our teenagers don't agree. They want more information, specifically about sexual intercourse, birth control, venereal disease, and giving birth. All are valid and important areas of knowledge for young people who have passed puberty.

What subjects do you wish you knew more about? (Listed in order of interest, rather than by %)

|  | All | Younger | Older |
| --- | --- | --- | --- |
| Sexual intercourse | 1 | 1 | 2* |
| Birth control | 2 | 2 | 1 |
| Venereal disease | 3 | 3 | 2* |
| Giving birth | 4 | 6 | 4 |
| The female body | 5 | 4† | 5 |
| The male body | 6 | 4† | 6 |

\* tied at second place
† tied at fourth place

There is only a slight difference between the age groups in terms of areas of interest. For the younger teenagers who are not yet physically familiar with the opposite sex, knowledge about the prospective sexual partner's body ranks fourth rather than last. But in general, younger and older teenagers share the same concerns, although a greater differentiation emerges when the list is broken down according to gender.

| Boys | Girls |
| --- | --- |
| Venereal disease | Birth control |
| The female body | Sexual intercourse |
| Sexual intercourse | Giving birth |
| Birth control | Venereal disease |
| The male body | The male body |
| Giving birth | The female body |

How do our adolescents get answers to these questions?

## Sex Education in School: Helpful or Not?

Certainly there is some definite value derived from these classes. Almost all teenagers agree that some form of sex education should be offered in schools. But an even larger number feel that the courses don't go far enough; that kids don't receive the kind of information they want. This may be due, in part, to their reticence in asking specific questions in class. But frequently, the teachers, the course of study, the school administration, or groups such as parents' associations limit the depth of the material taught.

| If you had sex education in school, was it: | All | 13–15 | 16–18 | Boys | Girls |
|---|---|---|---|---|---|
| Informative and helpful | 42% | 44% | 40% | 38% | 46% |
| Not very good because they didn't teach what you wanted to know, or because the teachers were embarrassed and didn't tell it straight | 58% | 56% | 60% | 62% | 54% |

What is clear is that teenagers want more information, and they want to be taught by teachers who understand not only the mechanics of sexual intercourse, but also the emotional complications involved. Adolescents applaud a teacher who is open and comfortable discussing sexual subjects.

"Most kids get their sex education on the streets but I have to say I got it in school. We had a great health teacher named Carol. She wanted us all to call her by her first name. Not 'Miss.' The kids loved her because you could really talk to her. She was fairly young and really open and she told you what you wanted to know." (Dan, 18)

"I was glad I had sex ed in school because my mom never told us anything. Our nurse in school is really free about it and that's good. When you are telling someone about it, there is nothing to be ashamed of." (Diane, 13)

In many schools, sex ed is taught by specialists in other areas such as physical education, and although some instructors are qualified, many are not. Their credentials are limited to their own experiences and personal beliefs. Many are uncomfortable with the subject and resent teaching it, and consequently their students do not get the benefit of a well-planned, incisive course. Our teenagers also point out that a good portion of the information should be offered in elementary school. As one seventeen-year-old says, "It's important to know things before you start making any decisions. Kids should know about contraceptives because it will play a big part in their lives. They should know about the birds and bees when they are fairly young. At least in fourth grade. They should know where babies come from. Some people are so much more sexually ahead of others at the same age. There are sexually active seventh-graders and they should know everything anybody can tell them."

Adolescents feel that if parents can't or won't talk about sex, schools should. Otherwise, friends become the primary source of information. And the facts that kids pick up in the streets may be vivid, but not necessarily accurate. So it is crucial that we give our kids the opportunity to learn the facts accurately.

Sixteen-year-old Meredith says, "I've learned a lot from school. The films and stuff were pretty good. At first the teacher asked if anyone had any questions. Well, no boy or girl is going to ask a question about having periods and things. School teaches you, but I think you're still afraid or embarrassed to ask. So you run home and read the little booklet they gave you. I learned a lot from my brother's booklet. There were things I didn't know about boys when I was in sixth grade, but when I read his booklet I knew. I felt more secure."

Meredith's comment points up the importance of teaching each sex about the other. Teenagers want co-educational classes instead of separate "health" classes where girls learn only about menstruation and giving birth, and boys discuss wet dreams and erections. They want to know about each other's problems and feelings, as well as basic anatomy. If they learned more about the physical, emotional, and psychological characteristics of the opposite sex, and if feelings could be exchanged in an atmosphere of open dialogue, perhaps a better understanding between the sexes would result.

Another value of a good sex education course is the common ground it provides. Both the experienced and the uninitiated discover they have a lot to learn. Most teenagers either pretend or actually believe that they know a great deal about sex. Those who pretend are often embarrassed to ask questions because they are exposing their ignorance. How comforting for them to find out that others are just as unenlightened. And even for those who think they know everything, a sex education course can offer some surprises. As Benjie, fifteen, comments: "Everybody knew slang words for everything, but in school we learned the technological names and we also talked about venereal disease and pregnancy. The class was really worthwhile. Everybody thought they knew everything, but we were surprised to find out there was a lot we didn't know."

Robert Kapel, a high school student, polled the students in his New York school to discover how much they thought they knew about human sexuality. His findings? As teenagers progressed from freshmen to seniors, the majority of them believed each year that they knew almost all there was to know about sex. However, each year a comparable majority also stated that they had learned a moderate to significant amount during the prior two years. Since peers were the primary sources of information, Kapel concluded that sex-education courses are essential in order to correct peer-to-peer misinformation and to increase accurate knowledge.

Unfortunately, school is sometimes the only place where adolescents can obtain the much-needed sexual information. How many of us would allow our children to drive a car without knowing something about safety precautions, mechanics, and the rules of the road! *Yet we expect our children to enter puberty knowing less about their bodies, sexuality, and responsible relationships than they do about automotive matters.*

## Do Parents Tell Kids What They Want to Know?

Since parents obviously are the preferred informational source, we wondered how many actually discuss sex with their teenagers. The answer can be encouraging or disheartening depending on your expectations and point of view. Although half of our respondents can go to their parents for sexual information, the other half believes family discussions are impossible.

The ease with which sex or any other subject can be discussed in a family depends upon the methods of communication that are established early in a child's life. Our kids approach us with literally thousands of questions long before they reach adolescence. If we use these occasions to encourage their curiosity and develop their intelligence, we will answer all questions readily and openly. But if we discourage the asking with such responses as, "You're too young

Do you feel comfortable discussing sex with one or both parents?

|  | All | 13–15 | 16–18 |
| --- | --- | --- | --- |
| Yes, usually, or sometimes | 48% | 46% | 51% |
| No | 52% | 54% | 49% |

to know that," we are, in effect, slamming the door on their intellectual curiosity.

Most parents are comfortable discussing siblings, school, friends, or relatives. But many do not find it as easy to talk about such intimate matters as sexual drives and feelings, and their kids are very aware of their discomfort. And by the time they reach adolescence, kids know which topics can and cannot be discussed in the family. Often, sex is a dangerous or delicate area, discussed superficially, if at all. Many teenagers report that their parents become suspicious and give them the third degree if sexual questions are raised.

"I never go to my parents to talk about sex. My mother would never let me do anything if I'm under her roof. She'd say, 'Either move out or don't do it. Don't ever let me find out about it.' I just wouldn't even tell her. I would feel dirty. I'd go to a free clinic if I wanted the pill or something like that." (Vivian, 15)

"All my sex education came from dating. You might call it 'on-the-spot training.' My parents would be so embarrassed to talk to me about sex." (Jim, 16)

"Never talked about sex with my parents. I can't imagine them even doing it. Having sex, I mean. They'd be very uncomfortable talking about it. So would I, with them." (Graham, 14)

## When Parents Refuse to Talk About Sex

Although adults must surely realize that the topic of sex is very much on their teenagers' minds, many parents prefer to ignore this, hoping the subject will not surface. If it does, they either refuse to offer information or slough it off jokingly. In some cases, they even ridicule, reprimand, or appear shocked and disappointed. Teenagers cannot understand how parents can react so negatively when their children are trying to be totally honest.

"When I felt I was ready, I told my mother I went to a doctor to get birth control. It was like a jolt to her. Her first reaction was that it was funny. Then she said, 'Oh, so you think you're grown now? You think you're ready for that kind of thing?' It really bothered me because I was coming to her. Not hiding it from her. It was something I wanted to rap about seriously. She tried to play it off. Later she said to me, 'So you want to have sex and act like a woman? So do something to prove that you're ready for all these things.' She meant doing better in school. She tried to tie school in with the other thing. I don't go for that." (Ellen, 16)

"No! No discussions with my mother. She thinks French kissing is against our religion, and petting is a definite no-no. She probably worries because her sister got pregnant before she was married." (Claire, 15)

## Some Parents Are Surprisingly Honest About Sex

On the brighter side, a number of kids surprised us with reports of their parents' willingness to be open and honest. One sixteen-year-old describes the change in her mother's attitude about discussing sex. At first her mother replied that "birds sang and bees buzzed," but now she is beginning to feel more comfortable. Susan concludes, "After our shaky start, I was afraid if I asked a question she'd be saying, 'I wonder why she wants to know that?' But she didn't. She just answers my questions and tells me what she thinks and what she's gone through. I've learned a lot from her. In fact, she's explained about relationships so well that I can pretty much tell what a guy wants when I go out with him. I know I shouldn't feel pressured to do something I don't want to do."

"I learned most of it in school, but my mom and I can talk, too. Like about being flat-chested and things. I always told my mom that when you get married, don't you feel stupid? Do you shut the bathroom door or what do you do? She said you're not ashamed of anything when you're married. I sure would be. I'd lock myself in the bathroom." (Vicky, 16)

"Most of my sex education came from my mom. Homosexuality is the only thing I can think of that I'd like to know more about. We've discussed things like birth control. I have a cousin that is very close to me. She had been going out with a guy for one year. It was her first real boyfriend. She got pregnant and had the baby. So I was talking to my mom about it and she said it's a shame that my cousin's mother never discussed birth control. My cousin still may have gotten pregnant, but at least it wouldn't have been an accident." (Rosie, 18)

A sixteen-year-old boy said his mother's approach was terrific. There were never any special discussions about sex; it was simply a part of everyday conversation. On one occasion when he was thirteen, he and a friend found some X-rated movie tins in the woods. He asked his mother if they could look at the films. His friend couldn't believe that Bob was actually discussing this with his mother. She said that they could view one as long as the three of them watched it together. Bob thought her response was very realistic. He said that she knew he and his friend would watch it one way or another and she preferred to be there so they could all talk about it. Bob recalls, "The movie was gross and boring and I couldn't imagine why anyone would want to have intercourse in front of a camera." The boys returned the films to the woods and that was the end of it.

If his mother had gone the "typical mother" route by saying, "No, of course you can't see it," Bob felt the whole thing could have been blown out of proportion. Instead, his mother's reaction precipitated a frank discussion about the differences between a loving sexual relationship and the kind of sex that is usually depicted in X-rated movies. Bob remarked that his father would not have approved of their viewing the film. "He could never be that open, but my mom just doesn't have any hangups."

Other parents might agree with Bob's father, but there are many teenagers who would appreciate the kind of rapport that Bob shares with his mother. However, this method only works when the lines of communication between parent and child are wide open. Bob's mother felt that both boys would react maturely to the "sit down, let's look and talk" approach.

## Books Can Help

Parents who can't bring themselves to talk about sex can and should encourage their kids to read about it. In some cases, this is a better approach than having a forced heart-to-heart talk which may prove embarrassing to both parent and child. However, the reading should continue beyond the "Where do babies come from?" stage. Sally, eighteen, tells us, "My mother told me about getting my period, but nothing else. In first grade I had a friend who taught me all the words. Later I figured out what the words meant. We also had books around the house so you didn't have to embarrass yourself by asking. I can remember reading one book about babies over and over again. Another time my mother went to a meeting where a doctor gave a sex lecture and she brought home the tape for me to listen to."

However, there is really no substitute for honest, unashamed dialogue, and seventeen-year-old Christopher explains why. "Parents have to be open with kids. Even when they're four or five years old they gotta know what 'fuck' means. Parents can't say. 'Oh, don't say that word. It doesn't mean anything. You shouldn't know that yet.' If kids are old enough to ask the question, they're old enough to receive an answer. If not, they'll find out the wrong way—from someone else."

Many of us grew up in homes where frank discussions of sex were not only forbidden but shameful. It takes time and effort to free ourselves of the embarrassment and anxiety that those attitudes breed. However, it is time well spent if it allows us to respond to our youngsters' questions candidly.

## Birth Control

Unwanted pregnancy is the persistent fear of both parents and teenagers. Therefore, we would expect that parents are giving their daughters and sons as much information as possible about contraception. Right? Wrong.

### Parents Still Don't Tell Their Kids About Birth Control

Almost three-quarters of our teenagers report that they and their parents have *never* discussed the matter at all. It seems as if sex, in general, is easier to talk about than the specific area of birth control. (Remember that 48% can discuss sex with parents.)

Some parents try to justify their avoidance of the subject by stating that their kids have never asked. However, kids are savvy enough to know which questions will lead to trouble if they're voiced, and naturally those are the questions that go unasked.

Birth control is a touchy subject because parents fear that discussing it is tantamount to condoning sexual intercourse for their kids. One seventeen-year-old girl states: "If I brought up the subject

Have you and your parents discussed birth control?

|  | All | Younger | Older |
|---|---|---|---|
| Yes | 29% | 28% | 29% |
| No | 71% | 72% | 71% |

of birth control, my mother would be sure I was having sex. She'd really panic so I just don't mention it. Of course, she'd panic even more if I got pregnant, which I did eight months ago, but she never knew."

Parents who avoid the subject of birth control are merely protecting themselves from the conflict of discussions. They are *not* protecting their children. In fact, their teenagers are more likely to begin a sexual relationship without adequate knowledge or protection. As fifteen-year-old Lucy says, "I wish I knew more about contraceptives. Nobody ever really sits down and talks to you about it. You hear kind of roundabout, but not everything you should know."

"I feel that sex is mostly part of the body and not the mind. It's something your body tells you to do. People have one set idea about teenage sex. I can understand how they feel with the statistics about teenage pregnancy. But it has to be accepted, and instead of saying sex is definitely wrong, teenagers need to be taught about birth control, normal sexuality, and love." (Connie, 15)

"I really want to know more about birth control. Some of the pros and cons and how different things affect you. Couple of years ago my mom said, 'When you need the pill, come to me.' But I don't want the pill because I know that messes you up. And right now I don't need it. But I feel I can handle intercourse. I'm trying to hold out because I'm only fifteen, but I don't know if I can. If I really did get into a serious relationship, then I probably would have sex despite the risks. I'd probably enter into it but I'd be really careful. There's a high risk." (Sally, 15)

Statistics show that one million teenagers are pregnant each year and many of them are no more than children themselves. As teenage pregnancy rates soar, birth-control information is almost as vital as food and clothing. In addition to information about contraception, we must also discuss loving relationships, marriage, religious convictions, moral beliefs, and whatever else we feel is important, while never losing sight of the fact that our teenagers may become sexually intimate whether or not we approve. Caring parents cannot afford to dwell in a fantasy world where their teenagers' sex lives are concerned.

## Boys or Girls—Who Gets More Information?

Are parents more likely to discuss birth control with sons or daughters? To find out, we broke down the teenagers' responses according to sex:

| Have you and your parents discussed birth control? | Boys | | Girls | |
|---|---|---|---|---|
| | 13–15 | 16–18 | 13–15 | 16–18 |
| Yes | 24% | 24% | 32% | 35% |
| No | 76% | 76% | 68% | 65% |

Only 1 out of 4 boys (regardless of age) has discussed birth control with his parents. Fathers often give brief instructions to their sons, such as, "Be careful. Protect yourself. Don't get a girl pregnant." But rarely do fathers (or mothers) explain in detail and in exact terms about birth-control methods, and the emotions and responsibilities that go with sexual activity. Boys may want specific information, but they are often reluctant to approach a parent because they don't want to admit their naïveté, or feel uncomfortable talking about intimate subjects.

Responsible parents should take the initiative before or as soon as they are aware that their teenage sons are becoming sexually active. Explanations about the use of condoms must be precise. Adolescents must be made aware of the dangers of venereal disease and how they can prevent it.

Parents do seem to fare slightly better with their daughters, as indicated by the higher percentage of "yes" responses from both age groups. This may be the result of the common bond that develops between mother and daughter, as each recognizes the mutual problems that women experience. Sara, eighteen, explains: "It's a lot easier for me to discuss sex and birth control with my mother just because she's female. I don't think it has anything to do with her beliefs. She just understands the feelings of a woman, like about premarital sex or abortion. I don't know what my father would do because I've never talked to him about it, but he's male and sort of on the other side."

However, Sara's experience is not the norm for the great majority of girls, and it's clear that we parents have to take a more active role with our daughters as well as our sons. We should not only be candid and specific about the various methods of birth control and how to use them, but we should also encourage our girls to discuss the subject with the family doctor, gynecologist or Planned Parenthood representative. When is such talk appropriate? There's no set age, but our daughters' physical maturity and dating activities offer useful clues.

We are not signaling acceptance of premarital sex when we initiate such discussions. We are simply letting our adolescents know that we are there for conversation and information.

Since it's obvious that teenagers aren't getting the information at home, we wondered how many actually use some form of birth control.

### More Don't Than Do: Nearly 6 Out of 10 Teenagers Do *Not* Use Birth-Control Techniques At All, or Only Sometimes

Teenagers who have intercourse regularly are more likely to use birth-control methods. Those who are not experienced and who have sex infrequently or sporadically are least likely to use contraceptives. Often, first experiences are spontaneous, so birth-control devices aren't available or utilized. And some girls feel that if they take precautions, the boy will think they were expecting sex and lose respect for them. If sexual contact isn't planned the girls don't feel as guilty.

| If you have intercourse, do you use some method of birth control? | |
|---|---|
| Yes | 41% |
| No | 36% |
| Usually or sometimes | 23% |

(No and Usually or sometimes: 59%)

Seventeen-year-old Rochelle expresses the view of many when she says, "No, I didn't use birth control the first time because it wasn't planned. It just sort of happened. But next time I will (or I should say, *he* will), because I was a little worried about that for a while." Girls such as Rochelle believe that their boyfriends should be responsible for birth-control procedures, but most boys feel it is the girl's responsibility. And in the face of such disagreement, there is a good chance that neither one will be protected.

## Who Are the Users?

Before the advent of the pill, the use or nonuse of birth-control procedures was left almost entirely up to the boy. Now, more and more girls are taking charge of their own bodies.

---

Older teenagers who use birth control methods:

| | |
|---|---|
| Boys 16–18 | 38% |
| Girls 16–18 | 50% |

---

If society encourages males and females to share equal responsibility for a baby, there might be less disparity between these percentages. But until that happens, girls will always run the greater risk.

We found that there is not much variation according to religion. Even many of the Catholic teenagers intend to use contraceptives. Teenage girls, in general, do not want to get pregnant. Stacy, sixteen, believes, "Sex with someone you love is beautiful. But you have to be careful. You can't just let your emotions take over and not protect yourself. Kids who have intercourse without birth control are crazy. That's the one thing I'm always worried about. Getting pregnant."

"Some of the time I use birth control; usually [he uses] a condom. I'm definitely going to go on the pill. I won't ask my mother, I'll tell her. One abortion is enough. I don't want another." (Adele, 17)

Although most teenage girls, even the ones who don't use birth control regularly, echo Stacy's and Adele's views about pregnancy, there are some girls who deliberately plan to get pregnant. Usually, such young women are unhappy and insecure and view pregnancy as a way of getting much-needed attention and love. Often, they are lonely and unpopular with their peers. In their eyes, a baby will be someone to love, someone who will love them back uncondition ally. Many also believe that motherhood will give them stature and set them apart from their peers who are still merely "children." Unfortunately, these are the girls who are least likely to be able to care for and raise a child. They have too many emotional problems of their own and many discover, too late, that responsibility for another human being is not the solution they had hoped it would be.

What about boys? How do they feel about the idea of preventing pregnancy? Those who are conscientious and mature are very definite about the importance of birth control.

Sydney, sixteen, comments: "I'm very careful. I use condoms. No way I want to get a girl pregnant." And one thirteen-year-old who is looking ahead states: "I haven't done it yet, but when I do I wouldn't want a girl to get pregnant, so I'd go to the drugstore and not tell my parents."

Other boys, however, are careless, sometimes to the point of irresponsibility. Santo, seventeen, boasts, "I'd never get someone pregnant. I get out in time. I got a reputation of being strong. Able to control myself. Pull out." And even after an unfortunate experience, one young man says, "No, I don't use anything and probably never will. That's how my girlfriend got pregnant—eventually."

## Pregnancy

### No More Shame, Hiding, or "I Better Get Married"

When girls decide what to do about unplanned pregnancy, self-determination is their motto. Since the girl bears the responsibility, she feels *she* should make the decision that's the best for her and the unplanned-for fetus.

### Girls' Reaction to Unplanned Pregnancy: Abort or Not?

More and more teenagers are keeping their babies. Of the one million teens who become pregnant each year, close to 600,000 give birth. Since 1960, the number of adolescent births has more than doubled.

Twelve years ago 8 out of 10 unmarried teenagers gave up their babies for adoption. Now only 2 out of 10 would follow that course. And of the adolescents we polled (not pregnant), 4 out of 10 say they would keep their babies—with or without a husband.

Girls: If you were pregnant and not married, would you:

|  | All | Younger | Older |
|---|---|---|---|
| Not marry the father, but still have the baby | 38% | 43% | 33% |
| Get an abortion | 28% | 17% | 38% |
| Have the baby and give it up for adoption | 21% | 23% | 20% |
| Marry the father even if you didn't love him or felt you were both too young | 13% | 17% | 9% |

Marrying "to give the baby a name" or for appearance's sake is not an attractive or reasonable alternative for most girls. They refuse to consider marrying the father if there is no love involved or if they are both too young. College-bound women particularly reject such a possibility. Obviously, they are going places, and they have no intention of being saddled with an unwanted husband. Across the board in all groups, old concepts of morality and female dependency are being firmly rejected.

"I might like a guy enough to go to bed with, but I might not like him enough to marry him. I wouldn't have a baby because I'm on the pill, but if I did, I still wouldn't marry him unless I really loved him." (Nancy, 17)

"My mother thinks I'm crazy because I told her if I ever got pregnant, I'd never get married if I was under twenty-five. There's too much I want to do first. I might have the baby, depending upon my financial situation, but I'd probably get an abortion. She can't understand that at all." (Phyllis, 16)

It is significant that the option of abortion is now accessible to them, increasing their range of choices. Our teenagers speak of *wanting* a child when they're ready—not *having* to have one.

"I would definitely have an abortion because I don't feel I'm ready to handle a kid mentally, physically, or financially. I don't want that obligation. There are too many things I want to do in life." (Jessica, 15)

"I thought I was pregnant, but this morning I got my friend, so I'm not. It would depend on who I got pregnant by. If I knew he was irresponsible and someone I could not trust, then I'd have an abortion. If it was someone responsible, who would help me, then I probably would have the baby." (Mary, 17)

We place primary emphasis on the older teenager here because she is more likely to find herself faced with this problem, and because she is shaping her attitudes about adult sexuality at this time.

Older girls recognize that pregnancy would create awesome complications. If they have plans for their future, or if they consider the consequences to the child (being born unwanted to a mother unprepared to offer a secure home) they favor either abortion or adoption. Some teenagers have witnessed the problems experienced by their pregnant friends and they don't want their lives to turn out similarly.

A great majority of them express a mature concern about the financial responsibilities of raising a child. They realize that they would be unable to support a baby. As Georgia, seventeen, says, "I wouldn't get pregnant, but if I did, I wouldn't have the baby unless I was financially and emotionally able to handle it (which I wouldn't be at this age). A baby would wreck your life, your career, your chances to be what you want. So abortion would be the only solution."

Some of our interviewees who have had abortions did so without parental knowledge. Adele, seventeen, reveals, "I had an abortion about two and a half months ago. My parents don't know. My three close friends know, plus one other girl at school. I've never had any problem with it. It's a trust; a bond that would be crushed if they told. Another one of my friends got an abortion last fall and so she understands. She was there with me." Obviously, Adele felt she could not confide in her parents, and many other teenagers share her belief.

### Do Parents React with Shock or Acceptance to an Unplanned Pregnancy?

In many cases, girls feel that it would be easier to withhold the truth than to face angry parents and suffer the consequences.

Eighteen-year-old Esther expresses the hopelessness some adolescents would feel if they found themselves pregnant and believed there was little, if any, help at home. She does not accept abortion and feels she would have to bear the child. Young women like Esther may be the ones who suffer most.

"I've thought about abortion a lot. It really scares me. At first, I thought that was the only easy way out but the more you think about it, how could you kill or do harm to someone who is part of you? If I got pregnant my mom's reaction would be totally *kaput* at me. She wouldn't have any respect for me. I know she wouldn't want me to have an abortion. I'd probably try to take care of the baby, which I couldn't at my age. My boyfriend wouldn't want to get married because we still have a long way to go. He would help out as much as he could. It would be like trying to row a boat without any paddles." (Esther, 18)

A fifteen-year-old tells us that if she found herself pregnant she wouldn't tell her mother until after she had the baby. She adds, "I'd leave home after it started to get noticed, and I'd have the kid and then come back. I wouldn't leave the burden on my mother. She'd be upset and furious."

Many pregnant teenagers are little more than children themselves, chronologically and emotionally. And when they become mothers, they have to relinquish a part of their own childhood, and give up the chance to experience carefree adolescence. Some are forced to drop out of school. Even those who stay in school have to watch their friends go off to parties while they stay home changing diapers and coping with a fretful baby. Many teenage mothers end up abusing their children because they're so frustrated and so ill-equipped to cope with the responsibility.

Among some ethnic groups in this country, especially those with extended family ties, illegitimate babies are raised by their grandmothers. Although this may be a welcome solution for the young mother at the time, it is not always good for the baby. We have seen many teenagers who are the product of such arrangements. By the time they reach adolescence, their grandparents are unable to handle their demands for independence. Their relationships with their natural mothers are usually inconsistent and strained, yet the mother may be forced to take on full responsibility at this most difficult time.

Few teenagers are sophisticated enough to make a rational decision about childbearing. The novelty of caring for an infant may seem appealing, but most cannot foresee the complications that the child would produce and encounter as the child of an unmarried young mother.

## Boys' Attitudes About Pregnancy: Abortion or Not?

Most teenage boys have strong opinions about the extent to which they would assume responsibility. A large number of them accept abortion as a reasonable solution. Like the girls, they are very much aware of the problems of an unwanted child. Some have had the experience of living without parents. Others just don't want the responsibility of a baby at this time in their lives. Stewart, sixteen, says, "One girl said that if she got pregnant, she wasn't going to get an abortion. I would try to convince her to. If not, I would tell her, 'Look, I'm not taking any responsibility for the kid. You're going to be on your own with it.' I'll pay for the abortion. But I don't think it's my responsibility to support the kid if she has it without me giving her permission." Harris, eighteen, believes in abortion for another reason. "I'm not against abortion. I consider it a choice. All I can picture is a kid growing up in an orphanage or jumping from foster home to foster home because nobody wants him. The hurt the kid must feel. Like, 'Why the hell did they let me live?' It's definitely the girl's choice."

Some teenage boys say they would accept responsibility for the child, but not to the point of entering into a marriage they don't want, or for which they feel unprepared. James, fifteen, says, "I'd take the girl to the hospital and get all that iron and potassium junk that she needs, have the baby and that would be that. No abortion. I'd go to work and give all the money to the baby. I'd support it but not marry the girl. That would be strung-out ridiculous!" And seventeen-year-old Bill comments: "First I'd see if the girl would have an abortion. If she wouldn't I'd tell my folks. We'd have to get together with her folks and talk about giving the baby up for adoption. It would be pretty tough. If she wanted to get married, I'd probably kill myself!" (He laughs.)

Such comments reinforce our belief in the necessity of providing adolescents with valid birth-control information, as well as giving them a solid understanding of the responsibilities involved when one becomes a sexually active individual. Sixteen-year-old Lou expresses the thoughts of many of the more caring and mature teenagers. He believes, "Sex is something you have to take seriously. If you have intercourse without birth control, you're just asking for trouble. You only want a baby when two people are married and in love. It shouldn't be an accident because the kid's the one that suffers."

## Living Together

### Why Nearly Three-Quarters of Today's Teenagers Would Live with Someone Before Marriage

It is worth noting that girls are still more cautious than boys. Their response seems to reflect what we noted earlier in this chapter; that the female is still more vulnerable, particularly since she has to assume the ultimate responsibility for an unplanned pregnancy.

Would you live with someone before (or instead of) getting married?

|  | All | 13–15-year-olds | 16–18-year-olds | Girls | Boys |
|---|---|---|---|---|---|
| Yes or maybe | 74% | 73% | 74% | 68% | 79% |
| No | 26% | 27% | 26% | 32% | 21% |

The living-together arrangement marks an impressive change in American attitudes. Far from believing themselves to be "living in sin," our teenagers state that living together is the most sensible procedure they know to test compatibility before making a permanent commitment. They say they don't want to wait until after they are married to discover they may have made a mistake. As fourteen-year-old Janet comments: "I'd want to know what a real living situation is. If I got married and then found out he snored or he slept weird or wanted to sleep in different rooms, I don't know if I'd like that or not. Suppose he did a whole bunch of weird stuff, like always having midnight snacks or doing strange things in the bathroom? If he was really different, I'd like to get used to it before I married him. That way I could find out if I like the way he lives."

Since many of our teenagers feel that sex is a prerequisite for marriage, they want to know if a potential mate will be a loving sexual partner. Danielle, fifteen, tells us, "I think if my parents had lived together first, they never would have gotten married. They don't get along at all. Sexually or any other way. It's better to find that all out before you get married and have kids. Then you're stuck." And Rosie, eighteen, explains: "I know I wouldn't get married as young as my parents. My boyfriend and I had sex ed together in the same class, and we had to fill out a marriage contract as part of the course. I sure found out certain views that he had that I didn't know about. Before you get married, you have to understand each other very well. That includes money, children, and personal habits that might drive you crazy later."

For some teenagers, living together would be a permanent arrangement. One seventeen-year-old comments that she would only get married if she decided to have children. "Otherwise," she continues, "I'd just live with someone. Maybe by that time it [illegitimacy] won't make any difference."

Those who reject the idea completely either feel living with someone is morally wrong or relish their independence to the extent that they would rather live alone.

"I haven't been brought up to think that I would live with someone first. But I don't look down on anyone who does, because if that's their thing, then let them do it. I would make sure the big things that I wanted to be said were said and agreed upon before we got married." (Isabelle, 16)

And one fourteen-year-old states his belief quite simply: "What's the use of living together? If you like each other, you get married!"

The living-together arrangement offers a good example of generational values in conflict. Many parents have told us of the dilemmas they face when their college-age sons and daughters, who have been openly living and/or sleeping with heterosexual companions, arrive home for visits. Can the parents accept the couple's sharing the same bed in the family home? Or do they insist that the couple adhere to the traditional values and sleep apart? This is one situation with which the majority of our own parents never had to cope. There's only one practical rule, and that's to agree on the arrangements in advance. If parents don't want the couple to sleep together, the couple should be told ahead of time so they can either abide by the "house rules" or make other plans.

## Marriage

### 90% of Today's Teens See Marriage in Their Future

Do adolescents' views about living together have any effect on their plans for marriage? Do they feel that marriage is unnecessary or undesirable? On the contrary. Only 10% of our respondents say

| At what age would you like to get married? | | |
|---|---|---|
| Not at all | 10% | |
| 18 to 21 | 17% | |
| 21 to 25 | 45% | |
| 25 to 30 | 23% | 90% |
| Over 30 | 5% | |

that they do not plan to get married. Most teenagers are as conventional as their parents and grandparents when it comes to marriage.

Nearly half of them would like to marry sometime between the ages of twenty-one and twenty-five. The alarmists who fear that teenage morality threatens the institution of marriage and family will find little support in these figures or in the comments of our respondents. Nine out of ten of the teenagers surveyed believe in marriage. Max, fifteen, states: "I'm all for marriage, but I'm all for living with the girl first before I get married. I want a very open marriage, but a very close one and I'd like to see it last till death do you part."

Once again, however, we see a difference between the sexes, along the lines that our society has established. More boys than girls reject the idea of marriage, and a significantly larger number of girls than boys indicate the wish to be married before the age of twenty-five. The wish for earlier marriage, however, is stronger with the younger teenagers. As they mature, the less they feel that they must marry early, and the more they realize that the world can be as open for them as it can be for young men.

"I said to myself a long time ago that I was going to get married when I was eighteen. Well, I'm eighteen now, and I'm not about to get married. Probably by the time I'm thirty I'll say to myself, 'Well, I haven't found the right person yet, so that's okay.' There's no special age you have to get married. I know my mother told me when she was twenty-one every girl thought they had to be married or they'd be old maids. Nowadays girls don't feel that way. They can work, have careers, and wait until the right guy comes along. Or never get married if they don't want to. I'd like to be married about twenty-five or twenty-six, but there's no big sweat if I'm not. I think women like my mother used to feel insecure if they weren't married by twenty-one. Like no one would ever want them. I don't feel that way." (Rebecca, 18)

"One thing I'm sure of is that I won't rush into getting married. I don't just want a sex machine. I want a guy who will love me and be considerate and we'll have a lot in common. I think people get divorced if they get bored with each other and don't have the same interests. I'm going to take my time and I don't care if all my friends get married, I want mine to last." (Beth, 17)

## Our Kids Have Realistic Expectations

Teenagers want marriage to work. They want to feel good about their marriage partners. They have no false notions about marrying someone and changing the person afterward. They want mutual respect in a relationship. Most of them want children, but only when they can afford them (and not too many). Above all, they don't want to marry until they've been on their own for a while. They want to feel fulfilled rather than trapped by the formal institution of marriage. One eighteen-year-old states: "Sure I want to get married. I can't see living alone for the rest of my life. I'd like to share things with a wife and maybe have two kids. But not for a while. I think a lot of divorces happen because people get married too young and don't know what they want. You have to experience a lot of things in life before you're ready to settle down." And another eighteen-year-old recognizes the financial responsibilities of marriage. He believes, "It's not how old you are, it's what you got. I want to have a house, money in the bank, a nice job I can rely on. Make sure I have a couple of G's in the bank. My father always made sure I had clothes on my back and enough to eat. That's the way I'm going to treat my kids."

## What Do They Want in a Marriage Partner?

Our teenagers want a compatible mate; someone to whom they can talk and with whom they can feel comfortable and share interests. They want a partner who is intelligent, understanding, interesting, and someone with a sense of humor. They set their sights high. Since teenagers are not rushing into marriage to satisfy their sexual needs, they can concentrate on qualities other than sexual ones when seeking a solid marriage partner. And that seems to us a most healthy trend.

"I'd like to get married at some later time to a girl who is plenty smart and has a great sense of humor. Sex is important, but I think a sense of humor is even more important. My parents laugh all the time and they always said that a sense of humor got them over the tough spots. My girlfriend makes me laugh a lot and we really have a lot in common. I don't know if I'll marry her, but I'll marry someone like her." (Norman, 17)

Although the group who rejects marriage is small, the reasons for choosing this path seem worth investigating. But first, a note of caution. Because these findings are based on limited numbers, no firm conclusions can be drawn. Still, it is interesting to discover the dangers these teenagers believe they are avoiding.

## Why Do Some Adolescents Reject Marriage?

---

If you don't want to get married, what are your reasons?

40% of the responses point up marriage as being too filled with arguments and hassles

35% don't want the responsibility of marriage

30% fear the loss of freedom in marriage

12% say it would interfere with careers

12% simply find marriage boring

(Some respondents checked more than one answer.)

---

In the first category, boys and girls are not too dissimilar. Reluctance to take on responsibility, however, is almost a totally male choice (50% vs. 4%). That is not surprising since men are still viewed as providers, and this responsibility weighs heavily upon young men. What *is* surprising, however, is that twice as many girls as boys fear the loss of freedom (44% vs. 22%). And similarly, twice as many girls fear that marriage will interfere with career plans (19% vs. 9%). Traditionally, the desire not to marry has been the male's prerogative—a result of his unwillingness to surrender freedom. But today, girls are just as worried about losing their individuality, and less concerned about the prospect of life without a permanent mate.

"I never really thought about getting married. I don't believe in marriage myself. Marriage is just a piece of paper. If you're not married, you could do as you please and wouldn't have to do what your husband says. Like, 'Stay home tonight with me.' You just go when you want to go when you're not married. So I don't know if I'll get married or not." (Elly, 17)

"I don't want to give up my freedom and probably a good career, for a man. My mother did it and I saw how she resented it. If I ever do get married, it would be to a man who wouldn't be threatened by my work. Maybe another lawyer. That's what I want to be." (Suzanne, 17)

Our daughters know that career goals are not only desirable but attainable. The women's liberation movement is not a new concept to these teenagers and they are increasingly protective of their right to pursue a career. For the young men, however, career freedom has always been available, and they are more concerned about the responsibilities that go along with career, home, and family. Both sexes protect their freedom, but each perceives the threat in a different way.

Some teenagers want to remain unmarried in order to preserve their sense of personal identity. They want time to be on their own for a while. Others would like to work in secluded areas such as mountains or forests, and therefore have no intention of getting married. We know many adolescents who are worried about their ability to succeed as adults, and who are shocked by the destructive competitiveness they see. They often fantasize returning to a more natural life. Some do follow this path, but far more begin to develop greater capacities for coping. They realize that they can function and succeed, and that nature will always be available for shorter but gratifying retreats. Then there are those teenagers who realize that maturity is a vital ingredient in a successful marriage, and they know they are not ready and may never be.

Adolescents who have been abused in some way would prefer remaining unattached because they're afraid of becoming close to someone who might mistreat them. Sherrie, eighteen, says, "Long relationships don't do anything but hurt me, so I try to keep out of long relationships. I've been hurt by too many people, so I like being by myself now. I don't want to get married and be used. I would just like to be by myself for the rest of my life 'cause I've been with enough people; been with enough guys, and I'd rather be into myself." And John, who is seventeen, believes, "If you can't live singly, you can't live marriedly, and I have enough trouble by myself."

## Fear of Repeating Parents' Mistakes

The most compelling reasons come from those who have experienced bitter divorces in their own families. They claim ample demonstration of the unworkability of marriage and they want no part of it. There is cynicism here, but they have evidence for their views, and they are not about to wade into what seems to be a swamp of trouble. Jerry, seventeen, explains: "I don't see what the use of marriage is. Okay, as something to bind you together through the hard times, but I can see what's going to happen to my sister and it's no good. She wants to get married to the guy she's living with and she takes so much mental battering from him. He ridicules her in front of people and makes her look dumb. He's not even divorced yet and she thinks that piece of paper will be more binding for her than it was for his other wife. She's crazy. He's got a couple of kids, too. My parents are divorced so I've seen a lot of unhappy marriages. Who needs it?"

Two other adolescents have equally strong feelings.

"Marriage is a lot of hassles. Especially if you have a lot of kids. The marriages I've seen my mother go through make me feel like I don't want to get married. I haven't seen one good marriage; something that really seems together, and it makes me just want to avoid that situation." (Helen, 15)

"I don't intend to get married for quite a while, until I'm thirty—if at all. The concept of marriage scares me. I've seen what my father's been through—three marriages. And I'm like my father in a lot of ways. First of all, I couldn't stick with one woman for that long a period of time. I don't really want to have kids that much because they get in the way. And if I did get a divorce, I wouldn't want to give up half of what I earned during my whole life to somebody I might not even be living with anymore. Now I take these things into consideration, and that's one of the main things that discourages me from getting married. Divorce and stuff." (Bert, 16)

On the other hand, teenagers whose parents have happy marriages believe that they, too, could have happy marriages in the future. Obviously, there will be changes in what is considered a family unit in years to come, but for the present, our kids feel as strongly as we do about building a life with one mate. And perhaps they are more realistic about the pitfalls and problems than we were at their age.

## Homosexuality

In recent years, gay-liberation forces have fought for and gained the acceptance of many straight people. And as a result of their struggle, many gays and bisexuals have a sense of self-respect for the first time in their lives. Hiding homosexuality in the closet is far less frequent than in the past, but the years of social oppression have taken their toll. It's difficult enough for adults to cope with discrimination and ostracism, but how do gay teenagers of both sexes handle feelings that society has labeled strange and inappropriate? How are they dealing with these drives and impulses?

Nine percent of our polled population have had a homosexual experience at some time in their lives. This figure is low in comparison to other studies, and we believe it is because our respondents did not rate as true homosexual experience the look-and-touch sexual play that is common among preadolescents. Only 5%, however, believe that they actually are, or could possibly be, gay. While some of these teenagers accept this preference, others are upset or confused about it and would like help in working out their uncertainties.

### The Conflicts

Those who are ashamed of their homosexual preference are less likely to be open about it. Most of them consider it private and do not think it is necessary to reveal their feelings. But we did hear from teenagers who have come to grips with their homosexuality and feel confident enough to talk about it. Those who have successful love relationships often discuss their preference and satisfaction quite openly. These young people are school dropouts, athletes, school successes, and teenagers from all socioeconomic levels. Their frank comments help to explain the conflict homosexuals face in trying to express their natural inclinations. Our participants' views can be very helpful to parents who think they might have a son or daughter with homosexual feelings, or to parents who just want a better understanding of this complex issue.

Adolescents are striving for identity. As they reach puberty, they experience a surge of sexual feelings that lead to many puzzling sensations and much experimentation. Sexual play with a friend of one's own sex is fairly common, and is by no means an indication of future adult homosexuality. But the pressures to grow into adulthood are strong, and include very clear expectations about sexual roles. Teenagers expect to be attracted to the opposite sex. When such an attraction doesn't materialize or if it is weak, a teenager may worry considerably about being "normal." This failure to fit into expected sexual patterns is shocking and frightening. On the one hand, the adolescent has certain drives and feelings. On the other, he or she faces a collection of standards that encourage heterosexuality, and discourage homosexuality through shame and ridicule.

Often the boy or girl will strive to deny or suppress the disapproved-of feelings. This often requires constant attention and caution. Although seventeen-year-old Kenneth has accepted his homosexuality, he's afraid to let his peers know because he fears they will think he has violated their sexual standards. "In my situation, you can't really have open friends. I wouldn't get high with friends because with the drugs the real me would come out. I am afraid to lose control in front of people—they'd know I was gay. I always looked at myself as a loner and a misfit and felt rejected by most kids my age. I sheltered myself from them and kept most things in. I'm just waiting for my type of person to come along. I was always afraid people would discover things about me."

The battle between inner reality and outer appearances takes time to work out. For some it is a lifelong conflict. Kenneth's struggle to come to grips with the distinctions leads him to attempt a self-definition, or hope, of bisexuality. "Maybe I was secretly planning the experience. It happened two years ago with a guy a year younger than me. As far back as I can remember, I had gay feelings. It's weird. I keep labeling myself as a bisexual because I am attracted to girls in a little way, but sometimes I don't know whether I'm saying that because maybe I can change. I've finally opened up to a few of my female friends and told them I think I'm gay. I've been avoiding one friend and I was going to break up our friendship and never see her again. But I figured, 'Well, I've got to start having friends; giving and taking and helping each other out.' So I told her and she accepted it."

Quite a few of the teenagers we spoke with feel that they have indeed been accepted. Although some of them have heterosexual relationships, they are convinced that they are more comfortable and interested in members of their own sex.

"I really would like to have a homosexual experience. There's no pressure from anyone else to have sex; just my own pressure.

Right now I don't feel any real attraction to the opposite sex but I wouldn't want to go through life without knowing what it was like. To see how the other half lives.

"I realized my sexuality about two years ago. I have some very close friends and we can discuss this. It turned out that my best friend for many years was gay and we found out together. That was nice and normal. I've had a lucky development. There's a girl I just met and she's gay. I've been accepted." (Alec, 16)

While some have made initial tentative explorations, others are standing back, uncertain of the intensity of their feelings. They are waiting to see what may develop.

"Every once in a while I wonder what it would be like to touch another girl and to be able to get her excited. But I've never done it and probably never will. I don't have any strong desires; just curiosity." (Betsy, 17)

"I know I'm not gay, but I have had gay feelings. Then I kind of said 'Well, what's wrong with me?' At least I don't think I am. So I just kind of turn myself off." (Kathy, 15)

"I feel I'm gay, but if a girl has the right personality, then I think I could have a sexual relationship. Everything rides on personality. I'm looking for a person I could really interact with. You know, understand each other without even speaking. I can see myself with either, so I don't feel too uncomfortable about it." (Steve, 17)

It is not unusual for a boy who does not fit into the typical "masculine" mold to doubt himself and wonder if he is homosexual. The doubt arises not because he has dominant homosexual fantasies, but because he believes he's not as macho as he thinks he ought to be. Philip, eighteen years old, says, "I'm not sure whether I'm calling myself gay because I'm not athletic and aggressive, or because I really am."

## Being Gay Is Harder

Going through the trauma of admitting and accepting one's homosexual drives is one phase in a difficult process. These teenagers have not found the easy access to loving and sexual relationships that are available to their heterosexual friends. Their first sexual experience may not occur until they're well into adolescence. For them, the beginning of shared sexuality can be a moment of exceptional pleasure and release from embarrassment and guilty isolation.

"It's nice to talk about it. It's very personal. I had three girlfriends before my first boyfriend. I had three girlfriends over the course of two years. I never had intercourse with them; I went, you might say, to third base, which was almost everything. I had one sexual experience with a guy about my age. I initiated it. I've known for a long time that I'm gay. By fourteen there was no question in my mind. Five days after I had the one relationship, I met another guy quite accidentally, and I've been going with him for three months. He's very sincere and I really am very much in love with him. We talk about our problems. He's twenty-five years old and I'm sixteen and there are problems that go along with it. There have been times when I've been scared by the whole thing, but as long as it's good for both of us, it's good.

"When the time comes when we have to break up because one of us is not getting what we need, or isn't able to give what the other needs, as long as we do it gently it's okay. I'm really afraid that someone might get it wrong. Like thinking a twenty-five-year-old is seducing a twelve-year-old. It's not like we met in a public urinal. We just happened to meet on the train as I was going home." (Thomas, 16)

"I think I could get into it; really enjoy a homosexual experience in the next few years. Then people you meet can accept things and don't get all bent out of shape over it and worry about being seen with you. Now you can't open up to anybody. Not being able to say anything to anybody is torture. I want to meet people like me and have a relationship. Now it's like I'm living in a fantasy world." (Andrew, 18)

The core of homosexual expression is not sexuality, but a full caring relationship in which sexuality takes the appropriate strong role it has in any adolescent love relationship. The freedom to reveal one's deepest and most intimately personal feelings to another, to discuss uncertainties and struggles; these are all part of the relationships gay teenagers seek. Because gay feelings are such a forbidden topic, these teenagers cry out for another person's understanding.

Many young women say that same-sex contacts can be less strained, more spontaneous and honest.

"I had a relationship with a girl for about two years. I was sixteen. It was all right, but after those two years I decided that it wasn't for me. It was a change, though. A lot of people don't understand. I'm a woman and she's a woman so if I have a problem, I could go to her and she can understand from a woman's point of view. It's the same thing with gay guys. They talk to each other and they understand where each other's head is at. To me, a woman can help more than a man." (Elvira, 18)

"I do want to get married and I want kids. But right now, I have to wait until my heart says I'm ready. I don't feel being with a girl is something crazy or something abnormal. I'm comfortable. They love me and care about me and at the same time they talk to me and understand me. When I try to go out with guys, all they want is to go to bed." (Sissy, 18)

Sometimes young men seek out nonsexual friendships with girls because such relationships permit a degree of openness not possible with image-conscious male peers. They want to talk freely without having to perform or fulfill preset masculine roles.

"I've told some of my female friends that I'm gay and they are very accepting. Boys pretend they're so macho that you could never tell them. They'd ridicule you. But girls understand and are much easier to talk to about that. They don't think less of me. Or if they do, at least they don't show it. I even think some girls like having gay male friends because they know they can talk to me and I won't come on to them." (Ted, 18)

"Most girls don't mind if you're gay, if you're their friend. I don't know if they feel like they have an advantage because you've shown a weakness or what, but they accept it more because they're not out to prove themselves to you. Most boys will not show any weakness. They're so afraid of showing anything less than total macho." (Andrew, 18)

And some boys who have not yet revealed their homosexuality find female friends "a cover." One such young man cultivated a friend who was perceived by peers as a bed-hopper. He says, "You see, you have to hang around girls to be accepted in high school and she was always all over me. So that's why I appreciated her. People couldn't understand how I could put up with her, but I used her as a cover."

## The Dilemma: To Hide or Reveal

Adolescents tell us of the problems in coming to terms with something that cannot be denied. It is important to recognize that many gays cannot exercise free choices; they simply are not sexually aroused by the opposite sex. What some heterosexuals may not realize is that contact with the opposite sex can be as undesirable for some of these teenagers as homosexual contact would be for straight teenagers. Parents who reject or condemn their children for being gay or bisexual erect a barrier that can become insurmountable. It is understandable that parents would be distressed at what they perceive as the limitations created by a homosexual life-style. For parents to add disdain and disapproval to their child's burden separates rather than unites the family. Although most teenagers would like to be honest with their parents, few actually are because they fear the aggravation and condemnation that might result.

"I don't think I'm prepared to go through years of aggravation. If I were to spill my guts now, I think I'd be risking my whole future because I'm depending on home for college support. My father always seems like a cool, easygoing person, but my sister, who has been around him more, says he's very impatient. He'll blow up at the slightest thing. So I was going to say something to him but I realized I better not." (Tom, 18)

Some adolescents do confide in close heterosexual friends. Others are not yet ready to share these feelings with anyone and honestly believe that it's no one's business.

"I have two close friends in school. There may be one other person who knows I'm gay. Someone else told, and I don't want this person to know because he's a real jerk. It's someone who gossips a lot. Although I'm not worried, it's not something that I need to share with these people. I would probably deny it because I'm not ready to deal with it right now. I've thought many times that I would like to talk to my father, who would be the perfect person to talk to because he's very understanding and sympathetic. But it's not something I'm ready to share. Now that I've got someone to talk to (the person I'm going with), it's relieved a lot of pressure." (Wayne, 16)

## Can Parents Accept Their Teenagers' Homosexuality?

Teenagers are not the only ones who are working out their problems. Parents are wrestling with their own feelings of shock and confusion. A major problem for most parents is their unfamiliarity with the causes and styles of homosexual life. While not wishing to be judgmental, they may nevertheless be repelled or frightened by what they perceive as an unnatural drive. Furthermore, they may deplore the "waste" of an attractive young girl or boy seeking a same-sex mate rather than marrying and becoming a parent. Doubts and fears about their own sexual adequacy or competency as a parent are sometimes aroused, leading to guilt. This in turn may provoke a forceful rejection of the child, in an effort to eradicate this "stain" and the guilt. Several boys speak of what the knowledge might do to their fathers' own sense of masculinity. They feel that Father would reject them in order to save face himself. It would embarrass him to admit that his son is gay because he feels it somehow reflects on him.

"I knew I was gay (although I didn't know what it really was) when I was five. I told my mother when I was about fifteen years old. She was kind of surprised, but she knew it for a long time, I think, because the way I walked and everything. When I was five, my older brother said, 'You're gay, you're gay.' And I said, 'Well, if it's me, it's me.' He understands, and my sister and mother do, too. But not my father. He's very old-fashioned and says he wants me to be a man. That's how he started hitting me and beating on me." (Ricardo, 17)

"I have two gay friends and a straight friend that know. It's perfectly fine with them, but my parents don't know. They want to be open, but with me being gay, it throws them off and we don't feel comfortable talking. My father would be very upset. My mother says he has a masculinity problem and he just hates gays. My mother wouldn't be too terrible. She's liberal and she'd understand and still love me. After the initial shock, it would be okay. I'm going to see my sister this weekend and I'm very close to her. I'll probably tell her. I'll probably tell my parents when I'm out of the house. I don't want to look at their guilty faces every morning when they wake up, especially my father. Eventually they'll know. I don't want to live in a closet." (Alec, 16)

## How Parents Can Help

Teenagers who can communicate with their parents in other areas are more likely to confide in them about the more personal issue of sexuality—provided they know the parents will not condemn or censure.

Those who are described by our interviewees as liberal parents can accept this "difference" in their adolescent. Some hope it will disappear when the "right girl" or "right boy" comes along, and they may be very disappointed when this change does not occur. Others have had to cope with lost ambitions, such as not having the satisfaction of grandchildren. Nobody's life can follow a clear and definite path, not even our own. And when we're dealing with the lives of others, particularly our own children, we must recognize how few certainties there are.

How parents react to the fact that their child is homosexual depends ultimately on the kind of relationship they wish to have with that child. If they want closeness and honesty, then they must opt to be supportive. Some gay-community organizations provide parent discussion groups and many of them offer excellent programs. They recognize that parents are subject to conflicts also. Those who are anxious to preserve the love and understanding of their children deserve help in doing so.

## How Straight Teenagers View Homosexuals

We asked all of our participants their feelings about homosexuals in general. The younger teenagers, especially boys, have negative feelings about being around people they view as gay. They don't want to be associated with them, perhaps because they feel threatened and worried that their own sexuality will be questioned. Guilt by association. Darren, fifteen, expresses the views of many younger teenagers. "Gays are all right as long as they just stay away from me. I guess if a friend of mine told me he was gay, I'd still be his friend. Well, you say you'd be his friend, but you know that you'd just ease away from him gradually and stay as far away from him as you can, eventually."

As they get older and learn more about homosexuality, some of their attitudes change. They may feel indifferent, more tolerant, or in some instances, sorry about the discrimination gays experience. However, all find it difficult to understand someone so different from themselves and the unfamiliar is usually treated with caution and distance. A characteristic of human relationships is that people establish and maintain connections with those who share common interests or goals. If gays and straights don't share any interests, the likelihood of close friendship is limited. However, if shared activities and experiences transcend sexual-preference differences, close contact can be maintained. Many teenagers consider it unfair to reject someone because of his or her sexual preferences and they assure us that such an issue would not influence their loyalty to a friend.

"I guess I could say I'd feel sorry for someone who's gay. If a friend of mine was, I would try to help her if she wanted the help. If she wanted to like other girls, I don't think my relationship with her would be any different. I would try to talk her out of it. I'm not afraid to tell anybody my opinion, but I wouldn't want to stand in anyone's way. I wouldn't want anyone standing in my way. That's just part of her life; part of her private life. It's also unfair to assume automatically that a person is gay. I will not take anybody's word for it. A lot of people think my boyfriend is gay because he wears pink shirts. What the heck. It doesn't bother me any. He keeps his shirt unbuttoned, too. So what? My opinion might be lowered a little bit because of what the people around the world are thinking. It's unfair. Being gay is natural, I guess, for some people." (Bernadette, 16)

Gay teenagers share all the concerns that other teenagers have. They are striving to feel strong and self-reliant, and to believe in themselves. They plan for college or drop out of high school in the same proportions as nongays. They seek and at the same time resist closeness to parents. They want to find a loving companion with whom they can talk freely and with whom they can enjoy physical contact.

We parents can make every effort to listen and comprehend. We can offer help, or accept the turning down of such an offer if that is the choice with which our gay son or daughter feels more comfortable. If we respect the individuality of each member of the family, we can create an atmosphere of love and trust, rather than deception and distance.

# 3

# Teenagers on Drinking and Drugs

---

- 1 out of 4 high schoolers drinks more than once a week
- 40% of teenagers smoke marijuana regularly
- 7 out of 10 high school teenagers have tried marijuana
- The majority feel that their parents know they drink, but only 29% say their parents know they smoke pot
- 50% will lie to parents about their pot use
- 55% say their parents have never discussed drugs
- 55% of all teenagers believe smoking pot is bad for their health; 68% of the nonsmokers believe this, while only 36% of the smokers think pot is dangerous
- 62% of the teenagers who drink believe drinking is bad for their health, yet they still drink

---

## Getting High

"The girls I hang around with drink because they want to. Nobody makes them do it. Some of my girlfriends will pull me away in school and say, 'Come on, let's go out in the hall. I have a bottle.' Or they'll say, 'Hey, Marc, let's get high. Do ya have any pot?' It's not like they feel they have to drink to stay in a certain group or anything. They're just bored, or they like it. I don't know which." (Marc, 16)

"Alcohol is easy to get. I never even bother to try a state store. I know enough older people who are willing to do it. I know that sounds awful; like they're willing to place more on friendship than doing what's right. My boss at work was getting it for me until he finally told me, 'No more.' Academically, this was the most important year for college. S.A.T.'s and achievements, and I have finals coming up. I know I probably didn't want to cope or deal with the situation. It's easier to get drunk and not worry about it. Then again, you wake up the next morning and it's still there." (Ollie, 16)

These are not the comments of a small or special sector of the teenage population. They are quotes from the average teenagers we interviewed in communities throughout the country. Girls, boys, athletes, students preparing for college. Whites, blacks, Protestants, Catholics, Jews. The children of doctors, lawyers, and company presidents, and the children of factory workers, clerks, and secretaries.

Our kids are getting high, and it's time we learned why and how directly from them.

## How Are They Getting High?

The most widely used intoxicants are liquor (whisky, beer, and wine) and marijuana. Drinking is the first choice for American teenagers, but marijuana is a close second. In the three months prior to interview, 66% of our teenagers had drunk beer, wine, or liquor, while 43% had smoked pot. By age, this breaks down as follows:

By age, in the past three months:

|  | 13–15-year-olds | 16–18-year-olds |
| --- | --- | --- |
| Beer, wine, or liquor | 53% | 78% |
| Marijuana | 32% | 55% |

Teenagers don't make the sharp distinction between smoking and drinking that adults do. They smoke or drink what they like and what is available. The legal restrictions are the same for both drinking and smoking if an individual is below the age of eighteen. But they know that the law deals more harshly with a sixteen-year-old caught with a joint than with a can of beer. They have also learned that parents make a similar distinction.

The high schooler who has a beer after a hard ball game on Saturday afternoon is not considered a drinker. Parents may even encourage moderate drinking at family affairs to train their youngsters how to drink and control their intake. Being labeled "a drinker" implies regular use of alcohol for more than casual social reasons.

Sharing a few six-packs or quarts with friends during weekends or getting drunk at Saturday night parties would be defined as drinking.

On the other hand, the teenager who comes home after a Saturday afternoon game and lights up a marijuana cigarette would be likely to evoke consternation in most American homes. He would be designated, accurately, as a pot smoker.

## Categorizing Drinkers and Smokers

We decided to identify "drinkers" as those who, by their own account, drink "more than once a week." When it came to choosing the pot smokers, we considered how society at large would be likely to distinguish between "smokers" and "nonsmokers." Would young people who smoke every other weekend or less at parties, or smoke two or three times a month, be considered pot smokers by their friends and parents? We thought so. Certainly the law would define them that way. And we found some confirmation for our judgment that smokers know who they are, because those who responded to the six different questions designed solely for pot smokers ranged from 43% to 49% of our total group.

In contrast, those responding to similar questions about drinking comprised 46% to 66% of the total group. This confirmed that the standards for identifying oneself as "drinker" were a lot less firm among teenagers than were those for considering oneself a "pot smoker."

Our teenagers deal with the question differently depending on the context. Anything to drink in the last three months? Two-thirds answer yes. But less than half report drinking more or less than once a week. How many of these are hard drinkers? We don't know because there's no agreed-upon definition of that. We do know that 1 out of 4 of the older group indicates they drink more than once a week. And boys tend to do more drinking than girls, but the difference is not great.

"When I was twelve or thirteen, my parents would ask if I'd like a glass of wine with dinner. I couldn't stand the way it tasted. A couple years later I came back and decided I really liked it. I guess my taste buds matured. I started drinking every weekend about a year ago. When I come home drunk, my parents don't know because they're asleep." (Mary Jo, 17)

"Every once in a while I'll say, 'The hell with it,' and get drunk.

Like if I've gotten through some tough exams." (Gregg, 17)

David, sixteen, tells us, "There was a period this year when even I could tell I was drinking a lot. There was a point for about two weeks when I was getting drunk at school, believe it or not, which can get you expelled. That was a dumb thing to do. But it was one of those days when there was nothing in particular to do except be with your friends. It always seems like everyone else does it, so it's okay."

## Teenage Drinking Habits

### Why and How They Drink

The reasons teenagers give are varied and they mirror adult reasons: enjoying the sensation, wanting to relax and forget problems, indulging because it's the primary activity at a party or other social grouping, or because of boredom. Jeb, seventeen, explains: "I like drinking with a girl or a friend, or if my brother's home we'll do it sometimes. It's just fun. I like stumbling around. Sometimes I'll drink to get rowdy or I get high sometimes when there's nothing else to do. If there's something to do, fine; I'll go out and do it. Otherwise, getting drunk is just another activity. I can't say anything else about it."

A fifteen-year-old whose parents allow him to drink beer at home in the hope that he won't drink outside (which he says isn't the case), comments: "I've never gotten drunk, but I would if I had a good reason to. Like if you're having troubles and getting confused and the pressure's just too much, then I guess it's not a bad idea to waste yourself for a day." And seventeen-year-old Andy's explanation is one any adult might give. "You always think of something to say when you're drinking. The things I say when I'm sober are usually just small talk. When I'm drunk I can start a real heavy conversation and I can relate better. Open and secure. I really like that feeling."

Many speak of knowing their limits, but very often it takes a series of bad drinking experiences before they temper their alcohol use. Jerome, sixteen, tells of getting very drunk and wrecking the car. "I was so sick afterward. At first I was laughing and having a good time. But later I wondered what I was doing. I had a 104 temperature and a hangover for two days. Now when I drink I know my limit. Enough to have an effect on me but never enough to make me sick. I used to drink everything. Beer, wine, vodka, everything, and I don't even like it. Just what it does to me."

## Where and at What Age Does Drinking Occur?

Many of our interviewees started to drink at twelve or thirteen (or younger). Some like Lisa, fourteen, are introduced to alcohol by family members. "My grandfather and father say that drinking one can of beer a day is very good for your health." And a sixteen-year-old whose father is a psychiatrist was initiated by a cousin.

"I'd never really touched alcohol before the winter two years ago. I had numerous experiences with it when my brother, who's three and a half years older, came home drunk and I'd have to clean up the vomit all over the place and put him in my bed which was near the bathroom. I thought that liquor held no appeal for me. The first time I got drunk, I was visiting cousins in Chicago, and my parents left. It was over Christmas vacation. My cousins were having a party and it was the first time I had ever taken a drink in my life. They were playing 'See how drunk you can get little cousin,' and I managed to get pretty drunk. It was like once it happened again, I really didn't care. Now I get drunk occasionally because I want to. I used to drink for the specific purpose of getting drunk. For two years I did that. I was drinking once or twice a week. Sometimes three times a week. It fluctuated. Maybe an occasional week where I didn't drink at all. I'm not sure the size of the bottles, but I drank about a quarter of a quart of hard alcohol on the average. I think there were times when I must have finished off half a quart, but those were the times I got sick. It would really ruin a day. There was one day my best friend and I went home and got drunk at nine o'clock in the morning. We had a bunch of free periods. It screwed up the whole day. It was really stupid." (Bobby, 16)

Others are introduced to alcohol by friends at parties, in school, or in the neighborhood. A few tell us that some of their friends' parents don't mind their teenagers drinking, and when they want to drink they go to their friends' houses.

The majority of teenagers have had a beer or a glass of wine at one time or another without becoming "drinkers," and most reach their own reasonable compromises between indulgence (or nonuse) and the requirements of their daily responsibilities. Adult experience often is helpful, as eighteen-year-old Rhonda tells us: "My parents set a pretty good example, I guess. They didn't lay down any heavy laws, but they didn't need to. You just need common sense to know how much or not at all."

However, 25% of the sixteen-to-eighteen-year-olds report drinking more than once a week. How do their parents react? Obviously, adults are aware of the rapid rise in teenage alcoholism, and most do worry about their teenagers' drinking habits. However, some tend to make light of the problem because they're so relieved that it is alcohol and not marijuana. Randy, fifteen, tells us, "I go to a party with a mug in my hand. It's obvious what I'm going to do with it. They don't say anything. I think they're glad it's not pot."

## Differing Adult Messages—More Panic About Pot

Parents worry more about marijuana use partly because they know so little about it. In contrast, most adults have experience with alcohol, and accept casual drinking as part of the social scene. Over the years, American society has developed a number of social rules about drinking: when to drink, how much, in what company under what circumstances. There are also separate rules for different social classes and for different age groups. When these rules are broken, an individual is said to have a drinking problem. There are specific words to describe the various styles of acceptable adult drinking behavior. "Getting high" is different from "having a couple of drinks." "Being social" differs from "getting bombed."

We impart these standards to our children along with all the other rules for appropriate social behavior. We teach them how to respect and converse with adults, how to work hard to earn money, how to dress properly for varied occasions, how to eat politely, and how to drink acceptably. School courses dealing with family life may even include discussions of these drinking regulations. However, this information in no way insures that teenagers will use alcohol in moderation.

Widespread use of marijuana is still so new, at least in adult society, that similar rules about its use don't exist. Consequently parents are much more apprehensive about pot use. Interestingly, many adolescents share these apprehensions and doubts. Their uncertainties frequently operate as an effective deterrent in the preadolescent years, when identification with parental attitudes is strongest. But when they begin to search for dependable guidelines for marijuana use, they usually come up empty. Few parents can give their teenagers a background of older-generation authentic information. They simply say, "Don't use it," which is understandable since parents do not want their children to become involved with yet another intoxicant. However, the result is that teenagers are on their own.

## Marijuana Use—Past and Present

### Pot Use in the 1960s

The following information provides insight into the background of marijuana usage that surged in the sixties and continues with even greater frequency among a portion of today's young people. We are in no way condoning marijuana use, but adults must realize that knowledge and understanding are necessary first steps in controlling its use.

In the sixties, teenage drug users felt that the warnings issued by the government and by the adult world in general were greatly exaggerated. They watched *Reefer Madness*, a film made in the 1930s, for laughs. Lacking data they believed to be reliable, the juvenile underground began to develop its own unwritten lexicon of information. For example, marijuana from certain countries was better than domestic varieties. Color, leaf vs. twig content, female or male plant, country of origin—these were some of the features that teenage consumers looked for.

Usually they would buy enough for a day or two. If they had sufficient amounts of ready cash, they might consider making a larger purchase, cutting it up into smaller amounts and selling those to friends in school. These "lids" were sometimes termed "nickels" or "dimes," referring to $5 or $10 purchases. A considerable entrepreneurship developed in some juvenile circles. A few teenagers might pool together a few hundred dollars and buy a pound of marijuana. It could then be divided up and resold in smaller quantities in high school or junior high school. Often the seller would look for no more profit than being able to obtain free grass for personal consumption. The search for new markets sometimes led senior high school students to introduce marijuana to junior high schoolers. Even fifth- and sixth-graders got involved, often via older siblings or friends.

One young entrepreneur, now a junior executive, recalled the evolution of his "business education" in those early days. "First we traded bubble-gum baseball cards. Then we started getting hold of pornographic magazines and selling to each other. Around seventh grade, one boy started rolling joints and selling them one at a time. By the time we were in high school, Quaaludes, acid, speed, and downers were hot market items in the bathroom and schoolyard."

As the drug business grew more sophisticated, regulations for use were established. Kids set their own standards—when to smoke; with whom; how much—depending upon their activities and goals and the results they hoped to achieve. And like any culturally determined set of principles for behavior, there were variations and even sharp differences in accordance with socioeconomic levels, geographical areas, and climatic conditions.

The sixties underground surfaced considerably in the seventies and eighties. Marijuana's presence is increasingly evident now, and there is very little mystery about it among the teenage population, except perhaps in terms of health effects. The decision to smoke or not is inescapable.

## Pot Use Today

Teenagers know who the smokers are and this information is rarely transmitted to teachers, parents, and other uninitiated adults. Smoking is not the exclusive practice of a fringe group. It is a regular pastime of many teenagers, and 70% of the older ones have tried it at some time.

## Adolescents' Social Rules for Smoking

Regulations regarding pot use are similar to adult rules about drinking. For extremely important activities, such as participation on school athletic teams, teenagers may refrain for the duration of the season. This rule may be relaxed at weekend parties, but the majority of athletes try not to drink or smoke. Physical condition is their top priority and they adhere to their coaches' ultimatums. Students who are preparing for critical examinations (such as Scholastic Aptitude Tests) generally don't smoke for the day or two preceding the exams. And those who are concerned about getting good grades in general may smoke only on weekends or not at all. Some students smoke after school or in the evening after finishing homework, but they value their good grades too much to go overboard. And there is an even larger group of teenagers who, for reasons we will discuss later, do not smoke at all.

Those who smoke excessively are termed "potheads" and placed in an unfavored category by the majority of their peers. In some circles, those who smoke on the way to school, or outside the school building, are considered potheads by those who seldom smoke or do not smoke at all. However, the definition of excessive use depends on the social circumstances of the school and the peer group. The term pothead may be used as one of criticism or derision in a school where pot is rarely used. In another school or setting where heavy pot smoking is the norm, pothead may be used affectionately by peers to denote "one of the gang."

Teenagers who have lost the power to concentrate or communicate effectively as a result of heavy drug use are sometimes referred to as "burnouts." This judgment is comparable to the adult society's rejection of a "drunkard."

## Who Smokes?

Who has tried pot?

|  | All | Boys | Girls |
|---|---|---|---|
| 13–15-year-olds | 42% | 47% | 37% |
| 16–18-year-olds | 70% | 74% | 67% |

Seven out of 10 teenagers have smoked by the time they reach the sixteen-to-eighteen age group. Even by the age of fifteen, 42% have experimented. Marijuana use crosses every racial, age, sex, and socioeconomic line.

Who still uses pot or hash?

|  | All | Boys | Girls |
|---|---|---|---|
| Ages 13–15 | 29% | 33% | 26% |
| Ages 16–18 | 49% | 54% | 44% |

About half of our high school students identify themselves as smokers, although only 23% smoke more than once a week. Note that boys are consistently more likely to smoke than are girls.

## Where Do They Get It?

According to our adolescents, there's easy access in schools and neighborhoods, and many report being turned on by relatives and friends of all ages, including peers, adults, and college-age friends. Pierce, fourteen, comments: "The first time I did it I was eleven, but I didn't do it that much. I was scared. Then I didn't do it for a year. When I was thirteen I started to smoke every day. But if I don't have it, I can go without it. My friends give it to me or I buy it sometimes. I have connections but I get it a lot at school, too." And others explain their sources:

"I smoke pot with my brother or sister and sometimes alone. It's sporadic. It started last summer, and I did it every weekend for two months. Now maybe I do it once every month. My brother got me started. I know that it's there and it's kind of a nice feeling." (Kate, 16)

"When I was dealing, I'd get the stuff from people at school and sell it to kids and one adult I knew. He's over fifty years old but he's really a cool guy. He's the only adult, though, because you could get in trouble selling to adults. I was making a hundred a week or more. Depends what I had. Sometimes I could cop two ounces of Hawaiian which is supposed to be really expensive. I got it maybe for $200 and I sold one ounce for $175. My mom caught me. She came in and saw my trunk full of all the stuff. She'd suspected I was dealing. I closed the trunk and ran out of the house. She called the police. They never really scared me because they're not going to bust a little-time dealer. They're not gonna throw me in juvenile hall because they caught me with maybe a quarter-pound. It's nothin' to them. It didn't upset me too much, but I almost flushed it down the toilet." (Syd 16)

## Why Do They Smoke?

### The Effects

Most report that they smoke because it feels good. They enjoy being high, relaxed, and temporarily free of depression, boredom, and worry about unpleasant problems. Curiosity may start them off, but the satisfaction they get leads to further use. Smoking is often referred to as "partying" when it is used just for fun or as a diversion. Eleanor, seventeen, comments: "If I don't have any myself, I'll only smoke it on weekends. If I have my own, I smoke it every day.

I get it in the neighborhood. I smoke to get high, and I can't see myself stopping except when I'm pregnant." And seventeen-year-old Grant says, "I smoke only for its effects. Not to be cool or for social reasons. I just like to party. I never smoked because of peer pressure, but just because I wanted to."

Some say that negative emotions disappear when they're high, so they're less likely to pick fights or get into trouble. And sixteen-year-old Mel feels it has helped him "mellow out his temper." He says: "I smoke every day, usually with people. One thing it has done to me is calm my temper down a lot. I used to have a very edgy temper; I'd really knock out somebody. I was having a lot of problems with my mother. We were always at each other's throats. My tolerance level is a lot higher now, even when I'm not partying."

Another sixteen-year-old tells us, "Most kids do things too much when they first start. Later they do things in moderation. But they have to make discoveries for themselves, and excesses are part of it. If a kid is totally happy and everything is going well, he probably won't overdo drugs or alcohol, or use them at all. But when he's feeling down and has problems, it's just easier to block them out with drugs. You feel happier. I admit it's stupid, but that's what happens."

### For Problems

Roger, seventeen, is realistic about using pot to block out his problems. "I like getting high. When I first started, around thirteen or fourteen, I did it with my friends. Once in a while now I'll do it by myself. It relaxes you a lot. If you have a lot of problems, you forget them. Not really forget, just put them aside for a little while. I use it as an escape." And Gwen, fifteen, who comes from a wealthy Eastern family, explains: "If it's a lousy, boring day and it's running badly, why not make it a good day? I've got nothing to lose."

Affluent teenagers may have different problems from adolescents in underprivileged areas, but drug use goes on with regularity in both sectors. And whether their families are poor, middle class, or wealthy, all teenagers share certain problems: divorce, unhappy parents, lack of love and attention, unsatisfying and turbulent relationships, school difficulties, and a host of other mental, physical, emotional, and psychological troubles that cause unhappiness and pain. For many of these young people drugs become a refuge.

One sixteen-year-old from a wealthy New England family was smoking heavily because she couldn't handle the academic pressure she faced. Her father, a doctor, insisted on A's from her. B's simply were not acceptable. She was taking six majors and was constantly tired and suffering from frequent colds. Her two brothers had received almost perfect S.A.T. scores, and she was expected to do likewise. When the pressure became unbearable, she stopped trying to please her parents (which she knew was impossible) and began smoking marijuana. Getting high not only relieved some of her tensions, but focused new attention on her as an "imperfect" individual—crying to be understood.

For a fourteen-year-old Chicago inner-city youth the motivation was different. Harry was the oldest of six children living with a working mother. School meant little to him and he was anxious to get out and go to work. He had a part-time job in a supermarket (he lied about his age to get the job) but when summer came he was out of work. There was nothing much to do but hang out with friends who were in the same boat. He felt frustrated and inadequate, and smoking grass eased his pain and boredom. He told us that the only time he felt happy was when he was stoned.

## How Strong Is Peer Pressure?

Many parents believe that peer pressure leads their youngsters into marijuana activity, and in some cases it does. But it is an ambiguous factor to measure. If we view it as an insidious plot to pull our kids into corrupting activities, it is indeed an evil of distressing proportions. However, it is also a vital aspect of adolescent growth. Peer respect for athletic skills encourages our kids to participate in sports. Similar respect (or in some cases, scorn) for scholastic achievement encourages (or discourages) students to get good grades. Peer pressure helps adolescents break away from prolonged dependency at home. It is, in fact, no more or less remarkable than peer pressure in the adult world. Let us not forget that we adults are often influenced by the judgments of friends and neighbors.

Deciding whether or not to smoke or drink as well as how much, when, and where, is not determined in any simple way. Many parents, however, see peer pressure as the determining factor and believe that they must apply their pressure as a counterweight. So we asked our respondents to rate the influence of peer pressure, at least in terms of their personal experience.

And the vast majority agree that it's not a major problem.

Do you feel pressure from other kids to:

|  | All | Younger | Older |
|---|---|---|---|
| Smoke pot | 13% | 14% | 12% |
| Drink | 10% | 10% | 10% |
| Neither | 77% | 76% | 78% |

(NOTE: We should consider these results in terms of whether teenagers believe the peer influence to be overly demanding on them.)

A few more boys than girls experience such pressure, which is not surprising since this survey indicates that boys press somewhat earlier and more vigorously against the barriers of convention than do girls.

Our respondents tell us that pressure does exist, and some adolescents do feel that it is a factor in introducing them to new experiences. However, others make a distinct point of saying that it does not have to be followed. These kids are proud of being able to stand up to pressure and make their own decisions.

## The Strength to Say No

Strong-willed kids resent and resist any efforts to influence them (including, in many cases, parental efforts). Sixteen-year-old Danny deals with pressure forcefully. "One kid tried to pressure me, and he was sorry. Real sorry. He kept trying and so I hit him and knocked out two of his teeth." And Lonnie Sue, fifteen years old, has seen the harmful effects of excessive drug use, and explains why she will not be pressured into compliance: "They don't pressure. One thing they know about me. They don't dare push me because they know I lose my temper very easily and I'm stubborn. You just have to be strong. One of my friends has a brother who started drugs on grass, then LSD, then coke. The brother kept pressuring my friend, and so did his friends, and sure enough, he started. He's really messed up now, and he was a nice kid in the beginning. It's a real shame."

"I'm really a secure person and never follow anyone. I know that sounds conceited, and I don't mean it that way. I just mean that drinking and drugs may be for kids who have to prove something, but I never felt I had to do that." (Anthony, 16)

"I never feel pressured. I just don't like to drink or smoke and no one could talk me into it. The other night I went to a party and you could tell that half the people there were drinking beer not because they liked it, but because it was just there and they thought it was the thing to do. I wanted soda and there wasn't any, so I went to the kitchen and got a glass of water. It's just stupid to drink." (Pam, 18)

Others say that they had some initial conflict about how to handle pressure at parties or elsewhere, but eventually either rejected it or went along with it only if they wanted to. One fourteen-year-old began smoking pot because her boyfriend did. She says, "I tried it but I didn't like it. I had been building up the desire to do it, so I did. But it was no big deal. It burns my throat so I probably won't do it again." Some, like seventeen-year-old Dan, try marijuana and just decide on their own whether or not to continue using it. "Just this year I started. Previous to that, I decided that I wasn't going to be pressured into it. I was just going to do it if it felt natural. If it happened, it happened. So I was at a party and it felt right to try it out. I like it, but only smoke on social occasions."

Robin, fifteen, admits that she started smoking because everyone else did. She continues: "Later on I began to think 'I don't like it. Why am I doing it?' So I don't anymore. And they don't care. I never had to do it in the first place. Your friends don't care if you do or don't." Many others point out that the climate has changed regarding peer pressure. They explain that the pressure is not as strong as it may have been a few years ago, although the younger kids probably feel it more than do high school kids.

"It's not even the 'in' thing anymore. It's just part of everybody's life almost. I'd like to say I won't ever smoke pot, but I can't be sure until the time comes. If and when I would, it wouldn't be because someone made me, but because I'd want to." (Katie, 14)

In short, although peer pressure exists and some teenagers are vulnerable to it, many others are not. We believe that peer pressure is more of a factor than most teenagers admit to, but there is no doubt that those who resist it are the adolescents who feel good about themselves, and who know that they will be accepted by friends regardless of their attitudes about drinking and smoking.

## Effects of Alcohol and Pot on Schoolwork

The majority of the teenagers who drink or smoke do not believe that either marijuana or alcohol has much effect on their ability to concentrate and achieve in school. (Of course, it is possible that many were not concentrating or achieving at very high levels before they started their drug or alcohol use.)

| School work is: | | |
| --- | --- | --- |
| | Pot Users | Drinkers |
| Worse | 14% | 27% |
| Better | 19% | 18% |
| The same | 67% | 55% |

However, one-quarter of the drinkers do believe that drinking interferes with schoolwork, as compared with only 14% of the pot smokers.

Frank, sixteen, describes the negative effect alcohol had on his schoolwork and family relationships. "I'm really a good student and managed an A average, which I was happy about. Then it fluctuated for a while and went way downhill. I was flunking every now and then and I was doing C's. Finally I just said, 'That's enough.' Also tensions were rising and I was short-tempered with my family. When you're high or drunk all the time, you don't want to hear anything from anybody. One day when I was straight, I sat back and said, 'I don't have to do this.' My grades are up now."

Many teenagers agree that pot can be as disruptive as alcohol, and they consider it particularly stupid to be stoned while in class. Some also feel that it hinders their concentration, making it difficult to complete homework. Claire, eighteen, says that it slows down her reflexes and impedes communication with other people, as well as making her so sleepy that she has little desire to work. It is this sense of disorientation, however temporary, that disturbs many smokers.

"I've been smoking a lot, but this has been my best year since maybe seventh grade. It's a really difficult school. I think, though, smoking has been damaging because if I get home at six o'clock and my parents are away for the evening, I'm going to smoke pot and then try to do my homework. It's a lost cause. It does foul up the short-term things you're supposed to do. I don't get them done." (Gregory, 16)

On the other hand, students who find pot relaxing say that they can handle schoolwork more readily when they smoke. Glenn, fourteen, tells us, "It depends. If I'm going into a class that I don't have to work in, I'll smoke. Sometimes I've done better in school because if I'm nervous about a test, I'll be more relaxed. But I think it changes my thought pattern. It's weird. They say you do worse, but in science I seem to do better."

"All I know is that a lot of my friends smoke pot and are average or above students. A's and B's. So I guess they're either brains or have found a way to handle it." (Bernie, 15)

"Smoking dope doesn't do anything to my schoolwork. It seems like when you're high, you think better. You start thinking about stuff you never even thought about before. It makes you wonder." (Jesse, 17)

### The Unmotivated

Many adolescents who attend school find little, if any, satisfaction or value in being there. They usually attend because they are forced to; because they cannot find employment and there is nothing else to do; because their friends are in school; or because they continue to hope that something worthwhile will happen if they keep going. Many of these students do not attend classes regularly so they see no reason to refrain from smoking whenever grass is available. In fact, some feel that being stoned is the only way to get through classes for which they are unprepared and uninterested. The less meaningful school becomes, the more likely they are to get high during the day. But smoking only increases their sense of alienation from school, and the efforts of concerned teachers seem to have little impact.

"I got stoned before I went to class in the morning. It made me tired. But I was ahead of everybody and they'd be talking about the same old things, and I got bored and restless. That's when cutting out of school started." (Angela, 18)

We are not excusing their drug use, but we are trying to point out their dilemma, as well as that of teachers who feel helpless to deal with the rise in drug and alcohol use among students. Fourteen-year-old Louise describes the situation that exists in many schools throughout the country: "The majority of kids in my school do it; I'd say ninety percent. But the teachers can't do anything about it. Pot's against the law so they try to stop it, but considering that almost everybody is doing it, they can't be policing all day. They're supposed to teach. One kid I know was smoking pot in the building and he got a three-day suspension, lost his open study and open campus until his junior year. The teacher asked him if he was still going to continue to smoke and he said, 'Yes.' So it didn't teach him anything."

Educators are constantly wrestling with drug and drinking problems, and some school systems are actively trying to devise methods for coping with the troubling situation. Some have had success with moderate policing, while others have run into Fourth Amendment difficulties concerning search and seizure. Many schools are trying a multifaceted approach, using special assembly programs, films, and reformed drug addicts, rock stars, and sports figures who meet with students in small groups to discuss the health issues of drug and alcohol use. And counseling can be a useful technique for those students who are responsive to the idea. In some instances, if school is important to a child, a threat of suspension might temporarily curb his or her use of pot. It's clear that neither parents nor educators (or other experts for that matter) have found an effective solution to the drug problem, even though we are exploring every avenue to control drug abuse in the schools and in our homes.

## Parental Knowledge of Adolescents' Pot and Alcohol Use

Just how much do parents know about their children's drug and drinking experiences, and how effective are their efforts at control?

| If you drink, do your parents know? | All | 13–15 | 16–18 |
| --- | --- | --- | --- |
| Yes | 46% | 38% | 55% |
| No | 27% | 30% | 25% |
| I don't know | 27% | 32% | 20% |

When drinking is the issue, 46% of the teenagers feel that their parents know. It is clear, however, that parents have no idea how much their kids are drinking. Claudia, eighteen, comments: "I tell them I don't drink much because I can't tell them the truth. I don't even like beer but if that's all there is, of course I'll drink it. They never know when I'm drunk because they're usually asleep and I don't leave them any telltale signs."

And one seventeen-year-old states: "Half the time parents have no idea because kids are pretty good at keeping things hidden. If you sleep over at a friend's house and get bombed or stoned, you just don't go home till you're sober. Your parents go around happy in their illusions that everything is okay. What a joke! Parents are really dumb if they think their kids aren't doing things just because they've never actually caught them in the act."

And when it comes to pot use, only 3 out of 10 teenagers believe that their parents know.

| If you smoke pot, do your parents know? | | | |
| --- | --- | --- | --- |
| | All | 13–15 | 16–18 |
| Yes | 29% | 24% | 33% |
| No | 38% | 38% | 38% |
| I don't know | 33% | 38% | 29% |

## Teenagers Feel More Compelled to Hide Their Pot Use Than Their Alcohol Use

One parent assured us that her fifteen-year-old son would never smoke marijuana because he came from a good family and had a strong moral upbringing. Her son, however, told a very different tale. He was not hesitant to confide that he had been smoking pot for two years and had managed to keep it from his parents. He was not a heavy user, but he realized how upset his parents would be if they knew he had even tried it, let alone used it occasionally. Milton, fifteen, states it simply: "Just because they're used to drinking, they don't think it's as bad as smoking, but I think it's worse. I've had a drink in front of them, but if I had a joint, they'd die." And Andrew, fourteen, concurs. "They really disapprove of the pot, but they don't mind me drinking. I can be more open with them about that."

The problem for teenagers is that they're trapped between two equally important opposing forces. On the one hand, they value parental approval and good relations. But they also want to experiment and move into new areas. Such behavior inevitably arouses some parental anxiety. However, when parents believe their teenagers' activities are necessary (such as an overnight hike with a youth group or a first date) their worry is tempered by the awareness that these activities are perfectly natural and good for growth. Drinking also may be seen as an inescapable rite of growing up. But few parents feel that way about marijuana.

In order to keep peace in the family and avoid the risk of punishment, many teenagers tell parents what they think parents want to hear. They may admit to some experimentation, but that's about all. Most kids who smoke or drink simply cover up how often, how much, and when they do it.

"My mother thinks I don't do it now because the doctor told me not to get high because I've been fainting. He said it was because I was smoking pot. I let her think I stopped." (Ruth, 18)

"They know I smoke, but they don't know how much. I'm scared to tell them. They ask me why I do it, but I just can't come straight out and say I do it because I like it. I wish I could say that, but I really think I'd hurt them, so I say nothing. My sister, who's twenty-two, was sticking up for me and giving my mother stuff like, 'The kids in school say you have to do it to hang around.' But that's not the reason." (Harvey, 14)

How then do parents really know whether or not their sons and daughters are smoking pot?

## Will Teenagers Lie or Tell the Truth If Asked?

If your parents ask you if you smoke pot, will you:

|  | Boys | Girls | Younger | Older |
|---|---|---|---|---|
| Tell them the truth | 52% | 50% | 45% | 55% |
| Lie to them | 48% | 50% | 55% | 45% |

Roughly, 50–50, although the younger ones seem to feel it is more necessary to lie. Conversely, the older they get the more likely they are to be honest, probably because they feel entitled to make their own decisions regardless of adult opinion. Stacy Ann, seventeen, comments: "My parents found out I smoke pot, but I don't think they worry about me too much. I'm seventeen, and don't feel I have to hide it or lie about it. They think I'm intelligent enough and responsible enough to handle it. As long as it's in moderation. It used to be a pretty big concern with my brother. They gave him a few talks. Now it's an understanding. They know that both of us are pretty much in control."

### The Honest Approach

Those who believe in honesty exhibit a certain forthrightness that demands respect even in the face of disapproval.

"My parents don't want me to smoke, although I'm sure they know I have. I'd give them a straight answer if they asked. They'd be disappointed but I'd explain I only do it if there's nothing else important to do, and I'm not hurting myself. I'm not ashamed of it." (Pierce, 17)

They also tell us that they are more inclined to be truthful if they think their parents can discuss the issue without getting excited. Amy, fifteen, says, "If my mom found out, I wouldn't lie to her. I think I'd say that I feel I can handle pot and that it's not too heavy for me. I'd tell her, 'Look, Mom. You know I don't get into things I feel I can't handle.' I'd consider the consequences. I told her a couple of years ago that if it ever came up that pot was around, I'd probably try it because I'd feel comfortable with it and I wouldn't get carried away. And if I felt it was absolutely necessary, I'd quit."

### Why Nearly 50% Resort to Lying

Many of those who would lie don't want their parents to think less of them. Nor do they want to upset their parents. Debbie, sixteen, explains that she told her mother (in a kidding way) that she smoked marijuana, but her mother didn't believe her. "I guess I wanted her to think I was kidding. I want to tell her the truth but I don't know if I could, because I'm afraid she would look down on me and I don't ever want her to do that."

More frequently, the expectation of arousing shock or panic reactions discourages honest communication. As Karl, fourteen, says, "There's no way I'd admit to my parents that I smoke pot. They'd have a heart attack. I'd rather tell the truth but I can't." And Linda believes her mother's reaction would also compel her to lie:

"I'd have to lie because I can't talk to my mom. She turns things upside down, inside out, and takes things for granted, things that aren't true. I told her my cousin was on pot and she said, 'What? You mean Joanie's on drugs? She's going to start on acid,' and all that other crap. Good Lord, the kid's only thirteen years old. I only told her to make conversation and she had a fit. Can you see her if she thought that it was me?" (Linda, 14)

But fear of punishment is the dominant reason for lying. Sometimes this fear is carried to extremes. One fifteen-year-old left home because she was so afraid that her father would beat her when he discovered she had been drinking. She and a friend were gone for forty-five days. She explains: "My parents spent $1,400 on a private investigator to find us, and of course the police were looking for us, too. When they found us, my mom was crying all over the place. On the way home they were trying to talk sense into us. And my dad was saying, 'Where did we go wrong?' And he cried. My dad didn't cry when his own father died. And that night (my dad's not gone to church for a long time) he went to church with us and took us all out for dinner. I think he thought I ran away to rebel against him. I was just scared what he'd do to me."

And a seventeen-year-old relates: "My father still doesn't know about the other drugs. He'd kill me. He thought the pot and drinking was bad enough. He doesn't realize that over half the kids in our school do it. He thinks there's one out of a thousand kids who do it, and they're criminals or something. He went berserk when he found out about it. He just went crazy. One night when I'd been drinking, he smelled it, and he beat me up real bad." (Arlene, 17)

## Parental Cover-Ups

Parents are guilty of cover-ups, too. Sometimes, one or both parents may be aware of a drinking or drug problem, but choose, for various reasons, to ignore the situation. Arlene's mother, for example, never told her husband about their daughter's use of drugs because she was so afraid of his reaction. And Barry's mother let the issue slide because she didn't want to incur his anger. Barry explains:

"There was one instance where I thought I was sensible enough to drink in the house when my mother was there. I think I must have had three small, strong drinks (I had a bottle in my room) and the next night my mother pulled me aside and said, 'Hey, let's talk about it,' which is unusual for my mother. We had a small conversation and that was it. It upset her no end. But she's never brought it up and she never mentioned it to my father. She's afraid of my anger against her if she ever told my father. I tend to be less toler-

ant of my mother and she's afraid of me getting angry at her."
(Barry, 16)

Barry's mother obviously thought that Barry's drinking was a serious problem, not just a one-time experiment. She should have discussed the situation with her husband, regardless of Barry's reaction. As responsible parents we can't let our kids' attitudes dictate
our behavior, particularly when we believe an action is justified on
our part.

When we ignore a situation or remain silent, we are, in effect,
endorsing the activity, or indicating that we really don't care
enough to try to solve the problem. Although teenagers may appreciate our reticence, they may also feel that we're not as dependable
and responsible as we should be, and they may lose respect for us.
Sol, sixteen, believes that his parents are not aware of the full extent
of his drinking because he hides it well, but as a result of a recent
incident, his father now knows that he drinks. He says, however,
that his father would rather not face the fact. "There was a time
two weeks ago when I got drunk. I came stumbling into the house
at three in the morning and my father was still up. As my father was
on the stairs, I opened the door with my key. He was just turning off
the light in the hallway so I didn't know if he saw me. Half of me
was thinking, 'He just doesn't want to look. He'd rather turn his
back because he doesn't *want* to know.' He never brought it up."

If parents are to be helpful to their adolescents, they must confront the issues and discuss them as a family, not as adversaries.
Limits and consequences have to be determined. If there is a real
problem, the adolescent must be helped to recognize it as such, and
professional help should be sought. Even then there is no guarantee
that the problem will diminish or stop, but at least if the situation is
faced, there is hope for a solution.

At some point in a teenager's life he or she must take responsibility for his or her own actions, and parents have to relinquish
control as well as guilt. When we feel we have done all we can, the
next move is the child's—for better or worse. This is not a copout. It
is a reality.

## What Happens When Parents Are Drinkers or Drug Users?

The issue takes on different connotations when parents themselves indulge heavily in alcohol or drug use. From their standpoint,
they may wish that their children did not drink or smoke, but they

cannot disapprove too vocally because of their own activities. It is a parental paradox comparable to the dilemma of cigarette smokers who strive to enforce "no smoking" regulations when their children take up the cigarette habit. They cannot really reprimand their kids without appearing hypocritical, as Allison, fifteen, attests: "My parents are so inconsistent. They say, 'Don't you dare drink outside this house, and no pot.' But when I tell them they should stop smoking cigarettes, they think that's different. My mom says, 'It's such a habit now. When I started I didn't know how bad smoking was for you. They didn't know back then.' If we tell parents we care about their health, they don't listen. So how can they expect us to listen to them? She says, 'You're lucky because you have the advantage of scientific information.' I tell her, 'So do you, now,' but it doesn't register. So I forget about talking to her and if she asks me if I smoke, I'll tell her a white lie. It's easier than arguing."

Fourteen-year-old Mandy says that her mother found signs of pot and went through her room. "She's never said anything to me. I think she smokes, too, so if she confronted me I'd embarrass her by asking her." And Adam believes: "The reason it's not such a big deal in our house is because my mother's friend smokes it. Now she can't berate us about it because her friend does it and she also uses Valiums and alcohol, which is not a good combination. Her friend's daughter gave us a little marijuana plant. My mom nursed it, put it in water, and it grew roots. How dare she tell me I can't smoke?" (Adam, 18)

In any case, if parents are drinkers or drug users, they should not be surprised if their children follow suit. Chris, sixteen, comments: "My parents know I smoke dope. They do, too. I've been smoking about two and a half years. Actually, I was totally against it. I didn't figure it was healthy so I wasn't messing with it until I saw my father had some stashed up in his closet. When I found my father with some smoke, I was a little upset, but I went ahead and gave it a try."

Occasionally, however, parental indulgence has the reverse effect. Teenagers may be so disgusted by their parents' behavior that they resolve to abstain.

## How Effective Is Parental Advice? What Are the Most Helpful Controls?

Since parents are so concerned about drug use, one might expect that they would make vigorous efforts to encourage abstinence or caution against overindulgence. We wondered how much dialogue was taking place between parents and teenagers, and if parental advice had much bearing on a young person's decision whether or not to smoke. We also wondered if the drug issue was similar to sex, in that some parents never discuss it for fear that doing so would give their children ideas they hadn't had before. We asked:

| | |
|---|---|
| What did your parents tell you about pot when you were younger? | |
| Nothing | 55% |
| They warned you about its dangers and told you not to use it | 30% |
| They warned you about its dangers, but left the decision about it up to you | 12% |
| They told you that using it once in a while was okay | 3% |

Over one-half of our respondents' parents do not discuss the matter at all. A few say that their parents don't know much about pot anyway, so they wouldn't have anything to offer. And some, like Carolyn and Joey, feel that their parents probably never thought it was necessary to talk about it.

"They haven't said anything because I guess they know I won't do it. None of my friends do so I'm not around it. Dad has said if I ever go to a party and they start getting out the drinks and pot, just say you don't want any and if it gets really bad, just call home and he'll come get me." (Carolyn, 16)

"There's really been no discussion about smoking or drinking in my family. I just don't do it. That's all. If I had kids, they could do it as long as they knew what it was gonna do to them. Then they probably wouldn't, either." (Joey, 14)

### Making the Goals Realistic

When parents do initiate discussions, are they effective? That depends upon many factors. Foremost is the question, "What are we after in talking to our children?" Teenagers say that if we insist on total abstinence, including experimentation, we are not facing reality. Howie, sixteen, states: "I guess they care a lot and I can understand why no parent wants their kid to smoke pot or drink. They've told me not to, but I think that's unrealistic. All kids are going to experiment. I'm sure when my father was in college he drank beer like crazy."

However, if we disapprove of marijuana use, we must tell our children how we feel. By discussing our views, we can give our adolescents the benefit of whatever knowledge we have, and they may respect our views enough to go along with them. Tommy, fifteen, says, "My parents just said, 'Stay away from it,' and I figure that it was good advice." Others share his views.

"All I know is my mom is against drugs. She's a nurse and she's seen people in the hospital who are heavy on drugs. She told me about that, and we talked a long time. She's crazy about a lot of things, but that's not one of them." (Carolyn, 14)

"My parents are pretty liberal and they told me if I drink or smoke, not to do it too much. It makes sense. I don't smoke pot and I drink very little. I don't know if it's because of what they said or if I just don't like it." (Geraldine, 17)

A slightly larger percentage of the nonpot users over the pot smokers said that their parents had warned them about use. So parents who do try to limit pot smoking may find some reassurance in that tendency, even though it is slight.

Other parents believe that the best approach is to follow up a discussion by emphasizing the confidence and trust they have in their adolescent's good judgment. Seventeen-year-old Chico tells us, "My father likes to read about medicine and things. If he sees an article on smoking or drinking, he just gives it to me to read. A lot of times parents know you're old enough to know, and you've got common sense. They don't have to go around bugging you all the time."

One eighteen-year-old boy feels he has the solution to parental worries about overindulgence in pot and/or alcohol. He says, "If parents say a flat-out, 'No, don't you dare,' then of course the kid is going to use that as a perfect means of rebellion. He'll smoke and drink but do it so his parents won't know. But with most kids, if you tell them you know that they'll probably try it, but you have confidence that they're smart enough to only do it once in a while or not at all, then the kid will usually respond to his parents' trust in him.

Plus, it's no big deal to 'get away with it' if there's nothing to get away with. This is what my parents did, and there was no sneaky joy to go against their wishes. I smoke occasionally at home, but my parents know I don't do any more than that. I think they handled it well with me."

Although many parents may not agree with this young man's philosophy, it does point out an alternate way of dealing with a sensitive situation. By revealing our teenagers' views on the various methods of handling this dilemma, we are presenting choices that may prove helpful and effective in your own family.

Perhaps the power that parents possess to help their children with these decisions is best revealed in these statistics.

| | Nonpot Users | Pot Users |
|---|---|---|
| My parents really listen to my ideas and really care what I think | 66% | 54% |
| My parents don't listen or they put down my ideas | 34% | 46% |

When our teenagers feel that we really listen and care, they are more likely to discuss the pot situation with us, and less likely to smoke. However, discussions must involve an exchange of ideas and viewpoints; our kids won't accept ultimatums. They are willing to listen to us, but they must reason it out for themselves. What we say has little *direct* influence. Only 11% report that their parents had any influence on their decision to stop smoking. And while they agree that open discussion is the most effective method (although its success is at best limited), they also agree that punishment only serves to drive their drug usage underground.

Sheila, sixteen, comments: "Even if I experimented with other drugs, I don't think my parents would yell or completely freak out. I know they'd by plenty upset. It would also disappoint them a little bit, but I don't think they'd give me a punishment. They'd know it wouldn't work. They'd talk to me about it and my mother would express her feelings. So would my dad. They'd ask me why I was doing it but they'd let it be up to me because they know I can handle myself. They know I smoked pot, but I wasn't a spaced-out kid. In the end they left it up to me because that's the only thing they could do. But they talked to me and told me what they really thought. We can talk pretty well."

Fifteen-year-old Laura's mother carried talking one step further. "My mother said she had enough faith in me that I would quit sooner or later, which I did. I quit when she sent me to camp in August. They had people from Teen Challenge there, boys and men that were on cocaine, heroin, and stuff like that. They said how they found that their faith in God could be more important than taking drugs. That really made an impression. If they can do that and they're on harder stuff than we are, we can do it."

Developing independence and learning how to make sound decisions is a complex process. Personal characteristics, social skills, relationships with peers and siblings, and numerous other factors are involved. Parents are only one part of the total picture.

## Other Reasons for Stopping (or Limiting) Pot Use

### Interference with Work
Many kids say that pot has an adverse effect on their work habits and goals. One young woman reports: "Last year I was getting high every day. Just recently I have so much work to do that I can't handle it all. So two weeks ago I stopped. I don't know for how long, but I have to get my head together." And Tyrone, fifteen, admits that smoking makes him lazy. He adds, "During the day I don't get high because I don't get done what I gotta do." And one sixteen-year-old says, "Maybe it's adolescence, maybe it's the pot, but I'm not as ambitious as I used to be."

### Lessening of Enjoyment
Quite a few mention that they use pot less as they get older because they've become bored with it. The urge to experiment is not as strong. "It doesn't thrill me. I used to do it often but I don't like it that much anymore. Probably by next year I won't even bother. I'll save my money," comments Fred, fifteen. And one sixteen-year-old, who began smoking at twelve, tells us, "I'm already pooping out. Now when I do it, it's at night to relax—the way my mother would have a gin and tonic."

### Recognition of Possible Deleterious Effects
In some cases, teenagers stop or cut down because they've had bad experiences, or because they have witnessed the results of excessive drug use by peers.

"I used to smoke two or three times a day. About a year ago I wasn't feeling so good, so I stopped. I don't need to do it because it really makes me feel lousy. Everybody says it's so great, and maybe for them it is. But not for me. After school I would go over to a friend's house and stay there till six o'clock and get high. Same thing every single day. They're still doing it, but I haven't seen them in a long time. They are people I want to stay away from. They remind me of a period in my life which wasn't the greatest. When I see them, they're blitzed all the time and I don't know how they can live like that. I know that sounds dumb coming from someone who did the same thing. But I can see they're not going anywhere. They're barely in school. I'm glad that's not my life anymore." (Rhoda, 18)

Sixteen-year-old Alex says that he began to see changes in himself. "I read in a psychology book that the way to know whether your child is using drugs is to watch ... (and they gave a list of things to watch for). One of them was if the child becomes sloppy or generally messy. I used to be 'Mr. Neat,' and my room became such a mess that I began to wonder. But I don't see myself ready to give up pot yet; in fact, I'm not so sure I ever will. I think it will get to the point where I won't *own* any or have any paraphernalia. But I'll cut down."

Cliff, who is eighteen, regrets the image he once had and explains how difficult it is for people to accept the fact that he has changed. "I was crazy. I had longer hair and was overweight, but nobody questioned me. They'd say, 'Ah, he's stoned; he's high,' and I would play the part. People say you change (which I have) but you never have a second chance to make a first impression. People still think of me as that way. That's why I'm leaving school."

The consequences of being discovered by parents, school authorities, or the police, frighten or discourage some teenagers, but for sixteen-year-old Ronald it took an unfortunate series of incidents involving a girlfriend to help him decide to limit his marijuana use. "A friend and I just last week figured that over the course of our lives we've probably smoked $400, between us, of pot. I thought, 'Oh, no. Think of what you can do with that money.' I'm just beginning to work my way into coming down. This was the first week that I told myself I'm not going to get high in school. (Which I've done once or twice a week in the past months.) I saw my old girlfriend get expelled from school because she was smoking pot in the back of the bus. She had been suspended for a week and then she was caught doing nitric oxide and had been expelled after that. I watched that happen, and it wasn't too pleasant and she had to go through a lot of pain with her parents."

We've heard from the pot smokers; now, let's find out why slightly less than half of our young people do not use marijuana.

## The Nonsmokers

### Why Don't They Smoke?

---

If you do not smoke pot, is it because . . .

| | |
|---|---|
| You're not sure what it might do to your health and mind | 27% |
| Your parents would really be upset if you used it | 10% |
| You just don't like it | 25% ⎫ |
| You've got too much else to do and it just doesn't interest you | 46% ⎭ 71% |

(Some marked more than one response)

---

When we broke down the results by age and sex there was not a great deal of difference.

---

If you do not smoke pot, is it because . . .

| | Boys | Girls | Younger | Older |
|---|---|---|---|---|
| You're not sure of effects on health and mind | 27% | 28% | 29% | 25% |
| Your parents would be upset | 9% | 11% | 12% | 7% |
| You just don't like it | 27% | 23% | 23% | 29% |
| You've got too much else to do; it just doesn't interest you | 42% | 49% | 47% | 46% |

---

Teenagers who are involved in activities that truly interest them feel that drugs or drinking will interfere. Anthony, sixteen, says, "I'm busy with school, music, sports, and my friends. Who needs all that other garbage?" Furthermore, they don't want to jeopardize their relationships with their parents and their own positive self-image. One eighteen-year-old has little conflict about her choice:

"It's not because I'm such a strong person or anything like that. No matter how much pressure, I know there's no way I would ever get into drugs because I know how much guilt I would feel if I did do it. My parents would be disappointed, and I would feel like I let myself down and that would bother me a lot." (Alma, 18)

Some just feel that it is a ridiculous, meaningless activity. Rob, sixteen, believes, "It's plain stupid to smoke pot or use any drugs. Any person in their right mind knows that. The only people I know who do it are insecure, bored kids who can't find anything else to do." Jake, sixteen, agrees. "I really think kids that smoke and drink a lot are rebelling against something, and I don't have anything to rebel against. My parents are pretty cool and I really have too much else to do. I know drugs have to mess up your body, so it's stupid to do them."

## The Health Issues

Some feel very strongly about the health issues. "It scares me. I think pot can affect your brain, and scientists don't know enough of the bad effects yet. By the time they find out it'll be too late if you're already using it," comments Scott, fifteen. And others express the belief that people who are fortunate enough to be born with healthy bodies are foolish to ruin them with drugs. Their experiences with friends who have suffered as a result of drug use enforce their convictions with an authority that no adult on the outside could equal.

"Never. I'll never smoke. I think it destroys your brain and ruins you. I have a lot of friends, ex-friends really, that smoke pot. I just don't like them anymore. They're light-heads." (Stanley, 16)

To the pot smokers, the health issue is a powerful but ambiguous influence. Some say that they recognize the health risks in both pot and drinking, but intend to continue anyway. Here is how they judge the issue in regard to marijuana:

Do you think smoking pot is bad for your health?

|  | All | Smokers | Nonsmokers |
|---|---|---|---|
| Yes | 55% | 36% | 68% |
| No | 26% | 47% | 14% |
| I don't know | 19% | 22% | 18% |

Note the difference in attitudes between smokers and non-smokers. While only 36% of the smokers believe pot is dangerous, 68% of the nonsmokers believe this. And although only 27% of the nonsmokers report that health reasons were an important influence on their decision not to smoke, there is evidence here that it has a larger influence on them than that number would indicate. However, concern about health does not appear to be a meaningful influence on the smokers, for even though 36% think that it's dangerous, they continue to smoke.

Some say they know its dangers but are reluctant to give it up because they like it too much. Others believe that they will cut down eventually, because they are seriously concerned about the health effects.

"I was smoking pot every day for three years. I started when I was fourteen. I've cut down a lot but I don't know if I'm going to stop. I've been reading some articles and I'm not sure whether or not pot can damage your brain, lungs, or reproductive system. So I've cut down, but not out." (Mel, 17)

"I'm a little uptight about it. I wish I knew more. I think it's important for kids to know what the responsibility is and what you're getting into. It's good to experiment if you can handle it. I am worried about the health aspect of it even though I use pot. I guess the health part keeps me away from other drugs." (Faye, 15)

Although new medical data about the effects of marijuana are brought to their attention every day, many teenagers believe that it's based more upon moral disapproval than scientific fact. Because there is so much conflicting information authorities have lost some of their credibility in the eyes of adolescents. They don't always believe the establishment position on certain health issues.

Most teenagers, however, do want reliable information, and, as one fifteen-year-old states: "I think a lot of stuff is printed to scare us. Nothing I've read has convinced me, but I'm willing to be convinced." Mal agrees and expresses his desire for help in making a decision.

"If there were medical facts put in front of me that said, 'This is bad for you and here's why,' then I'd consider it. Pot's probably not even as bad as cigarettes, or maybe just as bad, but look at all the people out there smoking cigarettes." (Mal, 15)

Sixteen-year-old Norris believes, "We're the experimental generation and that's unfortunate. I would love to have the information about the long-term effects."

Although the health issue will not deter some teenagers from smoking pot, it worries some of them to the extent that they will consider cutting down. And for other teenagers, uncertainty about pot's effect on their health is reason enough to abstain completely or smoke very little. Their comments suggest that a reliable and objective presentation of the health issues is the best information parents can offer their teenagers. However, if this information is colored by parental lectures, rules, and punishments, our data indicate that its usefulness would be considerably lessened.

## The Nondrinkers

### Why Don't They Drink?

Teenagers who oppose drinking express similar doubts and cautions. They criticize friends who drink as an escape. Some fear what drinking does to the body, and some state that their parents' abstinence has influenced their own decisions not to drink.

Those adolescents who have been exposed to alcoholism in their own families have firsthand experience of the real dangers of drinking, and they seem determined (at least for the present) not to fall into the same trap.

Nelson, fifteen, explains: "My brother died in a car accident and my father keeps telling me if I take drugs or drink, I'll end up like him. My uncle smokes tons of cigarettes and drinks, and my older sister does too, and my father is close to being an alcoholic. I look at them and know I don't want to be like them." And sixteen-year-old Kit observes, "I've seen drinking mess up my dad. I've never done drinking as a habit but I used to go to parties and drink out of other people's glasses. And I've been drunk maybe twice. But now I keep thinking about my dad and how it ruined him. I haven't had a drink for a long time. It makes me feel good to say, 'No!' I feel like I've conquered something."

Jack, eighteen, says, "My grandmother is an alcoholic and has a liver problem, and of course my mother drinks. And one night a friend of mine got completely bombed with a bottle of vodka. At the time I had a pen full of baby rats that were my pride and joy, and my friend poured half the bottle on the rats and killed them. That was six years ago and I still think about it. I only drink diet sodas."

## Health Issues and Drinking

Our statistics show that teenagers have stronger views about the harmful effects of drinking than they do about pot smoking.

| Do you think drinking is bad for your health? | | |
| --- | --- | --- |
| | Drinkers | Nondrinkers |
| Yes | 62% | 69% |
| No | 29% | 17% |
| I don't know | 9% | 14% |

Nearly 7 out of 10 of the nondrinkers believe drinking is harmful, but even 62% of the drinkers express the same view. This across-the-board agreement about the dangers of drinking may be due to the fact that there is a considerable amount of documentation about alcoholism and its effects. Even more important, the information given out by physicians and public agencies has been directed toward adults as well as toward adolescents. *Teenagers tend to put more faith in information aimed at the total population than they do in data which they believe are published for the express purpose of frightening them out of doing something of which adults disapprove.* In any case, teenagers who drink are well aware of the dangers to physical health. And yet, they continue to drink.

"I know for a fact that alcohol kills your brain cells and damages your liver. The main reason I have cut down is not because I'm worried about the physical damage. I saw changes in myself. At twelve o'clock I'd find myself lying on a sofa somewhere in a back room. I'd say, 'Just leave me alone!' There was a change in my friends and I realized something was going on that wasn't good. I still drink plenty, but not as much." (Frank, 17)

"I really like beer but I know it can be deadly stuff. You get to operating machinery like a car or something and you could really do some damage to yourself and to other people, to your mind and everything else. But I like the stuff." (Ned, 16)

"Drinking can kill you. Look at all the drunk drivers, the winos, the alcoholics. It's sad. Everybody knows how bad booze is but it seems like half the world still drinks. Two of my friends were killed in an auto accident caused by drinking, and yet the other night I got mad at my mother because she wouldn't let me have a keg of beer at a party at our house." (Benjie, 17)

## Harder Drugs

When we explore the issue of harder drugs, we are dealing with an area that provokes maximum anxiety for both teenagers and parents. Thirty-six percent state that they have never tried any drugs. Among the 56% (42% younger, 70% older) who have tried marijuana are many who have also experimented with speed (also known as "uppers"), depressants (also known as "downers"), LSD, Quaaludes, angel dust, cocaine, Valium, heroin, or methadone. We did not attempt an exhaustive list of all drugs since those available on the street are not always consistent with pharmacological descriptions.

It is clear, however, that there is considerably less involvement with other drugs than with marijuana. Speed and cocaine are the more popular, but they are experimented with by less than 20% of the teenage population, and actually used by less than 10%. This means that half of the experimenters decide to become users.

Teenagers usually seek advice from an experienced peer if they intend to go beyond liquor and marijuana. The hard drug experimenters look for some authoritative source of information regarding the long-term and short-term effects. Like any consumer, they may be concerned about using a "good" product, one that produces the desirable effect and is, at the same time, considered relatively safe. They say it is not possible for them to obtain this information from parents (who they think are inexperienced), or from physicians (who are unlikely to provide them with the facts). Once again, they rely on peers.

Because of past experience, the juvenile underground has begun to communicate information that serious brain damage can occur from glue sniffing; that continued ingestion of amphetamines can become dangerous; and that LSD can lead to very frightening experiences. Although cocaine is popular and not yet considered dangerous, it's unlikely to be used as regularly as marijuana by most teenagers because it is so expensive.

## Speaking from Experience

A few of our interviewees describe the painful realities of their former or present drug experiences. Some have only experimented; others have used drugs regularly. Edward, sixteen, tells us that he was warned about the effects of hard drugs, but had to find out for himself. "I've taken hard drugs two times in my life and don't want to do that again. I took speed once and acid once and had a bad experience with acid. My brother had told me not to touch it, but I kept asking him to get me some. He said, 'I know where it's at, and believe me, you don't want it.' But of course I had to go and try it and fall on my own face. I saw him at college a few weeks ago and told him, 'You were right!' "

Hard drug experimentation reaches across all levels of the socio-economic ladder. Quite a few teenagers speak of doing speed in order to stay up so they can complete school assignments or study for tests. And one sixteen-year-old says that his sister, who's obsessed with weight, gets amphetamines from her "legit doctor" who serves insecure females. "My sister would give me some and I also stole some when I worked in a pharmacy. It was nice and I was really winging, but it's not the kind of thing you want to do often. I've tried Quaaludes and had a few unpleasant experiences with them, although I think I would prefer them over alcohol. It's like drinking without the mess. But I don't do them now." Brenda, eighteen, says, "I've been into all kinds. Ups, downs, hash, acid, ludes, opium, methadone, tacs, speed, black beauties, heroin. Now, once in a while, I smoke marijuana. I'm glad I came off the others because I feel better. Not like I'm dreaming. You're not in the world when you're taking that stuff. I walked around the streets and felt that nobody could see me. I thought I was invisible, from another world, another planet. I liked that at the time because it made me feel better, but I don't like it now."

One fifteen-year-old explains why he believes some white teenagers try harder drugs: "You see, it's like this. A black family, when they're brought up, they know so much about it that they know what to mess with and what not to mess with. They're around it all the time. But a white family, when they're comin' up, they don't know about drugs and their friends could tell them, 'Do this, do that,' and they'll do it. The ghetto consists of winos and drug addicts, you know, acid-takers and all that. So a black family don't want their kids doin' all of that and they tell them not to, and show them what could happen. But a white family, when they get outside and their friends are drinking beer and someone puts something in it, they don't know anything about it. My brothers were always telling me, 'Whatever you do, don't touch no acid.' I see a lot of people trip out over acid and I know what it can do to people. That's why I know not to touch it. White kids who don't know, they try it." (Rory, 15)

Teenagers tell us that lack of money and bad previous experiences are the biggest deterrents to hard drug use. The word seems to have gotten around that angel dust is particularly dangerous. Only 1 out of 6 who have tried angel dust still smokes it. That is 2% of the teenage population—not large in percentage terms, but a significant number of all teenagers.

## Help with Drug and Drinking Problems

### Why They Don't Usually Go to Parents

When teenagers do encounter problems with alcohol or drugs, peers are their most likely source of help. They would rather handle it themselves by confiding in supportive friends or by seeking outside professional help. They feel that parents won't be able to understand, and are likely to disapprove or be hurt.

"I would always go to my close friends for help. I love my parents but there are some things your friends can help you with better than your parents. Mine are a little old-fashioned and they think, 'Other people's kids drink and smoke marijuana. Not mine.' It would hurt them too much." (Cindy, 18)

"I wouldn't go to a friend if I was in real trouble with drinking and drugs, although I have a tendency to go to friends for everything. It's not that they don't pay attention to what you say. It's just that they tell you what you want to hear, and that's not always helpful. I would definitely go to a professional if I couldn't do it on my own." (Hank, 16)

And one fifteen-year-old tells us, "If I knew my mom wouldn't go crazy, I'd go to her. That's what I'd like to do because you should be able to go to your family for help. But most parents would take a fit." And many agree that self-help, meaning recognition of their own problem, is an absolutely essential first step.

The adults who are cited most often as sources of help are those who have personal knowledge about drugs through their own experience; parents of other teenagers who are objective and calm enough to listen and help; and adult friends or professionals who are close enough to care, but not as emotionally involved as parents.

If we parents can listen and discuss the issues calmly, we are more likely to become their confidants. We will also be more likely to hear about our kids' problems before they become so serious that even peers can't cope.

## Guidelines for Parents

No matter what we parents do, our children may use drugs or alcohol. However, since open dialogue and information seem to be the most effective methods of control, we repeat the following guidelines for your consideration.

1. *Discuss all issues openly with your teenagers.* Encourage each person to state his or her feelings and to listen to the other's point of view. Let your children know you value their opinions, even if you do not agree with them. This is important because our survey shows that one major difference between nonsmokers and smokers is that far more nonsmokers believe that their parents listen to their ideas and care about what they think.

2. *Let your children know that you respect them and trust their good judgment and common sense.*

3. *Read, learn, and keep on top of new data and medical information.*

4. *Provide your children with responsible, pertinent information, unaccompanied by lectures and ultimatums.* Acknowledge the inconsistency of some of the previously issued information and the effect this has had on their faith in new information. Encourage them, however, to consider this new material as part of the whole

---

In our surveys, we asked only one question pertaining to cigarette smoking. The results are as follows: 37% of our teenagers smoke cigarettes—40% of the girls and 33% of the boys, with the largest number being the sixteen-to-eighteen-year-old females. Fifty-two percent of the older girls are cigarette smokers.

body of knowledge that will help them to come to rational judgments about marijuana.

5. *Assure them of your love and caring under all circumstances, even when they are not perfect.*

6. *Encourage them to participate in activities that interest them.*

## A Short Glossary of Drug Terms

**Pot, Grass, Herb, Weed, Smoke, Mary Jane, Cheeba, Cannabis, Ghanja, Bhang, Boo**—All are terms for marijuana. Specific usage may depend on geographical location, socioeconomic or racial identification of the user.

**Lid**—An amount of marijuana measured out, smaller than an ounce, for sale.

**Joint, Reefer, Stick**—A marijuana cigarette.

**Hashish or Hash**—The resin of the marijuana plant, more precisely of *Cannabis sativa* or hemp.

**Toke**—An inhalation from a marijuana cigarette. As a verb, to inhale.

**Roach**—The remainder or butt of a partially smoked marijuana cigarette.

**THC**—The active ingredient in *Cannabis sativa* which leads to the high. Sometimes sold in chemically produced pills.

**Burnout**—Someone whose personality has changed negatively as the perceived consequence of excessive drug usage.

**Narcs**—Law agents or those working with them whose job is to discover and report for arrest those who are using illegal drugs.

**LSD**—A hallucinogenic chemically constructed drug of strong potency.

**Acid**—LSD

**Trip**—The experience that follows ingestion of LSD or a comparable hallucinogenic. A "bad trip" is one in which the anxiety or fearful images have predominated.

**Speed**—Amphetamines. These operate as stimulants. Some terms referring to specific amphetamines are "bennies," "dex," "whites," "ups," and "black beauties."

**Head Shop**—A shop in which are sold, among other items, paraphernalia for smoking marijuana or hashish.

**Cocaine**—A white powder which produces a short but euphoric high. It is most frequently ingested by sniffing or "snorting."

**Quaaludes**—A sedative manufactured legally in pharmaceutical laboratories. Used for its high effect. Also known as "ludes."

**Downer**—A sedating or tranquilizing drug. Some terms are "reds," "sopors."

**Angel Dust**—An analgesic used on animals which, in powdered form, is customarily mixed with marijuana and smoked. Frequently reported to induce persistent psychotic states.

# 4

# Teenagers on School

---

- 60% study only to pass tests, not to learn
- 55% admit that they cheat
- 76% say teachers play favorites. 71% believe smart children are the ones most favored
- 54% say teachers don't care at all about students' ideas and opinions

---

## Grades, Grades, Grades

**W**e asked:

---

Do you study:

| | |
|---|---|
| To pass tests | 60% |
| To really learn | 40% |

---

Six out of 10 teenagers study to pass tests, which isn't surprising considering the great emphasis that educators and parents place on grades. According to many of our teenagers, studying is nothing more than intense preparation for the ultimate S.A.T. scores. Kenny is a sixteen-year-old who attends a Philadelphia public high school that prides itself on the number of graduates who enter top colleges. He says, "All I do is study for tests. It's always constant pressure and my parents are on my case every minute. I can honestly see why kids drop out and some even do more drastic things."

Kenny isn't planning to drop out. He's a strong student and copes with the pressure. But what is he learning?

Lucille is in the top 5% of her class. She plans a career in psychology and has to maintain a 3.0 average for the college she hopes to attend. She has developed an effective if unsatisfying method for surviving in the system.

"I've learned how to give a teacher whatever she wants. In tests and in everything else. I know what each one looks for, so to get a good grade I give it to them, even if it's not what I believe I should be doing. I wrote the worst paper in English and I knew it stunk, but I also knew it was the kind of crap the teacher loved." (Lucille, 18)

Other students are not as adaptable as Lucille. So how do they cope? They cheat.

## Cheating

### The Cheaters: Who Are They?

By their own admission, 55% of our teenagers cheat. This practice may not be as American as apple pie, but it comes close. Here are their reasons:

| If you cheat in school, why do you do it? | | |
|---|---|---|
| You don't cheat | | 45% |
| You don't have time to study | 24% | |
| It's easier than studying | 11% | 55% |
| Everyone else does it | 6% | |
| It's the only way you can get a better grade | 14% | |

For most teenagers the pressure to get good grades is constant. And when all their teachers demand results at the same time, many kids simply can't cope with the workload. As one fifteen-year-old explains: "Each teacher thinks they're the only ones giving homework and tests and they pile it on. It should be staggered so that you could take just one test a day and give it all you've got. But the way it is now, it's not humanly possible to study for all the tests, so one subject always gets the short end. So you end up cheating in the subject you didn't have time to study for."

In this matter of cheating, we see a collision between two sets of values: achievement and honesty. We tell our kids that excellent grades are crucial in order to get into a good college or land the right job. And they learn the lesson so well that if they cannot produce the necessary grades on their own, cheating seems to be the only way to live up to adult expectations (to get an A, B, or C) and compete successfully with the other students.

On the other hand, we also teach our kids a code of ethics that includes honesty and obedience to rules, and cheating disturbs us because it's so blatant a violation of that code. Yet how many of us cheat on our income tax returns or exceed speed limits when it suits our purpose? How many of us close our eyes to bribery and corruption in business and from our political leaders? As long as we adults continue to practice deception and downright dishonesty, is it any wonder that our teenagers learn how to bend the laws in order to make their lives easier?

In this collision of values, it seems that achievement wins out. Where, then, does that leave honesty? When our kids cheat, do they feel they are being dishonest, immoral, improper, or unethical?

## Guilty or Not?

Do you feel guilty when you cheat? (Answered only by those who report cheating)

| | | |
|---|---|---|
| Yes | | 42% |
| No | 27% | |
| Not exactly guilty, but afraid of being caught | 20% | 58% |
| Only if it's a big test or paper | 11% | |

Nearly 6 out of 10 students feel little or no guilt, because they can justify cheating for one reason or another. One seventeen-year-old explains that he wasn't willing to spend any time studying for a subject that didn't interest him, so he cheated instead. He was a good student, and he preferred to devote his efforts to the courses he liked. Others have similar feelings about their lack of guilt.

"There are some classes where everyone cheats. I used to take exams where absolutely everyone did. I've never done it alone or maliciously. I don't cheat on exams. In this school the emphasis is on grades and more grades and getting into college." (Lenore, 18)

"How can you feel guilty when they pressure you into getting good grades or else? I'd love to just take a course to really *learn* something and not feel pressured to do well in it. That would make school okay." (Debby, 17)

"I've cheated before. If you can get by with it, it's all right. When I decided to go to a class I had cut the day before, I didn't know about the test the teacher was giving. When I got there, she said, 'Ready for the test?' So I gave this girl a dollar and she gave me her notes and I cheated. I passed the test." (Elvera, 17)

What about those who do feel guilty? Some say that they just don't like themselves when they do it. Sixteen-year-old Doug explains: "Once in a while I will look at a person's paper. I don't like it, though. It makes me feel bad and I hate it in others. I really feel upset. I don't make notes but I go so far as looking at someone's paper." Others, like Clarence, fifteen, won't cheat at all because they believe it's wrong. "What good does cheating do? If you don't know the stuff, you may as well let the teacher know you don't know it. Maybe she can help you. I think more than half the kids in school do cheat, though."

Still others are afraid of being caught or believe it just doesn't work.

"I tried cheating a couple of times but it was no good. I was getting 40s and 50s in Spanish and I used to write answers on my pencils. I had three pencils. But it didn't work. I still got a 54. I didn't feel guilty, though. I just wish it had worked." (Donald, 16)

And eighteen-year-old Abby sums up the cheating situation with a classic comment: "At one time or another, most all kids cheat. If they applied themselves to learning as well as they apply themselves to cheating, they'd probably do very well."

None of us condones cheating. However, there is something out of balance in a system in which pressure is so intense that the satisfactions of learning are often superseded by the pressure to achieve, sometimes at the expense of honesty. As thirteen-year-old Sam tells us, "Grades are everything to my parents. 'What mark did you get on your math test? What mark did you get on your English paper?' I hate that!"

## School as a Social Setting

For most kids school is a necessary evil that has one major benefit: it's a prime place for socializing. In fact, for some it is the only positive aspect. Sixteen-year-old Veronica explains: "My entire life is really school. I don't mean the work, but my friends. My family life is falling apart, so I look forward to seeing my friends and talking to them. Also, it's the only place I can meet boys."

In school kids learn to function as learners, conformers, leaders, social rebellers, sexual beings, and athletic competitors. They discover how to get along and how to solve problems with little, if any, adult help. Indeed, since most adults do not really understand what teenagers face in school today, kids learn to devise their own solutions for survival.

"School is not my favorite thing but at least you get a chance to be with your friends. There are plenty of hassles though, because some of the kids are totally obnoxious. I've had lunch money stolen when I was younger, and I was picked on plenty even last year. But this year it's better. Last year one of the kids who's about six feet tall (I'm short) picked me up and held me over an open stairwell, two stories up. I was sure he was going to drop me down. But I stayed pretty cool and I guess it wasn't interesting enough for him since I didn't scream or anything, so he let me go. Later on I used to give him quarters so he became my 'protector' of sorts. If any of the other kids would go after me, he'd come to my rescue. It worked pretty well until he got kicked out of school. You really have to learn how to survive." (Joseph, 16)

There is no other nonfamily setting that consumes so much of our children's time, involves so much of their attention, and demands so much effort of them. For the average teenager, any prolonged absence means the disruption of social maturation and the development of true independence. In fact, for many kids the actual process of formalized classroom activity is secondary. But how they feel about classroom activity is largely dependent on their opinion of the teacher.

# Teachers

## What Makes a Teacher Good?

| What do you like best about a teacher? He or she: | |
| --- | --- |
| Is fair. Grades fairly and doesn't pick on certain kids | 40% |
| Knows the subject he or she is teaching | 27% |
| Is enthusiastic about the subject she or he is teaching | 26% |
| Will help kids with schoolwork or other problems . . . even after school | 26% |
| Likes kids | 22% |
| Gives almost no homework | 17% |
| Can keep discipline in the classroom | 10% |

Thirteen-to-fifteen-year-olds emphasize fairness, and they also want a teacher who likes kids and is willing to help them with problems. Younger girls are particularly vocal about these qualities since they focus on personal relationships more than do the younger boys. They also seem to be more sensitive about being picked on and embarrassed in the classroom.

For the sixteen-to-eighteen-year-olds, fairness also heads the list, but the college-bound teenagers place even greater emphasis on a teacher's knowledge and enthusiasm. These kids recognize that knowledge is the key to success in future academic life, and as they get older their attention focuses on the course material itself.

When teenagers complain about teachers, parents often suggest that they ignore the teacher's shortcomings and concentrate only on the subject matter. But it's advice our kids find hard to accept because virtually everything they learn in a classroom is filtered through the teacher's personality.

### Fairness Is Number One

We have all heard our kids complain about unfairness at home, so we often tend to minimize similar complaints about unfairness in school. Yet 76% believe that teachers show some sort of favoritism, and they all agree that it creates an uncomfortable classroom climate. Like Annette and Vicky, most kids don't like it, even when they're teacher's pet.

"Teachers all have pets. There's one girl in class that my math teacher really hates and he always picks on her. He says she cheats, when I know everyone in the class does. Everyone. It's so ridiculous. He even called her parents, but no one else's. It's so unfair." (Annette, 14)

"I can't stand an unfair teacher. There shouldn't be a different set of rules for certain kids. I get good grades in English, so he likes me. There are some kids he doesn't like and I could be doing the same thing as they're doing, but they get in trouble and I don't. I was talking to this girl in the back of the class and he doesn't like her. So she got a detention and nothing happened to me." (Vicky, 14)

| To whom do they show favoritism? | |
| --- | --- |
| Smart children | 71% |
| Whites | 15% |
| Blacks or other minorities | 9% |
| Children who are not smart | 5% |

### Smart Kids Get All the Advantages

"The ones who are favored are the ones who know the answers, who want to learn and listen," states sophomore Juliette. Since the primary purpose of school is to inspire students to learn and think on their own, those who conform most closely to that goal are seen as the favored ones. Jack, thirteen, says, "If you're really a good student, teachers will be nice to you. I always handed in my math assignments, but one time I forgot and he didn't give me a zero. It helps if you're bright." But the slower students resent such favoritism, particularly since they're the ones who really need the special attention.

### Sexual Attractions

Students who are sexually attractive to their teachers often receive special treatment. Penny, a maturely built fifteen-year-old, knows exactly why she gets her A's. "Our English teacher is the most unorganized, stupidest person. I haven't learned one thing in four quarters. I get A's in the class, but I don't learn. He flirts like crazy. He loves me and other girls and lets us do anything we want but he doesn't teach us anything." Diane agrees, and points out that both male and female teachers are guilty of this kind of favoritism.

"It always happens. Sometimes they favor the smartest ones, or the prettiest one, or female teachers like boys best sometimes, or gay teachers sometimes like kids the same sex. But I had one teacher, a man, who was in love with me. He always used to write notes to my parents on how I'm working good and how sweet I am. It was so silly." (Diane, 13)

### Racial Favoritism

Twenty-four percent of our teenagers say that racial favoritism exists, and 15% of those believe that whites benefit. Joyce is a white teenager who hopes to study engineering in college. She sees teachers who patronize minorities and she thinks such an attitude is distorted and inappropriate.

"Blacks are either discriminated against in school or treated with favoritism. No middle ground. In this school, teachers go overboard to prove they're not prejudiced. It's sort of liberal guilt. They also try to overrelate to them. One teacher spoke an hour on vocational schools because he thought that would interest the blacks. You have to just teach, not think about what race kids are. They don't have to be treated any differently because no matter where they're from they're acclimated to this school's situation and they have intellectual minds." (Joyce, 18)

In contrast, a Hispanic youngster from New York City believes that discrimination accounts for his failure to get the help he needs.

"I got a reading problem. I read at fifth-grade level. I'm in a special ed class for reading and math. But they're not teaching like they're supposed to. They're just giving me junk work. I like to read health books about the heart, arteries, and the way the body functions. Teachers don't like to help me. Maybe they're prejudiced, especially against blacks and Puerto Ricans. They like their own kind. (J.D., 17)

### The Apple Polishers Still Win Out

The kids who don't "make waves" and who learn how to handle teachers are way ahead of the game. Eighteen-year-old Billy knows the ropes and explains: "Teachers like the kids that psychologically bring them apples, pay them compliments, laugh hardest at jokes, do favors for them. The kid isn't really out to be friends with the teacher, in most cases, but they're out for the grade." He concludes, "I've done my share of teacher bullshitting."

A fourteen-year-old girl agrees. "If you're one of those people that just can't get along with teachers, then it's hard. Teachers don't like that kind of kid and they get lousy grades."

Many of our respondents feel that partiality is simply a part of human nature, and almost all kids accept it as a fact of school life. Nevertheless, they still do not condone it.

## Interesting Teachers Breed Interested Students

Teachers who are enthusiastic about their subjects draw high marks from students. In their classroom, learning can be a truly enjoyable, exciting experience. Terry, a mediocre but diligent seventeen-year-old, says, "If a teacher doesn't love what he is teaching, then he won't teach very well. You may know chemistry, but you've got to love those bloody molecules." Others agree.

"There are a few teachers that are really enthusiastic. If I get them, I'm lucky, because they make the course. That's the best quality in a teacher because if they've got that, then everything else pretty much comes. They can get the students interested and that's what counts." (Jane, 18)

"I have a teacher this year I think is superb. He's so interesting to listen to. He's a man of the world. He's been all over the place and you could sit there and marvel at the way he tells you everything. So different from teachers who just read out of books." (Jeff, 16)

## A Good Teacher Cares

Almost all teenagers express positive feelings about teachers who are willing to help with problems, both in school and after school hours. They like to feel that teachers are interested enough to answer questions and deal with issues that may not be part of the curriculum. They don't like teachers who merely present information and say, "It's your responsibility now." They want learning to be a joint venture. Doris is a seventeen-year-old black student who moved from a predominantly black school into one with a mixed racial population, and she started off with considerable apprehension. She explains: "When I first went to the new school I thought it was going to be so hard because there was mostly whites in the school. I'd never been around so many white people in my life and I didn't think I'd adjust. But after I got there, it was the best school I ever went to. Because of the teachers, mostly. They were really helpful. They had films and they'd go over sheets with us and explain everything, even the simplest little things. Gym and math were my favorites. I never have liked math before, but when I got there I learned to do some math problems I've never seen. I learned a lot."

A teacher's readiness to help is particularly important for slow or poor learners. After years of failure, embarrassment, and discouragement, these kids often pretend that they don't care about school. But they do want help. If a teacher seems unapproachable, uninterested, or impatient, slow learners are afraid to ask for the help they need. As one sixteen-year-old says, "Teachers don't have enough patience. They want you to remember things right away and if you don't, they make you feel stupid. So I don't even try."

Teenagers who aren't doing well in school are usually the ones who create disturbances, start arguments, refuse to follow instructions, or play class clown. Such behavior is both a cry for attention and a way for teenagers to avoid facing their feelings of inadequacy. It takes a great deal of patience and sensitivity to deal with these students, and many teachers simply give up. When that happens, the teenager is likely to give up too, and drop out. Peter, at seventeen, looks back on his experiences in schools in Midwestern cities, and recalls the one teacher who cared and the many who did not: "I always have to have somebody there to explain things to me. I asked for help but it seems like nobody really paid any attention to me. It got me upset so I said, 'Fuck this school. I don't need any of this bullshit,' and I just dropped out. I remember one good teacher. I even remember his name. He was a good man. He always used to sit by me and help me out, explain things to me. I'd say he was the only teacher that did that. I have my sister helping me with some of the work because she's very smart. Sometimes I get books and I sit down and read. I'm gonna give it another shot."

When we ask kids what troubles them about the system, they

are very specific. For example, they know when they are merely being "passed along," and although some may appreciate it for a while, the perceptive ones recognize how damaging this practice really is. When these adolescents leave school, they don't know the basics or understand simple concepts. Fortunately, some, like Florence, eighteen, take steps to correct the situation. "Teachers weren't really fair or right giving grades. They gave me passing grades because I was cooperative. I was always behaving. But they don't give a passing grade for what you know up here, in your head. To be honest with you, I don't know how I got to the tenth grade. Most of the tests I had I flunked. They passed me anyhow. They do that a lot. I felt happy because I passed, but then I didn't feel happy because I didn't really know anything. I think they should have given me a tutor or something to help me out. They were doing it because it was their job and they wanted to get paid, but they weren't really interested in teaching the kids. Some teachers really took the time and were interested. They said, 'Hey, you are not doing good. What's going on?' and I told them, 'I fall behind. The class is too fast.' They would put me into another class. Some don't really care whether you pass or fail. I dropped out of the tenth grade. I'm trying to get my diploma now, and I have to be tested to see what I know because I've been out of school for three years."

## When the Student Feels Liked by the Teacher

Our teenagers appreciate teachers who take the time to know each student. They want to be treated as individuals, not as faceless members of a larger group. And kids are especially pleased if teachers become friends. It can be a very rewarding experience for them. Nancy, seventeen, tells us, "I like a teacher who isn't so high and mighty. I have some teachers who are real friends, and they're totally cool. My creative writing teacher left school but we still keep in touch and write to each other. We even call each other up. I consider her a close friend. And she has a great sense of humor!"

Most of us have pleasant memories of teachers who were relaxed enough to show a sense of humor. Their amusing and sometimes outrageous anecdotes often livened up an otherwise unbearable class. As one fourteen-year-old boy states: "Why shouldn't learning be fun? If you can have a good time and still learn, that's terrific."

"A good teacher is someone who's not cut-and-dried. I have a biology teacher that's really fabulous. She jokes around and teaches at the same time. The kids listen and they pay attention and what she says sinks into your head because she makes you want to learn it." (Sander, 15)

"I like a teacher who does something she wants to do, isn't afraid to be herself, and doesn't worry what the other teachers would think. I had a psychology teacher who loved to sit on the floor with her shoes off. The other teachers used to talk about her and probably thought what she did was awful. But the kids loved her and the other teachers were probably jealous of her." (Ted, 18)

## Kids Want Discipline, but How Much?

Our respondents confirm that very little learning takes place unless a teacher is able to maintain discipline. When we asked them how teachers should handle rowdy students, their answer was usually, "Don't stand for it. Put them out." Many advocate talking to the troublemakers first in order to try to resolve the problem within the classroom. However, if that method fails, removal from the class is in order.

Thirteen-year-old Arthur prescribes yet another tactic: "I think teachers and regular kids should ignore rowdy kids because all they want is attention. I don't think sending them in the hall or to the principal's office is very good because they'll just act like idiots and show off. We've got a point system and at the beginning of the year the kids know that the more they act up, the lower their grade is. When report cards come out and they get a bad grade, they'll know next time not to do it."

If a teacher sets firm, fair standards early in the school year, the classroom situation will be stable, and conducive to learning. Kids may test the limits but will fall into line quickly if the teacher is firm. Although many students laugh and talk about the antics of disruptive students, few appreciate the havoc they cause. Taking advantage of a weak substitute teacher can be fun, but most students definitely do not want a steady diet of leniency.

"I feel sorry for teachers who can't control the class. You have to be strict. My math teacher has rules and if you disobey them, you're in trouble. But she's very fair." (Sonia, 14)

"I had one really hard teacher. She was in her fifties. She really knew what she was talking about and I liked her even though she was hard. The easy teachers you can walk all over, you're not going to learn anything from, so by the time you get to college, you won't know anything." (Judy, 15)

The teachers who command the least respect are the ones who are afraid to get tough for fear that kids won't like them. (The same holds true for parents who fear that setting limits will cause their children to love them less.) But teachers have to be equally careful not to set oppressive limits. A tense atmosphere is not conducive to learning, as Carlotta, seventeen, attests. "I don't like a teacher who is too strict. I have some who emphasize work too harshly and there's fear every time you go in the room. I think that's bad. It's okay to discipline kids but they shouldn't hate to enter your room. How can you learn if you're always scared? I have a friend who gets sick; I mean, literally, sick before almost every class with this teacher."

Some teachers use physical force and ridicule to discipline. Some punish an entire class when one student misbehaves. These are usually the teachers who are unable to maintain a high interest level in the classroom, and our kids deplore such methods. They all believe that an interesting instructor rarely has discipline problems.

Teenagers report that in some schools discipline is almost impossible to maintain, and many sympathize with their teachers. According to one sixteen-year-old girl, most teachers try to keep order, but after a while they lose their patience and she doesn't blame them. And a fourteen-year-old boy agrees that in his school there is no way to control the kids. He describes students' beating teachers in the hallways, slashing teachers' tires, and stealing their cars. He doesn't think it will change, and adds, "There are just some kids who will never respect authority, and sometimes they're the ones who end up in jail."

## Do Teachers Encourage Students to Think or to Parrot?

54% of the students say that teachers either don't care about hearing their ideas and opinions, or put down their views

46% say that teachers respect their ideas and opinions

Learning is a two-way process; an interchange of thoughts and ideas rather than a simple transfer of material from one head to another. Do all teachers encourage such interaction? Unfortunately not, according to our respondents.

Teenagers tell us that some teachers are too insecure about their own ideas to accept someone else's. Thus, any sort of two-way discussion is threatening. Should an open discussion spark controversy, it might disrupt the peaceful continuity of the classroom and the prescribed curriculum. Others say that teachers are so concerned about getting through the necessary material that they're afraid to take the time to hear the students' views. As one sixteen-year-old states: "Why should we take their views on a subject and not tell ours?"

In contrast, when a teacher encourages an exchange of opinions, students develop confidence in the validity of their ideas, and learning becomes a truly exciting experience.

"My social studies teacher was great. He had a terrific sense of humor and he loved to hear us get up and make fools of ourselves. He'd ask us what we thought about the President or Russia or the Arabs or anything, and he was really interested. He used to argue with us sometimes but nobody minded. One time I told him what an ass I thought Ted Kennedy was and we must have talked about it for an hour. It was great." (Tony, 17)

"I like teachers who take you for what you are and don't try to change you. Most of them play a role of molding and forming you. But the good ones forget all that crap and just talk to you and listen to what you have to say." (Todd, 16)

In short, teenagers do not respond to instructors who seem distant and unapproachable. They resent being talked down to; they are unhappy about being taught from outdated books; and they know when the quality of teaching is not up to standards they want or expect.

## Do Teachers Enjoy Teaching?

Surprisingly, 65% of teenagers say yes. Jodie is typical of those who believe that teachers like their jobs.

"I have a teacher who is sensational. You just know she loves what she's doing, and I really look forward to her class even though I don't like French. But she makes a real effort to keep it interesting. She brings in records of French singers and movies of Paris, and I think she relives her experiences in France when she's with us." (Jodie, 17)

Jodie is indeed fortunate to have the kind of teacher who makes school an adventure. But what about the remaining 35%? We may safely conclude that they feel they are spending their learning time with people who do not enjoy them or the subject matter. Kids are hard to fool. They know when teachers would prefer to be somewhere else, and many feel their teachers are in the classroom simply because they couldn't get a job in another field. One of our respondents tells us that some of her teachers would be better qualified as ski instructors, secretaries, or waiters. Another young lady believes, "Some teachers may have liked their jobs when they first started, but when they found out they didn't like it, they were too old to do anything else. I always hope I don't get the ones who wish they weren't teachers."

Ernie, a fifteen-year-old in a vocational program, condemns his school experience in sharp terms. "School stinks! I hate it. Our school is very strict. Teachers are there not because they want to be, but because they have to be. It's a way to make money."

However, many teenagers realize that teaching can be frustrating and ungratifying. One sixteen-year-old offers a very perceptive commentary on the plight of teachers. "Most of the teachers I had didn't seem to enjoy it. They looked like it was a very large pain in the ass by the third class. I'm sure they liked the idea of educating kids so I guess they liked teaching in general. But it seems like more teachers must have nervous breakdowns and go bitter, fast. I can't imagine having to put up with a class of screaming kids. Kids don't have any respect." (Al, 16)

Teachers who enjoy their work can contribute something special to a teenager's life. They have an unparalleled opportunity to encourage creativity, independent thought, and intellectual achievement. Our youngsters want the kind of first-rate instruction that can come only from bright, motivated teachers who deserve our respect and encouragement. Parents cannot afford to settle for mediocrity. When your child has a superior teacher, don't hesitate to compliment the teacher verbally and in writing and let the school know, too. A teacher, like any other individual, works harder when he or she knows that the work is appreciated.

Similarly, if you are dissatisfied with the quality of teaching, don't be afraid to express your misgivings and discuss your point of view with the teacher and/or other school authorities. If we do not take an active part in our children's education, how can we expect the quality of education to improve? We must let educators know that we care and that we are anxious to share in the total educational process.

## Tuning Out or Turning On

What can we do about teenagers who are "turned off" to school and learning, who are disinterested, who are not working up to their capabilities? The first step is to uncover the reason, and in most cases there's no simple answer. Sometimes parents themselves are at fault. With the best intentions in the world, parents tell their kids, "You have to learn to do things you don't like to do," and all too often school falls into that category. Parents foster this attitude because they want their teenagers to realize that schoolwork must take precedence over hobbies and pleasurable activities. But it can backfire if the kids begin to equate school with the sacrifice of all pleasure and fun.

Kevin, fifteen years old, was brought to the office of a psychologist. He had a record of thirty class cuts during the first half of the year, and had been neglecting his studies for many years. His parents described him as "lazy," but he had a great deal of energy for the activities that interested him. He collected comic books and had boxes filled with them, some as old as fifteen years. He had amazingly well-ordered files for his collection, with identifying dates and numbers on each book. He knew exactly what he owned and the market value of each. He corresponded with other collectors and maintained an active mail trading-and-selling business. He was also an avid hiker and camper and could identify plants and flowers as well as his science teacher could.

Kevin was not lazy; he simply refused to give up the things he really liked in order to succeed in school. Why did he think such a tradeoff was necessary? His parents had drilled into him the belief that the "enemy" was self-satisfaction, fun, and enjoyment, and these had to be fought by self-denial. Although his teachers had tried to tap his resources by making use of his organization abilities and encouraging his interest in science, it was too late. He had already tuned out school to protect himself.

His achievements elsewhere demonstrated that he had both ambition and motivation. He simply needed the right environment. The psychologist helped Kevin's parents to find a special program in a school that would allow his talents to expand into many areas. The process was a slow one and required skill and patience on the teacher's part. Kevin's defenses were strong, and he had to discover learning could be an adventure, not a chore, as his parents had insisted. Kevin's parents were urged not to pressure him, but to encourage his self-motivated curiosity. They had to develop faith in his ability to choose the right path for himself.

Learning disabilities often account for a student's withdrawal. Others have hearing or vision loss, and some suffer from mild neurological distress that affects concentration and subjects the child to distractions that are ignored by most other children. Often, these handicaps aren't properly diagnosed by parents or teachers, and a bright youngster can reach age thirteen or fourteen and still read four or five years below grade level. A child like this faces daily discouragement, and avoiding school may seem to be the only answer.

Some kids just do not function successfully in a system geared to top-level academic achievement. When A students get all the praise, the mediocre or slow student needs a lot of family or outside support to keep going.

The range of unidentified reasons for nonlearning is enormous. For example, Susan picked up knowledge rapidly and was already accustomed to family stardom by the time she entered first grade. She was a first-rate student until she encountered heavier competition from equally bright children. She was so shaken by being less than number one that she gave up, claiming that school was not important. But Susan was lucky. She was encouraged to enter an Alternative High School Program.

This type of program is being offered in the more progressive school systems throughout the country. It is particularly helpful for those students who are "turned off" to regular education because it's not challenging enough, or for those students who have had little success in the traditional classroom situation. Classes are small and teachers encourage class participation and offer students individual attention. The teenager considers the teachers as friends, very often referring to them on a first-name basis. The emphasis is on independent study of subjects that are particularly interesting and meaningful to the student. The basics are not neglected, but they are often presented more creatively. One class was having problems with math and the teacher suggested that they set up a school store. The kids managed the store, worked as cashiers, bought and sold merchandise (school supplies), maintained ledgers, and kept profit and loss statements. This practical application approach made the kids realize that knowledge of math was vital to success in the real world.

In Susan's program, the basics were covered, but she also concentrated on the areas she enjoyed: the history of the women's movement and filmmaking. In addition, Susan attended group "rap" sessions two days a week to discuss with her peers the fear of being a second-rater.

## Helping the Underachiever

Clearly, the reasons for poor school performance are complex and numerous. The standard explanations—"he's lazy," or "she's a slow developer"—are usually the wrong ones. Even the students pick them up and explain their difficulties in the same terms. But such facile answers rob the child of the help he so desperately needs. As soon as the child seems to lose interest or begins to flounder, an intensive diagnosis should be made. The longer the problem persists, the more difficult it will be to get the child back on the track. The massive absentee and dropout rates in the big-city schools are often attributed to school laxity, parent unconcern, juvenile abandon, or society's relaxed moral standards. Although these all play a part, an early effort to discover and remedy a child's learning difficulties is the only real solution.

## Guidelines for Parents

1. *Speak with your child to try to discover what he or she feels is the problem.*
2. *Listen to your child's complaints about the teachers, the curriculum, the other students.* They may be true. Teachers are not always right. The curriculum may, indeed, be boring or too difficult. Other students may be tormenting your youngster. Thirteen-year-old Don was so afraid of the boy who sat next to him in class that he started cutting the class. He didn't tell anyone because his father would have thought he was a sissy. He continued to cut until the school secretary called home and discussed the problem with Don's mother. After she talked to Don she met with a school counselor and had him transferred to another section.

Nathan, fifteen, seemed to have lost all interest in school. He kept complaining that his English teacher went over last year's material, and that his math teacher constantly made mistakes. His mother told him if that was the case he should do very well because he'd know the material inside out, even better than the teacher. Unfortunately, Nathan quickly became bored and stopped paying attention in class, and his grades suffered. By the middle of the year, Nathan's mother was worried and she investigated her son's claims. She discovered that the math teacher was being replaced, and that other parents were upset by the repetition in the English course. She and the other dissatisfied parents were instrumental in having the course revised.

3. *Don't hesitate to discuss your child's learning problem with school personnel: teachers, guidance counselors, principals, or coaches.* When parents and professional educators work as a team, they are more likely to come up with effective solutions. Talk about the course of study, the teenager's special interests, motivation (or lack of it), interaction with teachers and other students, and study habits. Check for hearing and vision deficiencies.

4. *Examine the home situation.* Are there new and unusual tensions and stresses? Unhappiness between parents? Disappointing love relationships? Does the teenager have too many out-of-school responsibilities, or too few to make him a responsible person? Are parents pressuring to the point of rebellion? All of these situations contribute to the underachieving problem.

5. *Seek professional help.* Have the teenager tested and counseled, if necessary. School difficulties may be the result of deeper emotional problems that will surface once the teenager feels comfortable talking with an objective third party. Dyslexia and other learning disabilities that may have been overlooked in school may be diagnosed by a therapist or a professional specializing in learning disabilities.

6. *None of these suggestions is foolproof, but they're worth a try.*

## What Happens When Parents Pressure Too Much?

Because our society places so much emphasis on achievement, it's natural that parents will pressure kids to succeed in school. When such pressure becomes overwhelming, teenagers fight back. Some may reject the pressures by claiming they don't care about college or high-paying jobs. Others refuse to discuss school at all because they hate the nagging that invariably accompanies such discussions.

"I'm not a super-brain, but I could get passing grades in school if I try. I work hard in school and I come home and expect to relax a little bit. Go visit some friends, whatever. But she says, 'You're not going out of this house.' She says that I have to stay in even when I don't have any homework. It's like, 'Woman, get off my case.' " (Wally, 15)

Myron, sixteen, gets annoyed when his mother constantly questions him about school as soon as he gets home. He doesn't want to talk about it, and compares his situation to his father's. He explains that his father gets the same treatment when he gets home from work, and it drives them both crazy. They look forward to being home and want to leave school and the office pressures behind them.

In many cases, parents simply are not aware of the pressures and general school policies with which their youngsters have to cope. Irene, fourteen, says that her mother is more understanding when she knows what's going on in school. "If I feel the teacher is putting too much pressure on me, and my mom says, 'Why can't you do good in this course?,' I'll get her to talk to the teacher. Then she'll understand what kind of person the teacher is and maybe she'll even sympathize with me. She's done it a couple of times and last time she said, 'Wow, this guy's a nut!' "

"If you say to your parents, 'Oh, I have so much work to do,' they won't say. 'Oh, that's too bad.' They say, 'Well, do it.' You want to express the fact that you're really bogged down and you can't stand it, but you can't get that across to them because you know that once you tell them, they'll keep nagging you to do it." (Miriam, 17)

Many parents feel that if their child does not perform well in school, this lack of excellence reflects on them. But such an attitude is counterproductive. Our kids have to learn that working produces results. As thirteen-year-old Monica states: "My parents don't give me a hard time because they know that if I don't work, it's my problem. If they bugged me about it, I'd probably resent it and end up studying less."

Like Monica, seventeen-year-old Simon recognizes that schoolwork is *his* job, not his mother's. At his instigation, he and his mother have worked out a compromise. "Every day for ten years my mother has been saying the same thing. 'Well, Simon, how was school? Do you have any homework? Any tests to study for?' Finally last year (and I don't know why I waited so long) I told her, 'Look, Ma. I hate when you ask me the same damn thing every day. If I have homework, I'll do it. If I have a test, I'll study for it. Don't bug me anymore. If I get good grades, promise me you'll never ask again. If I don't you can start asking.' And it worked. She's never said another word about it again."

Simon's solution is an effective one if parents can be sure that less bugging will lead to more studying. But that doesn't always happen, even if parents do adhere to the "get off my case" request. Some kids actually use parental nagging as an excuse to avoid facing other pressures and problems. By telling parents that it's their fault, that their incessant nagging makes studying impossible, kids take themselves off the hook. Thus, nagging may be adding to, rather than helping, the problem.

For parents, it's a "damned if I do, damned if I don't" situation. Will nagging help or will it hurt? Because they're not sure, many parents seesaw between the extremes: backing off in the hope that the child will tackle homework responsibly, and renewing pressure tactics when that doesn't work. This can turn into a frustrating process of reminding, encouraging, or suggesting, which usually creates conflict. What can we do?

We can find out why the teenager is neglecting homework or studying. However, don't always expect his or her cooperation in such an effort. Frequently, on some unconscious level, he or she is reluctant to do homework because it is easier not to study than to wrestle with feelings of stupidity and helplessness. But be persistent. When we understand the root of their problem, we can cope with it more effectively.

## School Scorecard

In view of all we've heard from our teenagers about teachers, grades, and pressure, how do they rate their total school experience?

| Do you feel that school is: | |
| --- | --- |
| Necessary | 42% |
| Boring | 27% |
| Puts too much pressure on kids | 22% |
| Interesting | 21% |
| Challenging | 19% |
| Frustrating | 15% |
| A waste of time | 9% |
| (Some respondents checked more than one answer) | |

Not surprisingly, only a little over 4 out of 10 believe that school is really necessary. We may take some comfort in the fact that only 9% consider it a waste of time. The positive responses still outweigh the negative, but it's a close contest. College-bound students more than any other group believe that school is necessary, but almost an equal number of them find school boring as find it interesting. The sixteen-to-eighteen-year-old boys find school the most boring, and the thirteen-to-fifteen-year-old girls consider it the most challenging.

How can we make school more appealing? By offering courses that interest our teenagers.

## Courses for Everyday Survival

| Which of these subjects do you wish your school offered: | |
| --- | --- |
| How to go about getting a job | 43% |
| Sex, marriage, and family planning | 35% |
| How to manage money | 26% |
| How to get along with people | 18% |
| House and car maintenance | 12% |
| How to raise children | 10% |

These rankings remain consistent for all our respondents regardless of age or sex with one exception; girls reverse the last two categories. These are solid, practical issues for the adolescent growing into adulthood. There is no doubt that kids should be taught English, math, science, history, and languages. But why not add courses that will teach kids how to survive and function in society? Many high school graduates cannot write a check. They don't know how to buy a house; what to look for in an apartment lease; how to budget and manage finances; how to administer simple first-aid procedures; how to write an effective resumé. Many schools are now offering courses in these practical areas, but many more are not. One eighteen-year-old from a private school comments on some of the problems of a public school education:

"Classes are too big and teachers are so poorly prepared. It's changing, but the kind of education they offer is so backward. They're teaching kids things that don't mean anything to them. It doesn't match up with their real-life situation, so they don't care about it. They're not going to listen to a course in ancient history, when all they really care about is getting a job when they get out. That's the beginning and it gets worse." (Annie, 18)

Some students would like to see more variety in the curriculum and would like to be able to choose courses of special interest to them. Jordan, seventeen, complains that he was "bumped" from two courses he had been looking forward to taking since he was a freshman. One was an English course on literature of the 1960s; the other, a psychology course. He explains; "I couldn't believe it. Finally I had found two courses that interested me. I had gone through four years of high school taking required courses I hated. Then the head of curriculum planning said that because so many kids wanted to take those two courses, some kids would have to be dropped because the classes were overloaded. Can you believe it? Instead of adding an extra course so everyone who wanted it could take it, they were thinking of dropping both courses because it created too much hassle! And then they wonder why kids hate school!"

It's something we adults should think about.

## More Than Just Books

Our teenagers want to be active participants in classes and in school as a whole. They talk about experimenting, touching, doing things instead of merely reading about them. They would also like to help develop and administer school policy.

"Kids shouldn't have to just sit and listen to lectures. In European history we spent a week playing a game called Diplomacy. It made the subject more realistic and easy to understand in a practical way. Otherwise, if you sit there and just take notes, it goes in one ear and out the other. You might get A's, but it's no help." (Tom, 16)

Many of them enjoy field trips and other out-of-school excursions that offer new and different experiences and involve them in activities beyond the purely academic. But not everyone agrees. Some believe that schools have too many extracurricular activities and neglect the real purpose of education.

"Schools are basically supposed to be something where you go to learn, prepare yourself for life, a job or whatever. Nowadays schools want to do so much to bring kids in, like they put in extra sports and activities just to attract more people. That doesn't do any good because you might have a kid who's a great basketball player, but never learns anything. Let's say he winds up in college (which he shouldn't) just because of basketball. Then if he doesn't make it, he has nowhere to go because he's not intelligent. The people who are not going to learn are going to mess it up for everybody else and they should be put out. I like learning, and some schools are better at that than others. I liked going to my junior high every day because it was a good school. It was for advanced kids and you didn't see anybody that would mess up the school. You had to do good and they wanted you to really learn. You worked together to make it a good school. Now you see kids smoking and people who don't want to go to school, and they stay outside all day. Maybe all kids who want to learn should go to special schools, and ones who don't care about learning should be lumped together and sent somewhere else. It's unrealistic, but it's a thought." (Paolo, 17)

### Single-Sex Schools

Many teenagers don't favor noncoeducational schools. Some parents think the schools are excellent because there are fewer distractions, but the teenagers themselves feel that single-sex schools create socially immature individuals. The younger adolescents do not look upon the schools as unfavorably as do the older ones, which is understandable since the opposite sex is not yet as important to the younger teenagers. Robert's comment is quite typical of the sixteen-to-eighteen-year age group, many of whom transfer to co-ed schools in their high school years. "All boys' schools should be outlawed," he claims. "It's unnatural. All boys' or all girls' schools create socially backward kids. There has to be normal contact between the sexes. I'd never send my kid to a school that wasn't co-ed. School might be tolerable if it was co-educational."

But whether or not a school is co-educational, the major complaints are the same: the pressures of the grading system; the heavy test and homework schedules; the teachers; the curriculum. However, one of our participants thinks she has a solution to the "I hate school" syndrome. Sally, fourteen, believes, "If kids took a year off from school and would go out and work and not live at their home, and if they had to feed themselves for a year, they'd see how much better it is in school. They'd see how many more people you meet in school and how much easier it is. Then they'd understand that if you learn more, you get a good chance at college and you'll be financially better off. You'll also feel better about yourself. I think that would work, to some extent at least."

## Is There Room for Individuality?

There are schools throughout the country that offer superb instruction, but many of our schools are beset by long-term conflicts that have never been resolved. They affirm their dedication to individuality and creativity, but that message is not coming across to the majority of our kids. Of course specific educational standards must be met, but let's leave room for the child who views things from a different perspective; the child who questions and doesn't accept pat answers.

What happens to those five- and six-year-olds who watch older siblings march off to school and can't wait to get there themselves? Where is the inquisitiveness and sheer joy of learning that leads preschoolers to bombard their parents with those "why" and "how" questions? All too often, that enthusiasm disappears or gets sidetracked as kids go through the structured educational system and emerge as "educated" teenagers. One seventeen-year-old senior who attends a private school tells us, "I can't believe my English teacher. We're studying the great thinkers and philosophers of the world like Plato and Socrates. So instead of giving us a test that would let us think (like asking us to interpret something), he gives us a test where we're supposed to spit out stuff—straight from the book. Just plain memorization. No thinking. The teacher is too damn lazy to dream up a test that's interesting and lets us use our brain. I guess that would be too hard for him to mark." But perhaps the saddest and most important comment comes from an eighteen-year-old girl who recognizes the power of educators to stimulate creativity or destroy it completely. Hers is a thought that is echoed by many young people we interviewed.

"The way school is now, it sits on any kind of individuality. It knocks all the energy out of you. When you write a really humorous, unique composition and the teacher shows no appreciation because you happen to misspell a few words or she happened to be looking for a more serious approach, it makes you realize how futile it all is. I stopped writing 'funny and clever' (which is my nature) and started to give her what she wanted: unhumorous and dull. Just like everybody else writes. I got A's like crazy, but so what? My parents were really disgusted. They said, 'There goes the future Woody Allen.' But we realized you have to play the game. Give them what they want. Maybe college will be different." (Joan, 18)

# 5

# Teenagers on Friends

• 88% of all teenagers will see their friends even if their parents
disapprove
• 72% of teenagers believe that when parents disapprove of their
friends, "bad influence" is the reason
• The majority of teenagers would never tell on a friend unless it
was a clear case of life-and-death

Young children need the security of a home in which Mother
and Father provide protection, reassurance, and total shelter;
not just physical shelter, but shelter from the competitiveness, de-
structiveness, and loneliness found in the uncaring world outside.
But as children get older they have to learn how to cope with that
outside world on their own. And if home and family become the
predominant arena for working out conflicts and struggles, the child
won't be able to handle adult experiences. That's why friendships
are so vital to growth. Our teenagers need connections with peers
who are experiencing the same phases and problems. Through their
friends our kids learn that they can survive apart from us. They
learn how to function as social beings while maintaining their individuality. And the friendships that are constructive are those which
permit the free exploration of both those critical needs.

## Everybody Needs a Friend

Parents are great for information and protection, but only another ten-year-old can share the delight of baseball cards, jokes

about ugly teachers, and the rare and wild excitement of experiencing something forbidden. Friendships teach children how to live and share in a world with others. Young children learn that there are people like them and different from them. And they learn that the "outside world" won't treat them with the special love and care that parents provide. In short, it's part of growing up.

Deciding whether to go along with or resist what a friend is doing is solid training for building one's own set of standards. Without that opportunity, children run the dangers of either rigidly following parental thinking or of automatically opposing it in order to express their feelings of independence.

Teenagers tend to seek friends according to their needs, and because their needs differ from ours, we do not always understand or approve of their choices.

"I would classify my friends as misfits. People that just don't fit into cliques. They're not party people. They're the ones that don't go out much. My mother didn't like a lot of them because she thought they were weird and obscure. I think the one thing she's glad about is that there's no drug scene. My little sister is into that now. So at least she knows I'm not doing that. But she thinks they're all juvenile delinquents and wishes I had more normal, 'better' friends. I've never had any. Misfits value their friends more; they invest a lot more in them because they can't have a lot of little acquaintances (like me, when I was fat and had a bad weight problem). Misfits have fewer but better friends. I consider my friends earthy people who I can talk to. I could never do that before. I'm not as lonely now." (Tom, 18)

"This friend and I were really tight, and my parents were having a fit. I liked him because he was a sensational dirt rider [motorcyclist] and he was the only one who could keep up with me at the track. That was the only reason we were friends, but my parents were always getting on my case about his drugs. They were so afraid he was going to influence me the wrong way, which was so dumb because if I was going to do drugs (which I don't), I would have done them with or without me knowing that friend. When I finally told them I had no intention of not riding with him, I think they got the picture." (Dennie, 16)

As Dennie's comment indicates, most teenagers enjoy friends who share their interests. Occasionally they do choose friends with totally different interests, or friends who have qualities that they themselves lack. A very shy child may hang out with a boisterous one in the hope that the friend's self-assurance will rub off on him. The rowdy child, meanwhile, may enjoy having an admirer and someone to push around. If a child is a newcomer to a neighborhood or school, he or she may latch onto the first person who appears to be friendly. In any case, an adolescent's choice of a friend is no more mysterious than an adult's.

## Parental Interference

### Nearly 9 Out of 10 Teenagers Refuse to Listen When Parents Complain About Friends or Try to Interfere

Eighty-eight percent of our respondents tell us loud and clear: "I'll see my friends regardless of what my parents say." Of these, 56% would try to talk their parents into changing their minds. They prefer to see their friends openly and would like to feel comfortable bringing them home. But if their parents continue to disapprove, they'll see their friends anyway. Only 12% would stop seeing their friends, and by the time they've reached age sixteen, the number of those who would go along with their parents drops to 9%.

Their outrage is evident. They have established their own criteria. They have made their connections and they're not about to let parents interfere. They're willing to talk about it, but only to convey their point of view.

"They always find something wrong with one of them. He either smokes pot or is black, or something else. I lost so many friends from them doing it. They'll say I can't see someone, so that means he can't come over to my house. That means I have to sneak out and they'll call the other house and find out I'm there. I should be able to pick my own friends. God, I'm sixteen." (Andy, 16)

"My mother should realize that if I think someone is a bad person, then I'm not going to be friends with them. My mother even said that she thinks she should pick the person I'm going to marry. Do you believe that?" (Sandra, 18)

How effectively do parents' reasons stand up under their teenagers' scrutiny?

### 72% Think That Parents Oppose Their Friends Because the Friends Are a Bad Influence

All parents want their children to have friends who are polite, who don't drink or smoke, who are kind, honest, and bright—in general, "good influences." We are so afraid that if our kids' friends are less than perfect, they will lead our children astray. But teenagers resent this reason because it implies that they are too weak to stand on their own, to hold on to their own convictions.

"Influence, influence. That's all my mom says. Parents don't think you have a brain of your own!" (Alexandria, 15)

"Another kid can't really make you do anything you don't want to do, but my mom doesn't understand that. I hung around with two kids who shoplifted quite a bit but there was no way I would do that. They knew it. They were two nice kids who had a problem. They finally got caught, which was good, and they're still my friends although I have to see them when my parents aren't around." (Susie, 17)

Cindy, sixteen, who ran away from home, feels that her parents object to all of her friends. "My mother blames my friends for everything I do. She thinks they talked me into leaving home. My mother always compared me to everyone else. I asked her not to. She would say, 'Oh, why can't you be like Mrs. Toros's daughter. She's so nice and has such nice friends. Instead, you're hanging around with those friends of yours.' To this day, I can't bring them home. She won't accept them."

It's a dilemma all parents face: we want to protect our kids and encourage their independence at the same time. But when our kids get into trouble, the urge to protect them intensifies and their friends can become convenient scapegoats, permitting us to explain or overlook objectionable behavior in our own children. When we do this we are, in effect, allowing our kids to escape responsibility for their own actions.

## Shifting the Focus

If our adolescents are smoking too much, running away, or cutting classes, and we can't deal with the problem, it's easy to blame their friends. "If it weren't for them, he wouldn't be caught up in those dangerous habits." Of course, children can and do influence one another adversely, but if we blame all our youngster's actions on peer influence we are fighting the wrong enemy. If we do succeed in breaking up a friendship, it's likely to be a meaningless victory, since our teenager will go on to form new friendships that answer precisely the same needs. And instead of uncovering and dealing with the real issues—our adolescent's needs and inner feelings—we create a barrier of resentment and distrust.

For example, Roger, fifteen, was having trouble keeping up with his schoolwork. He had failed two subjects. Instead of seeking help, he avoided the situation altogether by pretending that school didn't matter. He began to associate with kids who cut classes frequently and used drugs. But his new friends were not the real problem. Roger's feeling of inadequacy was the issue that had to be faced and resolved.

In some instances, our teenagers' actions may express their desire for a new image or identity. They are, after all, struggling to define themselves as individuals. A teenager who feels cramped by the good-boy image on which he prided himself when younger may become rebellious as a way of moving toward greater individuality.

Cliff will be sixteen in a few months. He had been the class "brain" throughout elementary and junior high schools. Growing up in a suburb of a large Southern city, he has known most of his classmates since kindergarten. His reputation as the class genius both hampered and supported him. His sports participation was limited. During the years when scholastic achievement was far less important than throwing a football or winning a playground fight, Cliff was teased and called "faggot" by many kids. When parties and dating started in junior high school, he was ignored. He had friends, but they were studious and unpopular. Now Cliff wants something different. He doesn't know how to break the mold, but he knows he has to become more daring. He came home drunk one night. A few weeks later his mother found marijuana rolling papers in his room.

How can his parents tell whether Cliff is permanently deserting the standards which were so important earlier, and which made his parents so proud of him? There is no complete answer to the question at this point in his involvement. His parents cannot simply press for a return to the behavior and friends he had in the past. He is trying to find out who he is. Just how he is going to do that is unclear to him and to his parents. But if they can support him in his exploration and recognize that he has to limit his total concentration on studying and conformity, he will be able to find his way without having to fight his parents in order to be free.

The desire to become friendly with kids who seem braver or more rebellious may be a sign that a teenager wants to accelerate the necessary separation from parents. If we try to dissolve the objectionable friendship by forbidding it, our condemnation may make it all the more attractive. However, if we address ourselves to the need that the friendship satisfies, we are in a better position to deal with the situation. *Ask your teenager what qualities he or she likes in the friend you worry about.* Hearing his or her views may give you additional insight into the reasons for the friendship.

You're more likely to strike a responsive chord by discussion and reasoning than by unyielding rule-setting. If you fear, for example, that your daughter will be sexually exploited and abused by an older and more experienced new boyfriend, discuss the situation with her and offer her your knowledge and help with contraception if that appears appropriate. In contrast, if you simply forbid the relationship, you have lost the opportunity to convey your viewpoint or discuss any questions she might have about the relationship.

### When Parents Say Friends Aren't "Good Enough"

Vince, a sixteen-year-old doctor's son, explains how he feels about his parents' desire to choose his friends. "As far as my father is concerned, none of them are good enough. He finds fault with most of my friends. He objects to my best friend because he doesn't have enough money. I don't give a shit though. I see who I want and tell him that I'm old enough to pick my friends and make my own mistakes. Actually, the ones he likes are the worst, but he doesn't know it. When they're around him they're polite and he thinks they're okay. The ones he doesn't like are really good kids."

If we look back on our own friendships, we can recall friends to whom our parents objected. Remember how we resented the suggestion that we give them up and choose "better" ones? Very often we knew all along that the so-called better friends were engaging in activities that would have shocked our parents. Are we so naïve as to believe that things are any different today just because they involve our own kids? Can't we remember that the quickest death-blow to a friendship was a parent's suggestion that a certain child would be a "nice" friend?

When we disapprove of our kids' friends because we fear that their family's problems may influence our own children, we are doing a great injustice to both our kids and their friends. Two six-teen-year-olds who live in urban areas explain their views.

"My best friend's parents are really messed up and my mom and dad don't think I should see her. What has her parents' problem got to do with her and with me? If anything, I should be even nicer to her. My parents are afraid her problems will rub off on me some-how. I told my mom that she needs a friend and we should help her, not desert her." (Marilyn, 16)

"One time my parents didn't want me to see a friend because the girl's brother had been in trouble. The girl's not bad just be-cause her brother is. She's really nice and I wanted to keep her but my mom didn't want me to associate with her. They always say, 'Be nice to people,' but they only mean it when it suits them." (Angela, 16)

## Other Parental Objections

What other reasons do parents offer for their objections? Ac-cording to our respondents: they just don't like the way the friends look (7%); the friends are of a different race or religion (4%); the friends are not smart (4%). And 13% say their parents give no rea-sons at all.

### Physical Appearance

The matter of appearance is ambiguous. Undeniably, the man-ner in which a person presents himself to the world is a nonverbal description of himself. In the past, wearing old clothes, long hair, or sloppy jeans, may have been a sign of disrespect or not caring. But today it may be a deliberate effort to state one's individuality (or in some instances conformity).

Sandy, fifteen, tells us, "My mom always tells me not to judge a book by its cover. But she judges my friends by the way they look. I think that's hypocritical!" Another teenager says that one of her friends is not allowed in the house because he looks sloppy and re-pairs cars. Her parents won't accept the fact that the young man also is interested in art, medicine, and family heirlooms. According to sixteen-year-old Jean, he is more well read than any member of her family, but he is rejected because of his appearance and Jean considers this extremely unfair.

Jesse, fifteen, gives another example: "I have a friend who but-ters up my mom and she loves him. He offers to help her around the house and she thinks he's the greatest kid. She should only know! But my best friend dresses kind of sloppy and his English isn't too good, but he's really a nice kid and a very good friend. All she sees about him is the way he looks. He doesn't do any of the things (like pot) that the friend my mom likes does. Parents really don't know how kids are with other kids. They just see them when they're around the house."

### Racial and Religious Prejudices

Occasionally, parents make judgments that are based on standards entirely different from those their teenagers hold. This is starkly illustrated when teenagers believe that adults reject their friends on racial or religious grounds. Our kids are sharp observers. Although we may rationalize our prejudices with any number of cushions, camouflages, or denials, our teenagers know our real feelings. The incidence of high school racial battling indicates that our youngsters certainly are not free of prejudices and racial hostilities. But teenagers don't like to think their parents are bigoted. They prefer to believe that parents are above that kind of narrow thinking.

"My mom couldn't stand my friend, Tania, even though she had only heard rumors about her from her friends. We're Protestant and Tania was one of my Jewish friends. I brought her home with me one day last week and my mother couldn't get over her. (She was raised on a kibbutz.) My mother thought she was so polite and 'cultured' and I think she even hopes some of it will rub off on me." (Patricia, 15)

"I've got a lot of black friends. One night my parents were having a party here when Winfield came home with me. My mother screamed, 'Get him out of the house right now, right now! My friends are here!' I totally object to any criticism and bigotry on their part. I said, 'No, we're staying right here; I'm not getting him out of the house.' They got really mad and threatened to ground me, but they didn't. They are not picking my friends for me." (Gregg, 15)

And one sixteen-year-old has difficulty understanding what he feels is an irrational and inconsistent prejudice. "I'm in a rock group and our singer is a girl I have wanted to date for a long time. When I first met her parents, they seemed like nice people despite all of the negative stories I had heard from Jill. When I asked her what her parents' initial reaction was to me, she told me they said I seemed like a nice boy. But when she told her parents that I was taking her to a movie, they said she must be joking, that they wouldn't allow her to see me because I wasn't Jewish enough. I thought Jewish was Jewish. Judaism is a religion, not a trait. You can be 'not strong enough' but I've never heard of being 'not Jewish enough.' I told Jill I'd talk to her parents so she wouldn't have to sneak out and see me, but she told me it was hopeless."

We are certainly not going to like all of our kids' friends. But when prejudice or fear affects our judgment, we have little chance for a successful relationship with our youngsters.

## Parental Motives

Since adolescents are overwhelmingly resistant to parental influence, what can we do if a friendship really seems dangerous?

First, we must examine our own motives and purposes. Bill's father restricted his son from spending time with a friend he considered "too wild" because of the friend's interest in riding motorcycles. It became clear that Bill's father's fear was based on what he knew of the motorcycle gangs in his high school days. Bill was enraged because he felt that his father didn't believe he was mature enough to handle himself in this heavily masculine activity. Friendship was not the real issue. It was merely a convenient vehicle for expressing this conflict. When Bill showed his father how dirt-bike racing differed from a motorcycle gang's activities, and demonstrated that he knew how to handle the cycle cautiously, his father's anxieties diminished and the "wild friends" were no longer an issue.

## When Intervention Is Justified

If a relationship clearly becomes destructive or denies an adolescent the right to be self-determining, parents should make every effort to terminate or adjust the relationship.

Maria, fifteen years old, had come with her parents and younger sister from Argentina four years earlier and had been swept up too quickly into city life in California. She fell in love with eighteen-year-old Matt, who had dropped out of school in tenth grade and was living wherever he could find a bed. When Maria found that she was pregnant, she ran off with Matt and disappeared for two months, calling weekly to let her parents know that she was safe. She and Matt were living in a room in the city, and he paid their way by dealing drugs on the street. Her parents felt that Maria was hurting herself beyond measure. They could not find her to reason with her so they turned to the police. When she was brought home, they sent her back to Argentina to have the baby. She lived with the maternal grandmother whom she had always loved. She completed her schooling there and returned to California two years later, more mature and in control of her life. She decided to enter college and plan a career. Maria's parents had a difficult time reaching that decision to intervene. Maria's immediate reaction was stormy and resentful, but now both she and her parents agree that they took the right step.

Billy, twelve years old, stole small sums of money from his parents. Each time a theft was discovered Billy was found at the local pizza and pinball parlor, treating his fourteen-year-old friend, Jack. The parents talked with Billy and let him know they understood his need for companionship. But they were adamant about setting limits on how to go about making friends; they let him know it did not include stealing in order to "buy" friendship. If he continued to steal, then he would not be permitted to see Jack. To some extent this stand worked successfully with Billy because he was only twelve. Our survey shows that the odds for success in imposing such rules drops drastically as kids get older.

Parents must weigh the consequences of protecting the adolescents' right to choose and judge, and protecting them from self-destructive behavior. In general, however, *it is better to err on the side of freedom for the adolescent.* We must be responsive to our own sense of ethical responsibility, and we can and should express our views with clarity. That does not mean, however, that we must pull out all stops to break up a disturbing friendship, particularly if, in the process, we turn our kids against us. If an objectionable friendship does lead to trouble, it is better that we be there in a reliable and nonvindictive role to provide necessary support and reassurance.

## Short-Lived Friendships

Many of the friendships that worry us are short-lived. Often our teenagers discover that a friend whom they revered at first meeting has fewer good qualities than originally displayed. Sometimes, just allowing an objectionable friendship to run its course will work better than all our efforts to terminate the association.

"I really thought my friend Denise was a super girl. My mom tried to tell me that she was two-faced and bitchy, but at the time I couldn't see it. I confided in her about the guy who I was going to ask to the junior dance. That night I found out she asked the same guy just so I couldn't ask him. I never spoke to her after that." (Joyce, 17)

"I had a friend that was such bad news! When he first came to school nobody knew him so I talked to him and he really hung on to me. But after he got some friends, he started to lie about me and turned some of my other friends against me. I think my parents were relieved when I stopped seeing him. They never said anything when we were friendly, but afterward my mom told me how glad she was that Tom and I had gone separate ways." (Arthur, 16)

Our children do hear our attitudes and opinions about their friends. But if we go beyond expressing our views and insist that our teenagers give up a certain friend, they will fight, resist and defy us in order to protect their right to make their own decisions.

## Platonic Friendships

### Unanticipated Fallout from the Sexual Revolution: Friendship Without Sex

Since sex between adolescents has become socially acceptable, our kids can enjoy nonsexual relationships without feeling strange. Sex is simply less of an issue for them because it's both permissible and available. Through platonic friendships, teenagers gain an opposite-sex confidant with whom conflicts or anxieties can be aired, including those of a sexual nature. "How to do it?" is a question that comes up regularly. How to ask a girl for a date, how to talk to a boy, how to appear relaxed and at ease when you're really scared about not having anything to say, how to kiss, how to feel, how to start having intercourse. No one answers these questions with more comfortable authority than an experienced older sibling who has just been through it all, or a close friend of the opposite sex who is willing to give candid information that no book, parent, or teacher can give quite as well. And teenagers also enjoy the opportunity to be close and open with someone without having to contend with the elements of competitiveness or bravado that they perceive in same-sex relationships.

The decline of gender stereotypes has fostered these friendships. Boys are no longer burdened by the necessity of proving their masculinity by making sexual passes at a girl they like. Today, they are free to be upset, saddened, fearful, or platonically affectionate with girls. Girls are also freer to avoid the rigid masquerades of the past.

They are no longer forced to deny their sexual drive or engage in subtle seductive charades. Nor is their sense of self-worth defined in terms of whether or not some boy finds them sexually desirable.

The comments of two seventeen-year-olds point out the advantages that today's adolescents see in this freedom from role restrictions. However, they also indicate that sexual stereotypes still exist.

"It's easier for me to talk to girls because they're usually more sympathetic and sensitive. If they see a weakness in you, they don't run you into the ground. If you put your cards on the table they'll accept your weaknesses as well as your pluses. Boys are so afraid of displaying any weakness. Girls aren't out to prove themselves to you. They don't play one-upmanship." (Gregory, 17)

"There is one very good friend who I tell all my problems to. We can talk about everything and I can get a male perspective on the situation. I feel more comfortable talking to him than to any of my girlfriends. There's no pettiness, no competitiveness, no sex, just real friendship. It may sound silly, but we consider each other best friends. We'd do anything for each other." (Joanne, 17)

## Cliques

Cliques are part of a continuum of teenage clustering that often emerges from their activities. Boy and Girl Scout troops, Little League baseball or football teams, and church youth groups are at one end of the scale. These are adult-supported groups and often are organized for the purpose of directing young people's activities. At the other end are gangs, which begin as relatively informal associations of youngsters who band together for mutual support and companionship. As the gang seeks to strengthen its internal bonds, it often adopts a more formal structure that includes certain goals. The gang might decide to serve the community by keeping strangers out of the neighborhood. It may even decide to battle other groups for neighborhood supremacy. The paramilitary structure that is popular can generate sadistic experimentation and exploitation. Gangs are sometimes both vicious and dangerous.

At the midpoint of these two extremes is the clique. A group becomes a clique when it takes on the aura of exclusiveness. The teenagers most obviously hurt by cliques are those who are excluded. But those in the center are also hurt, although in less obvious ways. They are limiting their range of friendships and denying themselves the chance to learn how people different from themselves think and operate. However, cliques do provide a secure and consistent support system away from home.

They also provide direct experience in forming the kind of exclusionary groups that are an accepted part of adult life. Groups confined to a particular race, religion, sex, socioeconomic level, or nationality, are characteristic of our society. And kids learn how "to separate" in their cliques. But young people are not as sophisticated as we are about the acceptance/rejection process. They are likely to be blunter and more hurtful in allowing peers in or out.

### How to Beat the Clique

The most effective means of battling the clique is to offer support at home and in other settings. Help your children seek out new and different social activities; help them explore their own creative interests and untapped talents. Sally, new in a school district, was delighted to be accepted in the inner circle of fourteen-year-olds. However, her previous interest in music diminished rapidly until her father determined that he could not let that happen. He discovered that there was a group of young people, as lively and popular as those in the clique, who had formed a rock group and played at church dances and local parties. Once Sally became involved with her new friends and music, she no longer needed the false security that clique exclusiveness offered. The same is true of children who feel left out of a particular group. Searching for two or three other children who share interests will lessen the pain of being excluded.

Cliques will continue as long as the shelter they provide is necessary. But when our kids can find support in a group whose activities are based on shared interests and creativity, their need to band together for exclusionary purposes will diminish.

## Loyalty to Friends

Although many parents believe that teenagers should depend on family loyalty rather than on friends, they would probably agree that adolescents need friends who will be there and stay there, regardless of what conditions may develop. Adults are not usually subject to verbal or physical threats from a group of peers. But many of our kids have to contend with this possibility in their school activities and out-of-school relationships. And gangs, cliques, clubs, fraternities, sororities, and small groups of friends provide outlets that meet the need for mutual support. Loyalty in those settings is an intensely valued quality.

## When Will Teenagers Tell on a Friend?

The nature of loyalty may be tested in many ways. Indeed, the dilemmas that teenagers face might challenge even the strongest adult. When do the majority feel that loyalty demands the breaking of a trust? Only when a friend seems dangerously self-destructive. Fifty-six percent of our teenagers would break the code of loyal silence if a friend was threatening to commit suicide.

Theresa, sixteen, explains it clearly. "If you know someone is going to kill themselves, you can't just sit by and let it happen. You'd never forgive yourself." That view is shared by many others. Sue, a seventeen-year-old Midwestern high school senior, says, "I'd never tell on a friend. Well, wait a minute. I shouldn't say never. Because last year my friend, Barbara, was really freaking out. She tried slashing her wrists once and I felt there was no way I could help her, so I told her mother. I didn't feel I was ratting or anything like that, because she needed help."

The dilemma is clear and Lila, though only fourteen, recognizes the complexities. "You have to be very careful. You might try to reach them and it doesn't work. You'd have to figure out what they'd do if you told."

## Boys vs. Girls

46% of boys would tell if a friend were threatening suicide
65% of girls would tell if a friend were threatening suicide

Once again, we are witnessing the macho "we can handle it ourselves" feeling that many males exhibit. Conversely, the caring and sympathetic qualities that women are encouraged to display make it easier for them to "tell" and go for help, especially when a crucial issue such as suicide is at stake. (We discuss the suicide problem in depth in Chapter 6.)

Far fewer teenagers will reveal a friend's drinking or drug problems to an outside source, and the difference between boys and girls is small, 17% and 20% respectively. Of course, the danger from drugs, though strong, is not as immediately life-threatening. Also, since drug usage is actually hidden from parents, the idea of calling in parental help seems almost heretical. Sara, eighteen, explains: "If a friend was having a real drug problem, or drinking for that matter, I'd tell him to get help from a drug abuse center or A.A., but if he didn't want help, that's his problem. I wouldn't tell anyone, especially not parents." Robert, who has used drugs himself, disagrees: "First I would talk to that friend and try to figure out why he's doing this to himself. Then I might go to his parents for his own good. I'd hope someone would do that for me."

Many don't believe it's possible to help unless the friend requests it. "I have two friends who are into drugs very heavily and all you can do is talk to them and try to show them what they're doing to themselves. But until they want to stop, themselves, there's nothing else you can do." (Sam, 17)

As for shoplifting, very few teens consider it serious enough to report to an outside source. Only 6% say they would do so. (See Chapter 10.)

There seem to be two separate societies living parallel to one another in the same space. Teenagers and adults exchange certain confidences and ideas across a self-imposed barrier. However, the most potentially explosive issues or the most intimate and private ones, are rarely revealed to the "other side." Adolescents don't tell adults about their sexual activities, their drug habits, their deepest feelings, or their problems. And adults keep their sexual habits, their finances, and their inner feelings under wraps, too.

The popular image of the "we all love each other, tell each other everything" nuclear family is pure American mythology. Yes, openness does exist in many families, and honest communication should be actively sought. But the bottom line is that both adolescents and adults are more comfortable and open with peers. Therefore, it shouldn't surprise us when our teenagers rely more on their friends for support and closeness than they do on us. Relax and acknowledge it as a natural step in their striving for identity and separateness.

# 6

# Teenagers on Themselves; Suicide; Their Worst Problems and Fears

---

- Nearly 7 out of 10 like themselves
- School is the number one teenage problem
- Loss of parents is teenagers' number one fear; more than twice as strong as their own fear of dying

---

**P**uberty is a period of astonishing physical transformation. **Over** a period of several months, the small twelve-year-old becomes a tall and lanky adolescent. After the summer vacation, a plump little girl reappears as an attractive teenager with a young woman's figure. All these changes—the start of menstruation, the growth of pubic and axillary hair, as well as facial hair in boys, the beginning of semen production and a host of other endocrinological and physical maturing steps—have a profound effect on the self-image of the child-turned-teenager.

But even more important than these physical changes is the teenager's growing need to experience sexual love and intimacy. Attracting the attention of the opposite sex becomes paramount, and suddenly the teenager is acutely aware of his or her own desirability in the eyes of peers. The eruption of acne causes shock and depression. The kid who didn't care how many days he wore the same pair of rotting jeans suddenly puts on carefully selected clean ones before leaving for school. The thirteen-year-old who hated to wash her hair begins to wash it every day, experimenting with different styles. Uncanny changes, progressing in uneven stages. The body may be too short, too tall, too fat or too skinny. Big breasts or no breasts. Too much or too little hair. The slow maturers feel discomfort and embarrassment because their bodies seem so different from their friends. The precociously mature adolescents feel equally uncomfortable and self-conscious as their peers envy or ridicule their physical endowments.

## Discovering the New Self

Accompanying all the changes is the unrelenting observation of self. They study their attitudes, their positive and negative features. They watch peers who are respected, popular, successful, and try to comprehend what qualities make them that way. They are in the process of trying to redefine themselves, to become comfortable with their new bodies, their new selves. It is a difficult time at best, but it may become even more confusing if physical changes aren't matched by corresponding changes in self-image. When family and friends respond to their new "outside" self and treat them differently, they may be propelled into situations for which they're not yet ready, especially if their "inside" self hasn't had time to catch up.

Elizabeth, an attractive fifteen-year-old, has lived in the same suburban community since she was nine, and has known the same group of classmates for the last six years. She had been an overweight child, unhappy and embarrassed at being called "porky" and "fatso." She retreated into her studies and television, and became an avid after-school soap-opera viewer. Between the ages of thirteen and fourteen, her metabolism changed, and with it the shape of her body. She is now sufficiently well built to be attractive to boys. She is not slender, but she no longer hears the nasty names of the past. The adjustment, however, has been difficult for her. She is delighted that she receives approving comments, but over the years she developed a set of "I don't care about them, they're all stupid" defenses. Underneath, she harbored a powerful self-hatred because she blamed herself for being "so ugly." Now the rules have changed, but Elizabeth cannot change herself with the same speed. She is shy and uncertain with other teenagers, finding herself tongue-tied and awkward when they joke and relax together.

Her habit of self-criticism is so strong that she now condemns herself for being quiet, afraid, and lacking in confidence. She would like to learn how to act differently, but that doesn't seem to work even though close girlfriends try to help her. Elizabeth needs time to become accustomed to herself as the attractive teenager she is, and decide the kind of person she wants to be in relation to other young people. And that's exactly what she is in the process of doing.

## Do They Like Themselves?

### Their Physical Selves

Since the changes teenagers experience are so rapid, and often so startling, their sense of themselves is bound to be affected. So we asked them how they felt about themselves, both physically and in general. Forty-four percent report that they're satisfied with their bodies. Of the 56% who are not, "too fat" was the most popular reason (22%), with "too short" running a close second, followed by "underdeveloped." Certainly this response is not surprising in our appearance-conscious country where, every day, we are subjected to barrages of copy to remind us to diet, to increase breast size, to develop muscles.

But more interesting than these responses are their thoughts about themselves as individuals: their personalities, the qualities they like best and least about themselves, the changes they'd like to see in themselves.

---

How do you feel about yourself?

| | | |
|---|---|---|
| You like yourself | | 68% |
| You don't like yourself | 10% | |
| You wish you were someone else | 14% | 32% |
| You sometimes think of suicide | 8% | |

---

### They Are Very Concerned with Qualities of Character

Nearly 7 out of 10 adolescents feel good about themselves. They judge themselves with a critical eye that often is remarkably free of pretense and superficiality. The qualities that they value most are those of character: to have one's own convictions and to hold them; to be reasonable and fair with others; to be self-sufficient; to be friendly, honest, and realistic. A tall order. Naturally, adolescents are no more free of inconsistencies than are adults. They find as many roadblocks as we do in their efforts to live up to what they want themselves to be. However, the qualities they particularly like in themselves reflect the ideals they hold and are striving to achieve.

"I'm glad I'm me, mostly because I see the way other people act; like I can't stand their closed-mindedness or their prejudice. I'm not so stupid as to be drawn into that kind of trap. I try to be careful with what I feel. Investigate my feelings; not be too quick to jump to conclusions. That way I can be pretty fair with myself and with other people." (Candy, 14)

"I know what I want, I have some sort of direction and I can take care of myself. My parents brought me up to handle plenty of responsibility, and that's good. I feel sure of myself and I like that feeling. Nobody can kick me around. I've got strength." (Edward, 16)

"I like myself to a point. I like the way I get along with people. Generally, it's easy for me to make friends. I also get along well with the girls. I like myself as a businessman because I don't let myself get cheated. Also I like my optimism. I never look on the bad side." (Bart, 16)

"Many people have told me how honest I am. They also know I can keep secrets. They always tell me something without worrying that I'll tell someone else." (Jan, 13)

## 32% Criticize Their Own Personality Failings

It will probably come as a shock to learn that teenagers are as tough on their own shortcomings as are the adults around them. They deplore their weakness at sticking to their own beliefs. They don't like being dependent; being too angry or critical of others; being lazy or unable to work toward goals. Robert doesn't like his tendency to fight. Evie dislikes her lack of patience. Others say they are too moody or that they don't work hard enough in school. And all of them want to overcome what they see as faults.

"My ability to understand is what I like. I'm starting to tolerate more. What I'd like to change is my tendency to sit back, let things slide and let other people make decisions. Maybe that comes from being the youngest in the family. I haven't really let myself be heard. I'd like to feel more secure." (Dale, 15)

"I haven't been too happy with myself. But lately I've sort of got back in the swing of things. I'm not my own best friend. I get into a lot of fights with myself. I can feel it inside me, just disagreeing a lot. I state my opinions and somebody will come up with theirs and change mine completely. I wish I could keep hold of mine for a little bit longer. I'm not very sure of myself." (Judy, 13)

"I'm too fat and I want to be a little taller. Also, I have such a soft heart, and I'm very emotional. I don't look at myself as someone who is outstanding. I'm dull. I guess I'm special to the people around me, but to myself I don't feel very special at all. I want to be someone special to myself." (Louise, 16)

## How Other People's Opinions Affect Self-Image

Self-image is the slowly crafted picture of oneself that each of us forms out of years of experience with others and with our own ways of feeling and functioning. It is continually developing and subject to constant molding. Some of the shaping is determined by how successfully we live up to the standards that we have set for ourselves. Another factor is the attitude others have about us. The younger the child, the more vulnerable she or he is to those outside reactions. Adolescents may often manifest the truculent "I don't care what anyone thinks" attitude, but underneath they are developing a self-image that stems, in part, from the way they think other people view them. If friends or parents constantly put them down, they begin to think they are not much good. Almost every individual shrinks under constant criticism and thrives on praise and appreciation.

Evelyn, an eighteen-year-old in Pennsylvania who is planning to enter nursing school, says, "When you've been through a lot of people cutting at you, it really affects you when that's all you hear all your life. It makes you think you're not worth anything." Evelyn's parents have lowered her confidence to such a point that Evelyn does not think she will succeed in a career. Barbara, seventeen, expresses similar feelings and hurts. "My father always called me 'little dummy' or 'shrimp.' I was the baby in the family and I'm sure he was only teasing, but when I was little I really believed him. In fact, I believed it for a long time. It wasn't until I met my boyfriend and he told me how smart he thought I was and that he didn't think I was too short, that I began to feel I was okay. Unless you're very secure and sure of who you are, you believe you are what people say."

Sometimes these feelings of degradation can be overcome by resisting someone else's definition and adopting, instead, one's own standards for self-evaluation. However, when this inner strength cannot be called upon, life's adversities may prove so overwhelming that the child seeks a way out.

## Suicide

In the midst of a momentary depression, many people may say, "I feel like jumping out the window" or "I studied two weeks for that exam, and if I don't get an A I'll kill myself." To most of us, it's just a figure of speech, and we have no intention of carrying it out. Children and teenagers, too, may use such phrases as a casual way of emphasizing how strongly they feel about a matter, and usually there's no real threat implied. But for some youngsters it's not just a meaningless phrase. These kids are so unhappy about their lives (at home, in school, socially), and see so little possibility of change that they believe it is not worth living in such emotional pain. They think "I might as well be dead," and warily tell parents of their desperation, perhaps hoping that the all-powerful parent will *do something* about it.

We are all aware of the rising suicide rate among teenagers. The sudden and self-inflicted death of a young boy or girl is a tragic shock whenever it happens. Why do they do it? Teenagers tell us that much of their turmoil comes from pressures with which they feel inadequate to deal; from discouragement and sadness that overcome their confidence; and from parents who are not sensitive to their problems.

### What Causes a Teenager to Think of Suicide

The thought of killing oneself may arise at times of intense loneliness or self-derogation. When the gap between "what I wish I were" and "what I seem to be" seems impossible to cross, suicide may become a way to punish one's self for being so insufficient. Alternatively, when unexpressed anger leads to an overwhelming inner rage and tension, the only escape may seem to be self-destruction. For a child who is angry at his or her parents, suicide may be a way of getting back at them, of "making them sorry."

In general, these suicidal impulses are more likely to lead to gestures than to fatal, self-destructive actions. Superficial razor cuts on the wrist, taking pills out of the medicine chest, driving too fast and consciously taking excessive risks—these are all pleas for help.

In contrast, when a teenager experiences long-term despair and depression, a cry of help may no longer be enough.

The teenager who knows long-term isolation from others (even when finding shallow social contact at bars or other public places); the one who has always experienced failure and feels that self-respect and self-appreciation are completely out of reach; the young person whose continual anxiety creates so much tension, sleeplessness, and strain as to make life unbearable; and finally, the one who feels desperately and unrelentingly worthless and undeserving—these are the ones who are in greatest danger and most in need of help. Even the affluent adolescent may believe that suicide is the only solution to feelings of hatred and disappointment. Death may seem preferable to failure and loneliness. This kind of desperation knows no socioeconomic boundaries. The child's countless monetary advantages mean very little when he is aching inside.

Jonathan is an eighteen-year-old from an upper-middle-class family whose parents constantly remind him that he was an accident. They have instilled in him the idea that he is totally worthless and will never amount to anything. He fervently believes this assessment, and has attempted suicide on numerous occasions. He has two very bright, high-achieving older brothers who were always held up as examples. (His own I.Q. is also very high.) He feels that his parents truly dislike him, and his father did, in fact, physically abuse him so badly that the boy was hospitalized several times. When he left home and stayed with a friend, his parents never tried to locate him.

In order for young people to recover from such pain, they have to know that they are not alone and unloved; that there is someone who is close enough to share or hear their anguish without denying, avoiding, or belittling their desperate feelings. In Jonathan's case, he found understanding and comfort from a family who allowed him to live with them until he went away to college. Their support gave him the confidence to get a job and work his way through school since his parents had refused to pay for his college education.

## The Importance of Listening

Because parents find it so painful to listen to their child's anguish they may be tempted to talk the child out of his or her feelings. Very often parents downplay and minimize the severity of a child's emotional pain. They resort to a "Cheer-up! Things can't be all that tough" approach. Bernard, seventeen, explains: "Every time I try to open up and tell my parents how depressed I am, my father gives me a 'look on the bright side' lecture. I know he means well, but I can't be optimistic and change the way I really feel. So now I don't tell him when I'm depressed (which is usually all the time)." Certainly there are times when this approach has merit, but more often what an adolescent needs is a parent who can listen and offer a strong, dependable and caring presence.

Many of the pressures of a teenager's life can lead to severe depression and we cannot afford to dismiss their problems lightly. There is nothing more painful, for example, than being ostracized or embarrassed by peers. One fifteen-year-old had been rejected by a boy she deeply loved, and who she believed loved her. The ex-boyfriend told his friends that she was a nymphomaniac, and school became a nightmare for the girl. She told us she had attempted suicide by overdosing on pills because she couldn't bear going back to school and being taunted by the other kids. Her mother insisted that she was just being silly. The girl felt totally at a loss, and believed that no one understood the depth of her feelings or really cared that her reputation was being ruined.

We need to be particularly alert to the possibility that professional help might be necessary if our child's depression lasts for days and weeks at a time. He or she may need someone outside the family to talk to. Counseling may also help the entire family reevaluate its methods of getting along, its mutual support systems, and its pressure tactics—all of which may contribute to the teenager's sense of desperation or well-being.

### Teenagers Speak Candidly About Their Suicide Attempts

"I always think about suicide. That's what bothers me. I always consider it a possibility. I've felt so apart from everybody else, but now I'm learning that there are people in this world like me. One time I had a whole bottle of phenobarbital. I took one. Then I sat there and said, 'I'll take one every five minutes until I keel over.' but the one put me to sleep and I woke up the next morning with the bottle in my hand. I thought, 'What if it's empty? Am I still alive?' I opened it up and they were all there. I ran to the bathroom and flushed them. I get so paranoid about being gay. I choose my friends by whether or not I think they'll accept me. I don't have any male friends because everything now is so macho. I can't relate to that. I was born without a male ego. I had no identity for a long while. I was a very fat, feminine kid, nonathletic. I couldn't identify with either male or female. I was like floating in space until twelfth grade. I've never liked the way I look. I'm obsessed with my weight. I weigh myself five, six times a day. I lost fifty pounds in three months by throwing up. I call it my 'holocaust of the body.' I was mentally out of it. I barely remember those three months. I would eat and vomit. I still think of myself as a fatty and I'll always think of myself that way. I cover myself up and wear ratty clothes. I'm still nervous with people and I'd like to change that. Be more sure of myself and not care so much what people think. I feel that if I open myself up to people, it gives them ammunition to use against me. I feel better about myself now, but I still think of suicide every once in a while." (Jack, 18)

(Jack lives with an alcoholic mother and aunt, and has a part-time father. There is very little communication in the family and Jack is pretty much on his own. He was into drugs at one time. He felt used by fair-weather friends, and built a wall around himself to shut out rejection. He considers himself a loner. He is bright, verbal, and aware of his problems. His gayness troubles him, and he suspects he may actually be bisexual. He is happy to leave high school and hopes to branch out into computer science.)

"Guess you can say I've tried it. I was bike riding, and I'm a good rider so I know all the dangers. I rode as fast as I could around the most dangerous curve, and tried to kill myself. My boyfriend knew about it and watched me the rest of the week. He thinks it's resolved now. I can't say that's true. I haven't tried it again, but I've thought seriously about it. My mother is at the root of my problem. It's the trust. I was getting talked to and lectured at but not getting any trust. I was also having trouble finding time to split with my boyfriend and my other friends. And it was the last week of finals. Too many conflicts at once. The week I tried to kill myself, I told a lot of people. More than I thought I would. I guess I wanted them all to stand behind me. I got a lot of phone calls. We have two phones, and if one was busy they'd call on the other one to see if I was still there. It was pretty comforting. I guess more people cared than I thought. I'm most afraid of lack of love, because without love, I think I would very honestly think about dying again. It's hard to exist without someone shining a lot of love on you. (Darcy, 13)

(Darcy is an exceedingly bright, verbal thirteen-year-old, intellectually mature beyond her years. There is a stepfamily situation that has produced great turmoil, and she was nearly seduced by a stepbrother. She is aware of her problems and at the time of our interview was desperately seeking professional help, which her family was reluctant to provide.)

"I've tried to commit suicide to get even with my mother. I've done crazy things like take pills, but she never knew about it. She's never home to see me go through these fits and torture myself. So the times I take 25 aspirins and 500 milligram pills, and my ears are ringing, she doesn't even know. Why do all that if no one's going to react to it? People don't try to reason with you. I only have one friend, a male, I can rap about it with. He doesn't think it's stupid. I already know taking all those pills is stupid. I don't need to be told that. I just want someone to understand what I'm feeling and try to relate to me. I don't really want to die; I just want to escape. I also thought if I'd end up in the hospital, she'd appreciate me more. Sometimes I think that some of the changes I'm going through are unique. I feel, 'Does anybody else go through this?' I ask myself if I'm crazy for feeling this way. 'Is there something wrong with me for feeling those desires; for hating my mother so much; for taking all those pills? Do I need to be in a mental institution?' I know it's just temporary and when I'm eighteen and out of here, it'll straighten itself out." (Anita, 15)

"Right after my mom died, and I was nine, I felt so lost. I tried to kill myself a couple of times. Once I swallowed a bottle of pills, and all it did was give me a stomachache. Once I tried to strangle myself, but it didn't work. I was suffocating so I stopped. I wouldn't do that anymore. No matter how bad things are, I can stick it out one more year until I'm eighteen and can leave." (Ruth, 17)

Ruth lives with four brothers and an abusive father. She was drinking heavily at fourteen, but doesn't anymore. She has run away six times, lived in foster homes, and if she runs away again she will be sent to a convent. So she is biding her time and eagerly awaiting her eighteenth birthday when she plans to join the army.)

The fact that our teenagers are perceptive and self-observant does not always protect them from anxiety and loneliness. Their problems can become too difficult to handle when they feel neither supported nor understood. At times, they may not even be able to explain their terrible sense of being lost and alone. What can we do? Listen, try to understand, and let them know we're on their side. Empathy is a powerful ingredient.

## What Are Their Most Bothersome Problems

| What bothers you the most? 13–15-year-olds | | What bothers you the most? 16–18-year-olds | |
|---|---|---|---|
| School | 30% | School | 29% |
| Brothers and sisters | 30% | Parents | 28% |
| Friends | 26% | Money | 24% |
| Parents | 23% | Friends | 22% |
| Money | 13% | Brothers and sisters | 21% |
| Drinking and drugs | 10% | Drinking or drugs | 9% |
| Sex | 9% | Sex | 7% |

### School Is the Worst

On the average, teenagers spent six hours a day in classes, two or more commuting and participating in school-associated activities, and an ample amount of time on homework. School is their equivalent of adult employment. It is also the most important place outside of home for virtually all adolescents. Friends are there. Sports are there. Competition is there. Students are constantly being reminded that their school performance will play a large part in determining their success in later life. Every day they are evaluated and measured. Every forty-five minutes or so they must demonstrate their punctuality or be punished for failing to do so. They must be attentive, polite, and obedient to teachers who, in their eyes, are insulting and patronizing and talk the greatest nonsense. If they don't behave in the ways expected, they are jeopardizing their grades, their future, and that inescapable threat—their record! Every ten weeks their compliance with the rules, their on-the-job achievement, and seemingly their intelligence are rated. What could be more detrimental to creativity and individuality? How many adults could stand that pressure in their jobs?

In addition, almost every outside activity or pleasure is evaluated in terms of "How will it affect Johnny's schoolwork?" Parents wonder whether Johnny is putting too many hours into his job at the fast-food place, or on the basketball team, or working on his car. They may feel that his outside activities are responsible for his poor school performance. Since we, as responsible adults, have spent years getting our kids to understand the necessity of succeeding in school, we may feel that we have achieved a part of our goal. From our standpoint, school ought to be a serious matter for them, and we want them to consider it that way.

However, as we have seen in Chapter 4, the school chapter, pressures from all sides (teachers, parents, peers, and their own pressures) weigh heavily upon them. Their discovery that other kids are smarter or more popular becomes most apparent in school settings. Since they believe overwhelmingly that teachers show favoritism toward the smart students, they begin to learn quite early who gets the goodies. If they're in the top academic group, they can bask in that satisfaction, although sometimes their own desire to be perfect creates additional pressures. If they are not on top, then the process of judging themselves "not as good as" or "tries hard but is only an average student" begins. The definitions they form of themselves start to take root, sometimes painfully. No wonder school is the number one problem area.

## Family Members Are Big Problems

When designating problem issues, teenagers rank brothers, sisters, and parents right up there with school. Siblings are most troublesome to the thirteen-to-fifteen-year-olds, whereas parents are the principal problem for the older teenagers.

The younger the child, the more space brothers and sisters occupy in his or her world. Because young children are still so tied to the family and dependent on parents, brothers and sisters may be viewed as intruders and competitors. However, as children mature, they expect less of their parents and more of themselves. Their boundaries expand and they find many of their satisfactions outside the home. The relative impact of siblings lessens, and as a problem siblings drop to fifth place among the sixteen-to-eighteen-year-olds. In fact, they may even become friends and confidants. Stan, a sixteen-year-old from a rural area in the Northwest, sums up the difference. "My brother and I used to fight all the time, but now that we're both older we're not wrestling over toys and physically abusing each other. We may do it verbally, but we get along okay for brothers. We even talk to each other civilly once in a while. I guess we'd miss each other if one of us went away."

From Sally's perspective as the eldest, she notes a similar change in her younger sister. "Me and my sister really used to hate each other. She was such a brat. She whined and cried to get attention all the time and she always took my things. Now she's thirteen, and I don't pay much attention to her. She's got her own friends and doesn't have to hang on me, and it's much better." (Sally, 18)

Concentration on friends is a sign of the teenager's emergence into the broader world. For younger teenagers, however, friends are still more of a problem than parents because they have yet to work out all the difficulties accompanying peer relationships. In contrast, for the sixteen-to-eighteen-year-olds, the reverse is true.

The problems that arise between parents and older teenagers are connected to the teenagers' movement away from our philosophies and attitudes, and into their own. They are gaining more independence and they see us as a continuing threat to it. They challenge our values and we, in turn, often confront them with their radical behavior. (See Chapter 1, on teenagers and parents, for a more thorough presentation of attitudes and conflicts.) Chip, who is in his last year of high school and plans to go on to a community college, points up the problems that have surfaced in his relationship with his mother.

"My mother thinks I'm a motorcycle bandit. I love riding and do it also because I can't afford a car. She thinks I'm reckless, but I ride my cycle more carefully than she drives her car. She also thinks my friends are hoods so I don't bring them home anymore. We rarely talk because we can't agree on much, so it's peaceful but unfriendly around the house." (Chip, 18)

"My mother has never experienced the things that I have. She's never run track, she never went out much, never traveled, never was exposed to any ideas except her family's, never wore makeup, doesn't know many of the things I know intellectually; yet she tries to tell me everything. It's so hard to make her understand that her beliefs are not my beliefs. She calls me a 'closet revolutionary.' Good Lord, I'm a conservative to my friends, but to my parents there's just no explaining." (Evelyn, 17)

"I have a real problem with my parents. Things are so much different than when they were my age and they can't understand the more liberal way the world is. I'm not into drugs at all, but they are so afraid all my friends are, and even though I try to explain that only one of them is, they won't believe me. They think I go to rock concerts to smoke pot. I have to tell them I'm going to a party if I want to go to a concert. And our political ideas are so far apart that it's tough to discuss that, and anything else, because they get so upset." (Raymond, 17)

## Teenagers Worry About Money

As adolescents get older, money rises from fifth place to third place. As they assert their independence, they have to take more responsibility for themselves and that means earning the money to do so. Dating is an expensive activity. Cars are demanding vehicles of convenience. Records, concerts, clothes, even drugs and beer, are all expensive items. Many do have jobs after school, on weekends, or during the summer, but very few say they find either the time or the opportunity to earn sufficient money.

"Who'll hire me at fifteen? I can't even get a job in a fast-food place, and that's the pits! I'd take it if they'd take me. I cut lawns and shovel snow but I wish I had a real job!" (George, 15)

"I have a heap of a car which I picked up for $75. But I can't afford the gas. I'm always running on empty and my girlfriend is always rarin' to go." (Scott, 18)

"Everyone says, 'You're eighteen. It should be easy for you to get a job.' Sure it would if I could work full-time. But I need really good grades to get into college so I've been hitting the books and that doesn't leave you much time for a job." (Art, 18)

Some steal or deal drugs when legitimate jobs are not available or not lucrative enough. Matthew is an entrepreneur, a self-admitted wheeler-dealer in the American tradition of free enterprise. He crosses over to the illegitimate side on occasion, but does so cautiously and within predetermined boundaries.

"Decent jobs are hard to get, so I get most of my money trading and selling things. I'll buy things for a certain price and I'll usually sell them for a lot more. Stuff like stereo equipment, radios, CB's, bikes. Occasionally I'd deal, but very rarely. I haven't done that for a while. Nothing hard; just pot. Hard drugs are one thing, but pot's another." (Matthew, 16)

Others, however, are casual about illegal activities. James, eighteen, tells us, "You gotta learn how to get money because one day you'll be on your own. I was selling drugs. I'd leave the house at six in the morning, come back about four-thirty with a pocketful of money. I was making $600 or $700 a day, selling black beauties and cocaine. I wish I was young again because now I'm eighteen and if I get caught, I could get a twenty-five-to-life sentence."

Al, now seventeen, was forced by the death of his parents to become one of the underground army of teenagers living on their own on the fringes of conventional society. He took money where he could find it, and banded together for survival with other runaways and abandoned children. "I was in the streets for a year, living in rundown buildings, ripping people off in order to feed myself and get clothes. I was fifteen. I don't like that because it's not me. That's not the way my mother taught me and I felt bad doing it. I joined a gang because I didn't have nobody else. On the streets it took a lot to live on. I never got nothing under $200. (Once I got $60.) We stuck up older people mainly. Black, white, Chinese. Kids didn't have enough money so why waste time on them when I could get somebody else that looked like he had money? We did it at night. Never take a chance out there on the street by yourself. So I always got two other guys and we split the money three ways. One would hold him while the other one's behind him, and the other one would go in his pocket. It was organized. When we got the money we would go and eat and buy whatever we needed. The girls would cook for us. Sooner or later I knew I'd get caught and I couldn't hack it no more, so that's when I turned myself in." Al's needs were for survival. His existence was basically spartan, but when there was enough money available, he and the others bought the same kind of pleasures that most teenagers seek out.

### Money—How They Spend It

Some form of entertainment, particularly music, is high on almost every list. Music is far more than diversion. It has become a means of relaxation, excitement, and creative expression. Todd calls it the "most important thing in my life" and explains: "The records, concerts, lights, the whole atmosphere. It's my salvation. If things bother me, I'll go into my room and lock the door; turn on the stereo and escape into my own world. I can just 'space.' Music is a lot cheaper than drugs and it's legal. Sometimes I'll smoke a little pot and space for a couple of hours, which is neat, but I don't need the pot. I'm a music freak. It's the place I'm happiest. So why not indulge my music habit even though it takes most of my cash, rather than a drug habit or some other form of meaningless entertainment?" (Todd, 18)

Teenagers who drive spend the largest percentage of their money on gasoline, repairs, and general maintenance. A great many others spend their cash on a variety of junk foods, with pizza, soft drinks, and hamburgers heading the list. Girls seem to spend more on clothing than boys do; and of course, teenage girls are invaluable to the cosmetics industry. Older teenagers would like to save money for trips, cars, stereos, and other expensive items that are often beyond their reach. But adolescents don't spend all their money on themselves. Gift-giving is not just an adult activity, as fifteen-year-old Marion explains: "I spend a lot of money on presents and my cash just flies right out the door. As soon as I save it, it's someone's birthday. That's where I think eighty-five percent of my money goes. I hate spending money on myself, but I love buying presents."

The majority of teenagers are free to spend their money as they choose. Apparently most parents agree that letting kids handle money on their own is good training. And, as might be expected, the older they get the fewer parental restrictions there are.

---

Do your parents allow you to spend and manage your money as you wish?

|  | All | 13–15-year-olds | 16–18-year-olds |
| --- | --- | --- | --- |
| Yes | 57% | 51% | 62% |
| No | 8% | 10% | 7% |
| Usually or sometimes | 35% | 39% | 31% |

---

### How Important Are Allowances?

Some teenagers, particularly the younger ones, would rather not have an allowance, and don't mind asking their parents for money whenever they need it. Fourteen-year-old Chris says, "They don't give me a regular weekly allowance, but every once in a while if my dad has a little extra money, he'll just give me a dollar bill. I like it that way because if I had an allowance, I probably wouldn't save it because I'd spend it knowing I was going to get more next week."

Others think that an allowance is very important, offering more independence and freedom to spend without having to report to parents. As one fifteen-year-old says, "How can you go to your mother and say, 'Hey, could you give me $10 because I want to buy you a birthday present?'" Many agree that an allowance provides useful experience in budgeting and managing their finances; something they will certainly have to do later on. We agree.

"I work as a waitress in a restaurant. It's fun sometimes. You work hard and get paid too little, but at least it's a job. I get $60 a month allowance and I have to pay for my own clothes, entertainment, everything. When I was little I got a nickel a week. At thirteen, we all got about 50 cents. But we always had some money to work with so we could learn to handle it. I really like that because I can manage myself." (Sally, 18)

Ron, who is eighteen, believes that his parents were helpful in teaching him the value of money. He explains: "We used to bug them to take us on the roller coaster. So they gave us each $2 and after we used that up, we had to spend our allowance money on rides. We soon learned that it didn't go far, and those rides translated into real money—at 75 cents a ride. As we got older, we watched my dad pay bills. He explained about electric and water bills, rent, car payments, department store payments, food bills, even the stock market. Kids should know all those things. We always went with my parents to help pick out a car. I remember they told us they could only spend $7,000 and we knew that amount of money wouldn't buy a Cadillac, by any means. We got a year-old Chevy with 12,000 miles on it and my dad explained why it was a good buy. We even knew when my dad lost his job one year. We've always had to work and I think it's a good thing. Even my younger brothers and sisters worked. When they couldn't get a real job, my mom would create jobs in the house (over and above their nonpaid work). These were special jobs they got paid for doing. She always let us do whatever we wanted with our money and most of us put it in the bank." (Ronald, 18)

What we are hearing is that managing and spending money are not the problems. Earning and keeping it are. Finally, we've hit upon a problem that we and our kids have in common!

In general, except for school, girls seem to be more bothered by all these problems than boys. This is not surprising since our culture encourages girls to be more sensitive, while boys are encouraged to shoulder burdens "like a man." Fortunately, changing attitudes about sexual equality have diminished this dichotomy. We are beginning to equip both boys and girls with comparable power to handle themselves in their surroundings and to solve problems accordingly. But we aren't there yet.

## What Are Their Greatest Fears?

Are our teenagers as frightened of the world situation as we sometimes believe they are—or should be? It has been theorized that the threat of nuclear annihilation has made our youth skeptical about their futures. Because some adults are afraid of this possibility, they believe that kids are driven to pursue immediate pleasures since the long-term ones seem so poorly guaranteed. To test the validity of this assumption we included the threat of nuclear war in a list of fears that our participants were asked to check. Our findings: Only 14% cite this as a major fear. Instead, what we discover is that these teenagers are not so very different from past generations. Reliance on parents is their preeminent source of security. Even greater than their fear of death is their fear of losing their parents.

---

What are your greatest fears?
The top three responses are:

| | |
|---|---|
| Losing your parents | 58% |
| Dying | 28% |
| Not getting a good job or being successful | 21% |

(Our participants chose more than one response in some cases)

---

## Losing Parents

Affection, reliability, dependency—all are reasons that lead teenagers to feel that parents are their anchor in a sometimes hostile world. Girls express this fear even more strongly than do the boys, which is not surprising, since girls of all ages tend to have a far greater attachment to their parents.

"My parents are a real pain most of the time, but I still would hate it if anything happened to them. I worry about that." (June, 16)

"I'm eighteen, but I'm still afraid of losing my parents. It would be such a devastating feeling of loneliness." (Martha, 18)

## Dying

There is very little difference between the sexes or age groups when dying is the issue. Many teenagers are afraid of both the pain that might accompany death and what might happen afterward.

"I'm afraid of dying. I don't think I'll get too old. I'll probably die in my forties or fifties. I'm afraid of what comes after. If I died right now, I know I'd go to hell because I do a lot of bad things. A lot of people say I'm a cold-blooded person. I'm just contrary. Sometimes Momma will tell me not to go somewhere and I'll go anyway. I've done a lot of wrong things." (Angelo, 17)

"Cancer scares me. I've seen it in my family and I don't want to die that way. But I'm more afraid of getting shot. Nowadays you can walk down the street and anything can happen. There are too many crazies out there." (Joe, 17)

## Lack of Jobs and Success

The fear of not getting a good job or being successful is expressed more often by the boys than the girls. Presumably this is a response to societal expectations that the male will be the money-earning head of the family. Although boys feel this pressure and react to it with greater apprehension, both sexes share it.

"I'm afraid of not making it when I'm on my own. Suppose I can't get a decent job and support myself and a family, if I have one?" (Jerry, 15)

"I'm afraid of people being smarter than me, and being able to outwit me. That way I don't have control and they can manipulate me. I want to be able to control my life and be successful." (Eve, 14)

The majority want to get ahead and make something of themselves. They are not only interested in being successful, but they care a great deal about working in a field that they truly enjoy. Many of them report that they would not want to remain in a job they didn't like, even if it paid well. They have seen their fathers and mothers working at jobs they hate, and the teenagers tell us they do not want to be trapped in the same way.

## Additional Fears

| | |
|---|---|
| Not doing well in school | 18% |
| Nuclear war | 14% |
| People not liking you | 12% |
| Getting cancer | 10% |
| Not getting married | 6% |
| Getting attacked or mugged | 6% |

Only a small percentage express any fear about remaining unmarried. Twenty years ago, this would not have been the case. But today's young people are not preoccupied with finding a permanent mate, and although they believe in marriage and hope to be married themselves at some time, they are not concerned about postponing it or even remaining single forever. Other fears, having to do with current experiences, are more pressing. They worry about being accepted. College-bound kids worry about being on their own. One eighteen-year-old states: "I know what kind of person I am, but I don't know how other people are going to react to me." Some are afraid of a run-in with the law, losing friends, or being in a bad accident. A few who are gay fear discovery. Others fear for their country. Jean, sixteen, says, "My biggest fear is that the United States is going to pot. The Russians are building up militarily and we're not keeping up. We're coming down." And one sixteen-year-old tells us, "I have very general fears, like awful things will happen that you can't control. The whole nuclear situation scares me. Somehow, if you get attacked on the street you have some sort of control. But things like bombs and wars—you're helpless. I'm afraid to be incapacitated. Like if I were in a wheelchair and couldn't do things for myself, but had to have people wait on me." (Jane, 16)

Today's teenagers are experiencing a world of infinitely more rapid technological change than their predecessors. They are challenged by new and diverse social customs and values. They are confronted daily by new facts and theories, and they must conjure up ways of dealing with threats and situations far beyond the imaginations of most other generations. Nevertheless, their judgments remain virtually constant with past generations and traditions. They value strength of character and integrity. They want to be able to take care of themselves without having to depend on others. They want their families to remain stable, and they want to be able to live peacefully and explore their futures. An impressive set of values and goals.

# 7

# Teenagers on Their Parents' Marriage; Divorce; One-Parent Families; Stepparents

---

• 81% think parents have a happy marriage to some degree, although this view is altered as teenagers (particularly girls) get older
• 75% think divorce is preferable to staying together if parents are truly unhappy
• More girls than boys favor divorce

---

### Parents' Marriage—Do Adolescents Know What's Really Going On?

**M**ost parents would like to believe that their teenagers remain innocently unaware of marital discord or conflict. Not so! When Mother and Father are angry at each other, their unhappiness affects the entire family. Teenagers know when Mom is upset or relaxed; when Dad is grumpy, happy, or worn out. What they don't know is why, because many parents try to conceal their marital problems and shrug off their children's questions.

Children catch on to this pattern of concealment and evasion at an early age. In fact, the whole family participates in a conspiracy of silence when everyone pretends that Dad is content even though he gets drunk every evening and falls asleep in front of the TV. Everyone tacitly agrees to ignore the problem and, most important of all, everyone agrees to act as though there is no such agreement. For many families, this process is an instinctive method of survival;

by pretending everything's fine, they hope everything really will be fine. For example, Mother may suspect Father has a lover, but "for the sake of the children," nothing is said. Father comes home late or not at all three nights a week. Sounds of an argument and crying are heard, and Mother is quiet and tight-lipped in the morning. When the children ask what's wrong, they are told that nothing is wrong; that Mother and Father were just talking to each other too loudly the night before; that there is no need to worry because everything is just fine. By avoiding a confrontation, parents protect themselves as well as their children.

By late childhood, kids learn that they are not supposed to observe what is taking place. They are expected to pretend that they think their parents are always happy and loving. In fact, we believe that a "happy marriage" is one of those moral concepts that is "meant to be," like loving one's mother or believing in God, which may account for the following statistics.

When we asked, "Do you think your parents have a happy marriage?," only 19% said "No." Of the 81% who responded affirmatively, 70% said "Yes" or "Usually," while the remaining 11% offered a less positive "Sometimes." Thirteen-to-fifteen-year-old girls profess more than any others that their parents are happy. However, as the chart indicates, by the time they reach age sixteen, they are not quite so idealistic.

|  | Girls 13–15 | Girls 16–18 | Boys 13–15 | Boys 16–18 |
|---|---|---|---|---|
| Definitely yes, parents have a happy marriage | 60% | 47% | 51% | 51% |
| No, parents do not have a happy marriage | 17% | 23% | 17% | 20% |

## What Makes a Good Marriage? Why Don't Some Work?

When adolescents describe their parents' marriage, they generally focus on the patterns and routines their parents have established to maintain peaceful coexistence. When these patterns keep the peace effectively, teenagers consider the marriage successful. On the other hand, relationships that are characterized by any of the following problems make no sense to our kids whatsoever:

—Constant arguing
—Violence and physical abuse
—Domination by one spouse
—Lack of communication
—Settling for boredom and permanent unhappiness

## Communication

Our teenagers believe that a natural exchange of thoughts and feelings is the basis for a happy marriage. They recognize the value of open dialogue, whether it is between parent and child, husband and wife, or friends. Teenagers are just beginning to experience and explore adult emotions and to discover the exquisitely painful ambiguities by which people communicate with each other. Therefore, talk is very important to them. Endless phone conversations with peers are devoted to sharing and analyzing their thoughts and feelings. From a teenager's perspective, parents must be friends who like each other and can talk to each other if a marital relationship is to survive.

When parents don't communicate, teenagers are puzzled. How can people live together that way? Why would they want to? Our kids have not yet learned about the persistence of habit, or the compromises adults make to cope with their fear of loneliness. Stanley, a fourteen-year-old from a small town in the East, says, "My parents like each other sometimes, but I think to have a good marriage you have to like each other most of the time. They don't talk to each other about really important things. I think they just tolerate each other." Sometimes they are perceptive enough to pinpoint the reasons for their parents' distance. Dominique, fourteen, explains: "My parents used to communicate more. My father talks but doesn't really listen. He'll just say, 'Yeah, yeah,' and he tunes out my mother. He thinks she talks too much. It's his fault, too, for not telling her he's not interested. I guess he's afraid he'll hurt her feelings."

Our kids are disturbed by this lack of mutual interest because they're afraid they will be tuned out in the same way. Clyde, a runaway who has appeared before Family Court, says that the hatred between his parents permeated the household and affected the kids severely:

"One time my father didn't talk to my mother for two years. I wouldn't want that if I got married. I also don't want to have kids growing up like me. It might go wrong the same way it went wrong for me. I didn't go wrong. My mother and father did. They hated each other and I think they hated us, too. I think that's why I run away so much, and end up in homes." (Clyde, 13)

This pattern of total noncommunication occurs more frequently than most of us realize. One eighteen-year-old tells us that she hadn't heard her parents say a word to each other in four years. And Faye, seventeen, describes a similar situation. "Lately my parents can't talk at all. They're not as close as they used to be. Because of my mother. She's a very religious person and is even more religious now and my father kind of resents that. She doesn't spend as much time with him as she used to. Right now my father's not speaking to my mother and that bothers me."

A striking contrast is offered by Patricia, fifteen, whose parents get along so well together that she believes "they'd be lost without each other." She explains: "My mother even picks out all my father's clothes and does everything for him. He consults with her about where to go out to eat and what to buy; how to fix things around the house. He tells her all about his work. He tells her everything."

### Parents Must Have Their Freedom, Too

Sharing is a valued quality, but dependency is not. Most adolescents agree that each partner must have the freedom to pursue his or her own interests and activities. Is this really possible? One seventeen-year-old thinks that is exactly why his parents are happy. He says that they don't get in each other's way, that they give each other space: "If my mom wants to go someplace and my father doesn't, he tells her to just go, and vice versa. They both have different interests, so if my mom wants to go to a museum and my father doesn't want to, it's okay. Or if he wants to play tennis all day, she never says anything. They do plenty of other things together and I think sometimes it's better if parents aren't together all the time. I'd go crazy being around someone all day long."

Our teenagers don't intend to fall prey to the kind of relationships Carlee and Jeanette describe:

"My father has to have my mother's attention at all times. He won't even let her read a book. If you want to know the truth he barely lets her breathe. I don't know how she stands it. If she talks on the phone for more than two minutes, he yells at her to get off. She doesn't have any life of her own and I think it stinks. She caters to him and gives in to everything he wants. No way I'd ever wait on my husband like that." (Carlee, 18)

"My parents' marriage was very one-sided. My dad did the things he wanted to do, with no questions asked. My mom stayed home, cleaned and cooked. If she went somewhere, it was always, 'Where are you going? What time will you be home? How much money did you spend?' It wasn't a giving relationship at all." (Jeanette, 16)

Paul, seventeen, believes that his parents may have to separate in order to resolve their differences. However, he realizes that it's their decision to make and he is very supportive. "My parents argue mainly about places they want to go. They're constantly on the move in their minds. My father has always wanted to do different things: everything from panning for gold to sailing around the world, and my mother is kind of insecure so they argue about what they want to do. She settles for what she has, and my father is constantly looking for something better. If my mother gets really pissed and starts calling him names, which has happened a couple of times (like after a recent move), my father knows it's just tension. She has to get it out somehow. And my mother's the same way. They've never said stuff like, 'I'm never talking to you again.' They're going to separate soon after we all leave, because they want to do their thing. My mother wants to live on a beach, kind of alone, and my father wants to roam around: get an old Chinese junk or something and sail around the world. They'll see each other. My mother can get along great on half of my father's retirement, and my father can do it too, on the other half. Whenever my mother needs something, I'm sure my father's going to be the one to take care of it. They got to lead their own lives after everybody's raised."

### Arguments Are Natural, but Violence Isn't

Kids witness many family arguments and they often judge their parents' marriage in terms of how such disputes are settled. As one seventeen-year-old states: "Their arguments come out loud and noisy, but the settlement comes out quiet." Some believe that parents who argue in private can spare their children distress. Brett, thirteen, tells us, "I never heard my parents yell at each other. I guess the big arguments are usually in private. They talk about things and make up that way, which I think is right. They never hold a grudge, either. My parents are older and have old-country ways, but I think they have a good marriage."

For the most part, disagreements should be aired, not pushed under the rug just because family members fear confrontation.

Learning how to handle arguments without damaging the other person or the relationship is a valuable lesson for adolescents on the threshold of adulthood. But when arguments are constant or violent, children know that the marriage is in trouble. It is frightening for them to see violence erupt between their parents, as Kay, seventeen, tells us: "One time my mother invited a lot of people to the house and my father didn't like that. They started fighting and it was really loud and violent. I was upstairs and was so scared that I hid in the closet with my brother and we both cried." And for fifteen-year-old Phil and his two sisters, home provides no sense of stability and security. He believes in no uncertain terms that his parents have a poor marriage. He says, "First they argue, then they hit. My father punches my mother and sometimes she's scared to hit him back. One time she called my uncle to help her; him and my father was fighting and it was awful. I get scared when my parents fight. Usually my father throws her out and she takes us to my grandmother. That's a lousy marriage!"

### Domination vs. Partnership

Although our kids don't approve of violent arguments, they do think that parents should stand up to each other. When one parent consistently dominates the other or forces the other into the role of perennial peacekeeper, they consider such behavior unfair. Sonia, fifteen, from an affluent Eastern family, remembers a drawing she made when she was a little girl, in which her father was a big black cat who took up the whole page. Her mother was depicted as a little gray mouse who cowered in a corner. She continues, "I would show the drawing to them. 'Mommy, this is you; Daddy, this is you!' So I must have sensed something even back then. I felt my father mostly dominated her and treated her poorly. There was never much communication or love between them." And Amy, sixteen, shares similar sentiments. "A friend of mine has a mother who does all the yelling and her dad kind of just sits back. I don't know how he does it, although sometimes I've seen him walk away and leave her talking to herself."

Quite a few of our interviewees tell us that their mothers always have to check out any decision with their fathers. Such behavior puzzles them. It doesn't match their view of marriage as a true partnership of equals. In their eyes, neither parents' word should be "law"; both should carry equal decision-making power. Although they understand that important family matters must be discussed and agreed upon by both parents, they feel that in routine situations the parent who is present should be able to make decisions without consulting the other. "My mom has as much sense as my father. She's even older than he is. Why does she always have to ask him things?" wonders one thirteen-year-old. "Sometimes I think it's a copout."

## How Do Teenagers' Attitudes About Parental Happiness Correspond to What They Want in Their Own Future?

There is no doubt that young people draw on their parents' marital experiences to determine what they want from their own marriages. Obviously, kids who think their parents have a bad marriage want something very different for themselves. But just as often, teenagers who believe their parents are happy find flaws in the relationship that they themselves couldn't tolerate.

"I could never stand a marriage like my parents'. I guess they're fine for each other, but I wouldn't want to live like that because I like to speak what's on my mind. My mother doesn't, and she usually concedes to my father. I guess my mother just figures, 'Why fight?' Maybe it's good because then there aren't so many drastic fights and they can stay married longer, but I don't know how she stands giving in all the time. I'd have to speak out!" (Belinda, 18)

Another eighteen-year-old tells us, "I'll never be a submissive wife like my mother. Never!" And Josh, sixteen, says, "My parents yell and yell and when they fight for real they throw lamps and things. It doesn't bother me because that's life. But I know I won't do that when and if I get married."

The majority want to be closer to their mates and communicate more effectively than they feel their parents do. A number also plan to have fewer children. One sixteen-year-old comments: "My parents are happy, but I think if they had it to do all over again, they would have had just two of us. That's all I want." The girls who have seen their fathers stay out at night vow to marry husbands who will be good family men. Those who view their parents' marriage as boring want more excitement in their own marriages. Patty, who is eighteen, speaks for some of the older teenagers when she says, "I know it can't be all perfect, I'm not unrealistic, but I feel most marriages are stagnant. I'd want someone very smart and very kind. My parents are kind to each other but there's no spark. They don't share many interests and their life is made up of nothing but routines. I want more than that. Maybe if my mother worked and got out in the world, it would be different. Or if they both took courses at night or something. They're both smart people but I think they've given in to the monotony of marriage."

In contrast, there are those who believe that their parents have a fine marriage. One seventeen-year-old explains why she would be happy in a situation similar to her parents':

"I really would like a marriage like my parents'. Their marriage isn't perfect but I guess none are except in the movies. But they genuinely care about each other, miss each other, and I never heard them say things they'd be sorry for later. I guess that's what real love is and I'd sure like to have it someday." (Terry, 17)

Your teenager may not assess every aspect of your marriage accurately, but you can bet he or she will come very close. Ask your teenagers what they think of your marriage. The feedback will be interesting.

## Divorce

### Those Who Say "Yes" to Divorce

Loss of parents ranks as our youngsters' greatest fear, and we know that splitting up the family is enormously painful for them. Nevertheless, under certain circumstances, teenagers definitely condone divorce, although they usually come to such a conclusion warily.

---

Do you ever think it would be better for parents to get a divorce rather than stay together?

| | |
|---|---|
| Yes | 75% |
| No | 25% |

---

Three out of 4 teenagers believe that divorce is justified if: parents argue all the time; physical violence is involved; one or both parents are unfaithful. We parents have to recognize that for our youngsters there are circumstances even worse than a family breakup; situations in which the home atmosphere can become so poisoned that divorce seems preferable. As seventeen-year-old Lisa says, "You wouldn't stay in a house that's on fire if you could get out." Seventeen-year-old Matthew agrees. "If things are really getting rotten, I think divorce is right. I wouldn't want my parents to, but they're happy. If they weren't, though, it's their life, and it's too short to spend it with someone you're always fighting with."

Girls, as a group, are more decisive then boys in condoning divorce when violence or unfaithfulness is involved.

---

• 55% of girls 13–18 say divorce is necessary if there is violence; only 42% of the boys agree
• 50% of girls 13–18 say divorce is necessary if there is unfaithfulness; only 34% of the boys agree

---

The older the girls, the more they hold those views.

| | Boys | | Girls | |
|---|---|---|---|---|
| | 13–15 | 16–18 | 13–15 | 16–18 |
| Favor divorce if violence is involved | 42% | 43% | 52% | 59% |
| Favor divorce if unfaithfulness is involved | 33% | 36% | 43% | 56% |

By the time they reach adolescence, both boys and girls understand that women are more likely to be victimized by violence or infidelity, and girls in particular identify with mothers who have suffered in these ways. As the naïve, preadolescent girl gradually becomes a woman, she learns what it means to live in a culture that practices sexual politics. Often, it can be a bitter lesson, as seventeen-year-old Suzy attests: "My father was having a bunch of affairs. When my mother was in the hospital having my younger sister, he was out with somebody else. I don't blame her for divorcing him. I think if I was her, I would have killed him!"

Claire and Trev are equally vehement about this issue, although Claire, like many girls her age, is less inclined to believe that divorce is the solution. For her, it's definitely a last resort, permissible only if the children are being harmed.

"One time my father went out and didn't come back for two days. He was drunk. My mom was mad and said, 'Papa, you forgot you even had a family.' I was afraid they might get divorced then. My mom called my grandmother and told her we were going to be on a morning flight to California because my father wanted a divorce. My mom was in really bad shape. She was crying. Finally, my father came to his senses and said he was sorry. I only think divorce should be if a parent is beating up the children. If it starts small, let it go. But if it continues, then the child should be separated from the parent who is hitting all the time. I don't like the idea of divorce, but you can't have a parent beating up kids." (Claire, 13)

"My father (he's actually my stepfather) is the kind that likes to be with other women on the weekends and he likes to stay out. Then when he comes back, my mother accepts him and forgives him. They don't get along at all. A year ago I saw my stepfather in a disco with this lady who lives upstairs. I called my mother and said, 'Your husband is in a disco with a woman!' She ran to the disco and there was a big argument. She said, 'I'm going to leave you,' but a week later they're back together again. He doesn't talk to her; he just uses her. She's a fool, but I feel sorry for her." (Trev, 17)

The number of boys (regardless of age) who disapprove of infidelity suggests that they have enough empathy to identify with their mothers' position. Fifteen-year-old Eric knew what his father's absences meant, and he can't find any reason to defend him: "When I was younger, my father was never around anyway. He'd come home for supper and then go out. So I never saw him much at all. My father wanted a divorce because he wanted his freedom. He was running around with many other women throughout their whole marriage, and even on their honeymoon. That's bad news! For me, if there weren't any kids, and my wife was unfaithful, I might consider divorce."

Although most of the teens we interviewed spoke only about their fathers' infidelities, we are certain that they would feel as strongly if their mothers were unfaithful.

### Divorce Is Not for Everyone

For 25% of our respondents, divorce simply isn't an option—under any circumstances. Some cite religious beliefs to justify this viewpoint, but what comes through most poignantly is the emotional trauma they would experience. As fourteen-year-old William states: "I'm part of both of them and I couldn't choose. If my parents got a divorce, I would go crazy. Sometimes if I even think of it, I start crying. But I guess if it happened, I'd have to accept it."

Many cling to the conviction that problems can be solved if parents make a real effort. When Eileen's parents did not follow through with a threatened divorce she was pleased, and even though she wonders whether that was the right decision, she remains firmly antidivorce.

"My parents have problems. They were going to get divorced when I was in seventh grade. I wanted my daddy back, and I got him. I don't know if that was the right thing or not. It probably would have been easier if they had gotten a divorce. But I still care about my dad even though he's a pain. If I was married, I wouldn't get a divorce if there were just fights. If he was beating me, I'd recommend him to psychiatric help and turn him into an abuse center. I'd try and work it out first and if he kept beating me, I'd say, 'Let's get separated for a while,' and hope that would work." (Eileen, 15)

For these kids, divorce may be inevitable, but it's never desirable. It means the destruction of their fantasies of the "happily-ever-after" family. It means choosing between two much-loved parents; deciding who is right, who is at fault, and who is the more reliable. And it may often mean rejection. Therefore, it's not surprising that teenagers want and expect parents to take every step possible to avoid divorce. They deplore rash actions and decisions made in anger. As Debbie, fifteen years old, expresses it: "They should put some effort into trying to get together. Then if it just doesn't work out, I can understand it if they part."

## Children Are Divorced, Too

In the midst of their own anger and pain, divorcing parents sometimes forget that their children are ending relationships, too. And unlike their parents, kids have not freely chosen to do so. Nor do they have an adult's years of experience to draw on to help them reshape their lives. Therefore, it is vitally important that parents explain exactly what's happening and why. Children must be told that they are not responsible, that there's nothing they could or should have done to prevent the divorce. And they desperately need to be reassured that each parent will continue to love them and spend time with them whenever possible. They want to know the truth and they appreciate parents who level with them. Evasions or half-truths have a way of coming back to haunt parents, and they do not give the child the security and answers that he or she needs. "Divorce is the pits," states an eighteen-year-old. "I don't think I was affected too badly, but all I knew was that this man who was taking us out on Saturdays wasn't coming around anymore.

They should have told us the whole truth." Three others share their feelings:

"I don't disapprove of the divorce but I believe that parents shouldn't just spring it on their kids. I had to find out from my grandmother when my parents got divorced. We came up from Florida when I was eleven. Mom was just settling into the house and we spent a lot of time with my grandmother. She told us. I thought my parents were just spending some time away from each other, but my mom just moved away and took us." (Mary, 16)

"I remember the day it happened. It was a summer day and there was a new car in the driveway. I came in and said, 'Oh, you got a new car!' Mom said, 'Yes, it's Daddy's car and he's leaving. He's not going to live here anymore, but he'll come back and see you.' I was six at the time. I didn't really understand what they were talking about. Then I saw my dad start to cry. I was shocked. I didn't cry then but I'm sure I cried afterward. He kissed me and held me and then walked out. That was the last time he lived here. I see him every two to four weeks. Later on I understood that he wasn't easy to live with so I guess my mother is happier, but she's pretty down on life." (Fran, 14)

"One night my father just left. My parents didn't fight at all. That was probably the problem. No one in the family expected it. It shocked everyone; friends, family, including me. I was young and didn't understand what divorce was. They told me, at first, that Daddy was leaving for a little while so it wasn't like he was going away and we'd never see him again. It was sort of a gradual thing. I saw him a lot. He lives in a different city now, but I used to see him every weekend so it wasn't so terrible. They didn't talk about it because they didn't think it was anything to discuss. They were just very different people who married too young and outgrew each other. They talk together all the time. It was a very sociable divorce." (Barbara, 18)

## Sharing and Helping One Another

A separation is always painful, but it can be made less so. If feelings are shared, if realities are discussed and preparations are made, the process becomes one in which all take part. "We talked a lot. We could see the divorce coming," says one seventeen-year-old whose parents did talk about their problems with her. And Hildy, sixteen, contrasts her experience with that of a friend's: "I think if parents are honest about divorce, I mean explain to their kids what's happening, it's less of a sad thing. My friend's parents never discussed their divorce with her, and it was a heartbreaking situation. I still don't think she's over it. But my parents talked to us for a long time and helped us understand their feelings and how even though they cared for each other, they just couldn't live together. They're really good friends now. I never want to get divorced but if my husband and I couldn't get along and we had to split, I'd handle it the way my parents did."

## After the Divorce

The adaptability of the human animal is nowhere more evident than in the postdivorce adjustments that children make. Once the split-up is a reality, and the pain of the actual severing is over, new assessments are possible. The children of divorced parents are less likely to say, "No, never" to divorce than those living with both parents. They have been there. They remember the discord, the long silences, and the tensions. "To tell you the truth, I was for it," comments one seventeen-year-old. "I figured, 'There's not going to be any more fighting between these two.' It's a hassle having parents who are like that all the time." A sixteen-year-old concurs: "I offered to pay for half of my parents' marriage counseling, but when it still didn't work, I gave up. I'm glad they split, though. It's a lot better for me now."

Kids realize that people cannot and should not put up with a relationship that is continually painful and destructive. As sixteen-year-old Tracy observes: "It's good my parents got divorced because as much as I loved them both, I saw a lot of hurt between them and it hurt us, too. When there's lots of fighting, even behind closed doors, the kids know. I would have liked things to work out instead, but I think I've grown up okay this way. My parents weren't good friends. I don't think they really knew each other. My dad liked my mom a little, but she didn't like him at all. It's better they're not together anymore." Tracy is determined that she and her husband will share their feelings, and she concludes, "Although half of my friends have parents who are divorced, I hope that when I'm married we'll stay together. I know nobody thinks they'll get divorced when they're first married, and I know divorce is not the end of the world—I survived—but I'll be darned sure of a good relationship before I'm married, and then I'll really try to keep it together."

## More Changes After Divorce

After the breakup new tensions may arise as family members struggle to cope with and adapt to the changes in the family structure. A child may become the recipient of disturbed or angry outbursts that were previously directed at the now-absent partner. Sometimes, parents use their children to work out their own feelings of loneliness and resentment. Diane, who is fifteen, tells us, "My father used to beat the shit out of my mother. It scared me because I didn't understand it. But since I'm living with her, I really hate her and blame a lot of the divorce on her. I don't feel that my mother deserved my father. He probably had to knock the hell out of her. It gets to the point where a person can only take so much. I think she gets mad at me sometimes because I remind her of him. When my mother and me got into an argument today, I told her, 'You're driving everybody away from you. Stop and think why you don't have anybody.' She got very upset and smacked me. She hit me a couple of times. She always thinks that's the way to solve things." And Jean, fourteen, says, "The hard thing is when my mother has problems and takes them out on me because she doesn't have a husband to take it out on." Parents must be particularly careful not to use their children as scapegoats for their own hurts. The darts must be aimed at the right target, not the nearest one at hand.

Another major change occurs when parents begin to play the singles game. Teenagers are often jealous when Mother or Father becomes involved with someone new, someone who might even become a stepparent. Mother may be spending a great deal more time and money on herself during this transitional period, and teenagers often resent both her absence and her preoccupation with the elements of her new life. There may also be jealousy if the parent dates more often than the teenager. And when a parent affects a personality change in order to impress a new date, many teenagers have reactions similar to seventeen-year-old Tom's: "My mom was so phony when she started dating. She dressed and acted like she was eighteen, and it was so embarrassing. She took disco lessons and was on the phone more than I was. She's mellowed out since."

But a particularly disrupting change for teenagers is the loss of financial security.

## When Father Doesn't Pay

Some of the kids describe themselves as pawns in their parents' money battles, often having to call their fathers when checks don't come in. Randy, an eleventh-grader, works in a fast-food restaurant after school. He feels he would not have to work so hard if his father were fulfilling his responsibilities, and he doesn't hesitate to express his opinions: "I don't think of anything about my father that I like. I don't really hate him, but I just don't like him. He's really out of the picture, not supporting us or anything, and I think that stinks. He's really a nothing."

The abandoning father is an unfortunate reality in the lives of many teenagers, occurring far more frequently than the abandoning mother (although we are hearing more and more about runaway mothers). Younger children are not aware of the financial problems created by nonsupport, but the older ones are often incensed and hurt by what they perceive as rejection and neglect by their fathers.

"I was a little kid when my mother and father split up. They were separated because he wouldn't pay the hospital bills. I was always in the hospital. Then just last year she got a divorce. And I say 'Good riddance' to him. I hate his guts because he left me. He never paid for anything and left my mom with all the bills. My mom cut his face out of all her wedding pictures." (Sue Ann, 16)

Father's failure to make any attempt to provide for his children is an indication to them that he doesn't really care. Nan, sixteen years old, weighs what each of her parents means to her in terms of whether they care enough to be there for her and her brother. "My father doesn't support me or my brother. I guess at first it hurt, but now I've got to the point where it doesn't bother me. I've accepted that he doesn't care. Maybe he has his own life to live, but he doesn't want to take time to include us in it. He doesn't have any good qualities left, although my mother says we shouldn't stop loving him. He always took care of us and put his family first, but now it's not that way. When things got bad, he gave up. My mom has always been there and taken care of us. She always comes through. I respect the fact that she hasn't given me everything. I don't think that parents should just hand you things. I think you should have to work for them."

Bert, sixteen, is mature enough to discuss his father's faults objectively: "I don't think he could handle the responsibilities of being a parent and that's one of the reasons they broke up." At the same time, however, he's still very bitter about his father's neglect. He explains: "I really resent that he has a lot of money (my mom doesn't have any) and he won't support us." Children of divorce are saying, "If Father wants to be considered my parent, he had better love me, help me, work with me, and fulfill his responsibilities to me." They want their fathers to be a part of their lives, and if they do let him go, it is only under extreme provocation and with great sorrow.

The distance between father and child may be intensified by divorce agreements that give one parent full custody while the other receives subsidiary status at best. Joint custody is one solution to this problem, and it is an increasingly popular choice. Clearly, children suffer least when both parents continue to function as full-time parents, rather than occasional visitors. If pressure has to be invoked to force a parent to accept his or her responsibility, the child may receive financial support but little else of value.

## One-Parent Families

Twenty-six percent of our respondents are living with one parent, usually their mother. And single mothers are more likely to work. According to our data, 77% work as compared to only 62% in two-parent families. Whether teenagers live with one parent or two, there are no differences in their attitudes or behavior in any of the categories we measured except one. More teenagers in one-parent families (51%) have had sexual intercourse than have those living with two parents (42%). The simplest explanation is that they spend more time at home on their own. Yet, this difference in sexual activity is not great; only 9%. The fact that there are no measurable differences in all the other categories suggests that living with one parent does not have any effect on normal adolescent development.

## Living With One Parent Can Be a Relief

| | |
|---|---|
| If you are living with one parent, how do you feel about it? | |
| Like it because it's less of a hassle than when both parents were together | 32% |
| Hope that parents will get married again | 24% |
| Miss the other parent | 24% |
| Don't think about it because it has always been that way | 18% |
| Feel embarrassed and different living with only one parent | 9% |

About one-third are relieved to be free of the arguments and stresses that they encountered prior to their parents' breakup. Their comments indicate that their new life-style is more relaxed. Joanie, fifteen, tells us, "Now that my mom and I are alone together, it's really peaceful. I don't have two parents telling me what to do all the time. I don't have to wait for my mother to consult with my father, or vice versa. They never agreed anyway! Now when I ask my mother a question, she answers. It's a lot easier now."

And a seventeen-year-old from the South observes: "The only difference I can see living with my mom alone is that my sister, who's nine, tends to be more affectionate toward guys. I think she misses my father more than I do. But then again, she never knew what he did to my mother. She only remembers the good times because she was always asleep when they argued and hit." (Sophie, 17)

Many of the teenagers say that they have more freedom and independence. There's no evidence that their life-styles or behavior change, but they like the fact that there are fewer restrictions and authoritarian rules. As sixteen-year-old Allen says, "I've got a lot more freedom now and my mother says I'm the man of the house. There's nobody that can tell me what to do, either physically or verbally, and you feel a lot more sure of yourself. My brother feels the same way. I don't really think he liked having my dad around either." One eighteen-year-old, who lives with his mother and grandmother, enjoys being the only male in the house. "My grandmother takes the father role but they both still have that womanness in them which isn't able to push teenage kids around. And that's nice because I'm a lot more free."

## The Disadvantages of Living with One Parent

Despite Father's strictness many adolescents miss him, and deeply wish that he was still with them. Jeanette, fourteen, says, "You know how they say, 'You're your mother's son and your father's daughter.' Well, I'd like to be closer to a man; I get along better with guys than with women." Her comments and those of eighteen-year-old Tess emphasize the adolescent's need for both parents. "I didn't like living with one parent. Before the divorce, I had a very nice family life and my parents got along very well. It was one less person to give you attention, to listen to, to be with. I didn't like the idea that the unity of the family was disrupted. You're always hoping at that age that your parents will get back together again. It's not until you are eleven or twelve that you understand that Daddy won't be back."

The younger teenagers who live with one parent express more of a sense of embarrassment about being "different" than do the other adolescents. Because they are more attached to the family and its activities, they feel left out when they see their friends being close to or involved with their fathers, especially on those occasions when the absent parent would ordinarily be involved (father/son, father/daughter activities). They also find it difficult to answer questions about the missing parent. As one thirteen-year-old says, "It really embarrasses me when people don't know my parents are divorced and they ask me something about my father, like, 'Do you look like your father?' How should I know? He split when I was born. If they're strangers I just say, 'I don't have a father.' Then you should see their faces!"

Usually by the time they reach age sixteen or seventeen, they are aware of the number of others who share their circumstances.

"I miss my father, but I know my parents were unhappy together so I guess it was the best thing that they split. It's no big deal living with just my mom. I didn't like it as much when I was younger because the other kids would talk about their fathers, and I couldn't. But now a lot of the kids I know have parents who are divorced." (John, 16)

## Remarriage

### Some Teenagers Are All for It

Once teenagers have accepted the reality of divorce and adjusted to life with one parent, they may begin looking for a new "resident" father or mother to complete the family. Often, this wish is motivated by loneliness. One fifteen-year-old wanted her mother to remarry a particular man who had sons because she very much wanted stepbrothers. Another says, "I loved it when my mom started to see people again, as long as I knew my father was gone for good. It was nice to have people around. I'm an only child. All her dates were nice to me."

Many teenagers feel that it's their responsibility to make sure that their parent's life is not empty and lonely. They may be troubled because they are having fun with friends while Mom is obviously alone and bereft of male companionship. Linda, who enjoys a sense of close kinship with a number of nearby relatives, worries about her mother.

"My mom is afraid of growing old by herself and she feels that every responsibility is on her. Sometimes that's one reason we don't get along. My grandma just got married recently and she's sixty-seven. Boy, she's like sixteen again! It's really changed her a lot. What my mom needs is someone to say, 'I'm here, you don't have to worry.' If someone was there, it would also take the pressure off of me. Sometimes I'm more of a mother to her. I tell her, 'Mom, it's all right. We'll manage.' " (Linda, 17)

And Jack's wish for his mother is honest and compassionate; he truly wants her to be happy.

"I'd like my mother to get married again, not because I want a father, but because she needs somebody. You see, *our* lives are *her* life. I don't open up to her about my personal feelings so she doesn't have anything to do, nobody to relate to. It would be nice for her to have somebody." (Jack, 17)

But they're not only worried about their mothers. Fathers get lonely also, and two of our teenagers express concern for their fathers.

"When my father got married again, I just loved his new wife. (I didn't live with him.) I was very happy for him. I used to worry about him because he doesn't cook, doesn't take care of himself, so I was very pleased at the time that there was someone to take care of him. It wasn't until after they were married a year that she turned sour, much to the chagrin of the family." (Joyce, 18)

"My mother died when I was nine and my father was so upset. He didn't smile for a long time and he didn't start dating other women for about two years. But he's over it now and I wish he'd get married again. I know how happy he was when my mom was around." (Jennifer, 17)

In contrast, some adolescents, mainly girls, celebrate their mothers' newfound freedom from unpleasant subordination to a husband. "My mother is really independent and I don't think she'll get married again," states Suzy, eighteen. "Actually, I don't blame her. She and my father had a 'friendly' divorce, but I can see how much happier she is not having to answer to someone all the time. He always wanted her home and she wanted to work. She's really bright and has a master's degree and my father just expected her to vegetate. But you never can tell. I wouldn't mind a stepfather."

## Stepparents

### How Will the New Parent Treat Me?

A stepparent may be fantasized as a savior of the family, Mother's needed companion, a replacement for the absent parent, or an unwelcome intruder. Whether or not a stepparent will be accepted in the long run depends upon the nature of the relationship that he or she can establish with the adolescent. "Now my mother lives with a man and things are pretty good," states Charles, sixteen. "I was unsure about it at first, both the situation *and* the man. I was much younger and I used to have fantasies about someone on a motorcycle taking me away and kidnapping me. We did have some trouble, and still do, just because of personalities. He's a powerful person."

If the stepparent tries to take over, trouble will develop, as two sixteen-year-olds explain:

"If it was the right guy, and he likes me and I like him, then she might get married again. As long as he wasn't poor, I wouldn't mind it. And he can't boss me around. That is the main thing. If he'd boss me around he'd get it right back from me. He'd have to know he's not going to be the boss in the house. I'm going to be just as bossy as he would be." (Alex, 16)

"Joe, my stepfather, says he's going to bring up this daughter (me) the same as his other one. The way he punished her, that's how he'll punish me. How does he know I'll do the same things she did? You can't compare kids. I resent that." (Becky, 16)

Family relationships change when a stepparent is introduced into the family unit. Although parent and child may not get along perfectly, they have established a life-style and a pattern of interaction that is comfortable and familiar to both. But when the new parent arrives, the child is suddenly thrust into unfamiliar territory. His life-style may change, and his relationship with his parent will certainly be different. And he begins to worry: Will my mother's love for her new husband deprive me of her love? Will there be enough love to go around? The child may vie for the stepparent's attention, either with other siblings or with the original parent. It is not an easy situation, as Dean, seventeen, points out. In her case, it worked out well, although it took quite a while. She explains: "At first when I was thirteen, my stepfather and I didn't get along very well. This lasted about a year and my mother didn't marry him right away. But now I'm closer to him than I am to my father. We get along almost better than he and my mother. But it was a difficult period, sixth and seventh grades. We are very similar and we competed, not consciously, but we did. We were both very aggressive and independent and all those things clashed. We were both pulling at my mother a lot. I didn't have a sister or brother to balance any of this off; it was either me alone, or with my mother, and I had to adjust. In the beginning of a relationship of a man and a woman, they want to spend time together, alone. You don't want to have a child right when you first meet your husband; but there I was. Now, though, it's fine."

Another young woman, eighteen, has learned what adult love is all about by watching her mother and stepfather together. She says they are "really in love," and she would like what they have. "My parents met each other when they were thirty-five, and they really knew who they were and what they wanted. Their relationship is beautiful."

There has been no experience of loss for either of these young women. Their stepfathers have supplemented and expanded their families, and given their mothers a fuller, more satisfying life. And each teenager enjoys a gratifying relationship with a new parent. In contrast, when there is no real effort at rapprochement or when the stepparent fails to take on the responsibilities of being a parent, trouble ensues.

The most irresponsible and devastating situation occurs when a stepparent abuses a child in some way. Such behavior leaves emotional scars that are not easily erased.

## The Stepfather as Seducer

"My stepfather and I don't communicate. We don't talk to each other. Not only because of what he's done to me, but what he's doing to my family. He chased me all over the house and he tried to abuse me sexually. I feel he turned my family against me because when I told my mother what he did, he said it was all bullshit. I was eight years old. He tried again when I was twelve. I pushed him away and he didn't bother me that way again, although he always had his hands on me and tried to kiss me. He said he wanted to marry me and have kids with me. At age twelve! It was a very frightening feeling. Then at fifteen, I left." (Trini, 17)

In similar cases, when a stepparent tries to abuse a child sexually, the natural parent may ignore the problem or insist that it did not happen. Why? Generally because the mother has conflicting desires. She's afraid of jeopardizing her marriage, while at the same time she wants to protect her child. If fear of losing her husband is her dominant concern, she may be unwilling to confront him, and allows the abusive situation to continue. Even if she does discuss it, the stepfather may deny it and the incident will be pushed aside quickly by the two of them. But not by the child. Trini ran away, as do many abused children. However, other children cannot and the abuse may continue, unnoticed or purposely ignored by the other parent or members of the family.

If a youngster complains of being abused (telling a parent he or she is being fondled or played with), the situation should be investigated even if the parent suspects the child may be lying. Talk about it. Get professional help. No adult relationship is so important that it supersedes the well-being of a child.

In most cases, however, teenagers who don't get along with stepparents have less serious grounds for complaint. For some, dislike stems from personality differences or jealousy. Kate, fifteen, states: "Once my mother gets with my stepfather, she's totally different. She always agrees with him about everything, no matter what we say. That really gets me mad. When she's around him, I find I can't be in the same mood as I can when we're alone. She's two different people. I guess she wants to prove things to him because they've just started to be married. She wants to impress him."

And other teenagers, like eighteen-year-old Doris, honestly believe their parents made a mistake in marrying the stepparent. "It was great when the three of us and my mom were by ourselves. But last year she married Jim, and I hate it. I'm not jealous or anything like that. It's just that he takes advantage of her and she can't see it. I can understand that she was lonely and wanted somebody, but why him? Maybe he was the only one around but I sure can't wait till next year when I can move out."

## Stepbrothers and Stepsisters

### Are Stepsiblings Pains or Pleasures?

Children who are thrown together when their parents marry have as many problems to work out as do their parents. (At least the parents have the advantage of loving each other and wanting to be together.) Issues involving partiality, sharing, comparisons, achievements, and personality traits can provoke streams of irritation. These are inevitable to some degree because individuals who are forced to live together are bound to have some conflicts. Therefore, it is particularly important for the children to have the freedom to preserve the friends and interests they had earlier so they won't experience a sense of loss. Stepsiblings are, after all, strangers to each other unless there has been a prolonged premarital relationship. They will have to work out between themselves the ways in which they can get along, but the adjustment period may be easier if they can turn to old, familiar friends for comfort. Stepparents can ease the transition by getting to know each child and treating him or her as a unique individual. They must avoid slotting their own children or their stepchildren into predefined roles such as "good kid," "bad kid," "selfish," or "nasty." The temptation to categorize kids in this fashion is particularly strong in combined families, and can only lead to trouble. Frederick, a sixteen-year-old whose father recently remarried, accepts the marriage but bemoans the presence of a stepsister. "At first it was okay, before my dad and her mother got married. We were really friendly before she became my stepsister.

As soon as she got to be my stepsister, she turned into a total bitch. For a while we hated each other. Then we'd like each other for a little while. Stepkids are trouble. If she started getting treated better than me, then the jealousy would show. I lived with my father for a while, but went back to my mother because I couldn't stand it."

Only or lonely children may look forward to the companionship that a ready-made brother or sister can offer. Often, they get their wish, but sometimes, as Darcy's story indicates, they discover they were better off when they were alone. She innocently stumbled into a most touchy situation with her stepbrother:

"Something happened last year that was very bad. I don't know what you call it—a love affair or something. I was lied to and hurt. I was used by my stepbrother. I haven't talked to him since, just a few times in the past month. Maybe since I couldn't talk to my mother, I found I could talk with him again. But I'll never forgive him for doing what he did. It wasn't exactly—I don't know how to explain it. He approached me, sexually. It was like a boyfriend-girlfriend thing. It would have gone on to worse things that I didn't like at all. My mother found out right in time. My stepbrother was always lying. I knew he was, but I was too young to understand. I was eleven, twelve. Since he said he loved me, I thought I must love him, too. I automatically assumed that one deserved the other. That's not the way it was at all. It took my mother to find that out." (Darcy, 13)

The comments of these young people indicate that the stepfamily situation is not an easy one for either children or parents. It takes time for family members to test each other and explore feelings, routines, and conflicting personalities. But when a caring relationship is established between stepparent and teenager, teenagers feel that they're not losing a natural parent. Instead they're gaining an extra parent—and a new friend as well!

## Guidelines for Stepparents

1. *Don't rush.* Give the family a chance to get to know you before you start setting up new rules.

2. *Try to become familiar with each child's personality, likes, dislikes, talents and problems, before "moving in" with your ideas about discipline and childrearing.*

**3.** *Let the kids know you are there to help and to listen.* They'll come to you when they are ready.

**4.** *Don't compare your own natural children with your new children.* Treat them equally, but respect their individual differences.

**5.** *Love.*

# 8

# Teenagers on Brothers and Sisters

---

- 82% like their brothers and sisters most of the time
- Only 3% don't like them at all
- Lack of privacy is the number one complaint among children with brothers or sisters

---

## The Love/Hate Relationship

**A**sk any teenager to describe his or her feelings about a sibling and you're sure to hear a barrage of emotions: affection, irritation, excitement, frustration, genuine love, profound hate. It's a relationship that can't be summed up easily. From infancy upward, siblings seem to love and hate one another simultaneously. Toddlers suggest that a newly arrived infant is really an unnecessary addition who should be returned. Yet even as they launch a campaign to get rid of the unwelcome intruder, they stand guard at the baby's crib, caressing, singing, protecting, loving.

That ambivalence continues. Love and hate. Love between siblings because they are family, because they share so much together, because they support one another and present a united front against the common enemy—parents. Tom, eighteen, describes this phenomenon. "My sister and I get along great now. We didn't use to, but we've kind of joined forces in the house to make a louder voice against my mom's drinking." And Troy, thirteen, comments: "If my father hits me, my oldest sister will stick up for me." Because parents are the ones who judge, reward, and punish, they usually can't become confidants or friends. But siblings can. They can share secrets with one another, or discuss escapades that can't be revealed to parents.

And yet there is hate—because of the very nature of the relationship. Siblings compete for attention, for privileges, for love; they manipulate each other as they struggle for power. Although it can be a boon to have a companion and ally right at home, there are times when the relationship backfires. Vengeful siblings who tattle or try to "get even" can be a real threat. In fact, disputes between brothers and sisters are among the thorniest and most unyielding of family problems. Parents struggle to resolve arguments that can never be settled. They seek the path of fairness through a thicket of "It's her fault," "I didn't start it," and other endless accusations. They are constantly wondering how brothers and sisters (who are supposed to love each other) can fight so vehemently. But is there any reason to expect perfect harmony between individuals just because they are blood relatives? Actually, it is often more difficult to get along with people who share some of our characteristics and who know all our shortcomings and pressure points.

When children rely on the family for companionship and intimacy, problems between brothers and sisters intensify. Sibling relationships become the focal point for handling all the problems of "getting along" that would otherwise be worked out with friends.

Relationships with siblings also provide a convenient stage on which to act out various tensions. For example, if a child is annoyed or angry with his parents, he may pick a fight with a brother or sister. When a boyfriend doesn't call, a sibling often bears the brunt of his sister's disappointment. If a teenager is failing a subject in school or feels inadequate or unpopular, pushing around a younger brother or sister can be an easy way to restore pride.

Jimmy, who is now seventeen, says that when he was in junior high school and feeling miserable about being new in town and friendless, his favorite activity was beating up his kid brother. "He was a pain, but I used to get really sadistic with him. I'm sorry now, because I think I was taking out all my frustrations on him. But then he used to really bug me."

Siblings also function as role models and as experienced adventurers who know the ropes and can offer advice. The younger child who insists on tagging along when her older sister goes to the movies with friends is trying to pull strength and support from the most logical place. She may be silently asking the questions, "How do I grow up?" "How do I find friends?" "What do I do when friends get mad at me? Show me. Protect me." When she is lucky enough to have someone who has just been through it all, the wisest path is to stay close to her.

Of course, such dependency can become unhealthy if it lasts too long because the younger child won't learn to develop self-reliance. When this seems to be taking place it is important that parents be alert, and help the younger one to define herself or himself.

Elaine, nine years old and the youngest of three sisters, had no friends of her own to play with after school. She was shy and apprehensive about being away from home. Over the years, she had become accustomed to depending on her middle sister, Nell, for companionship. Nell always had good ideas. When Nell entered adolescence she began to find more friends her own age to be with. She complained that Elaine was always underfoot, and she began to push her away when friends were around. Elaine became increasingly unhappy. She struggled to cling to Nell because she felt she had few inner resources and no one else to turn to. But Elaine's parents were wise. They realized that they had always considered her "the baby" and had not encouraged her to be independent. They began making efforts to show her that she had unique interests and abilities. When Elaine finally told her mother that she was lonely and afraid to make friends, her mother encouraged her to join a Brownie group and take up swimming, a sport at which she excelled. The process of individuation had begun for her in earnest, with parental support.

To discover the depth of the love/hate relationship, we asked:

| Do you like your brothers or sisters? | | |
|---|---|---|
| Yes | 64% | ⎫ |
| Usually | 18% | ⎬ 97% |
| Sometimes | 15% | ⎭ |
| No | | 3% |

These are probably surprising statistics for most parents who are convinced that their bickering children truly dislike each other and will never achieve even a reasonable amount of tolerance. However, it is clear that we all need the love and support of family members, sometimes more than we realize.

Family ties definitely supersede temporary annoyances, jealousies, competition, and resentment. Brothers and sisters may fight for territory, for control, for affection and attention, but in the long run they expect of each other and give to each other a degree of dependability that may go far beyond friendship. Sophie, thirteen, says, "At times my sisters and brothers have arguments and I say I hate their guts, but I don't mean it. We really love each other."

## The Major Sibling Problems

| | |
|---|---|
| Lack of privacy | 40% |
| Getting away with things | 30% |
| Teasing | 17% |
| Favoritism | 15% |
| (Some chose more than one answer) | |

### Lack of Privacy Cited by 4 Out of 10

Teenagers treasure their privacy and they resent siblings who intrude: the little brother who pesters his older sister when she's with her friends; the brother who wanders into his sister's room without knocking; the sister who borrows clothes, books, or records without asking. Christy, thirteen, says that her three older brothers never respected her privacy. "They'd go into my desk and take whatever they wanted. And they'd always cut in on my phone conversations when they wanted to use the phone. But," she admits, "now they're in college, I get kind of lonely." And Barbara, fifteen, complains about her younger sister: "My sister is nine and we don't get along. She's a pain. If I do something she has to know what I'm doing and she sleeps in my room even though she has a room to herself. So I usually don't get privacy from her."

### 3 Out of 10 Believe Siblings Get Away with Things They Shouldn't

This is a common complaint among older siblings who feel that kid brothers or sisters have privileges they didn't have when they were younger. Roz, eighteen, explains: "Sometimes I resent the way the relationship is between my mom and my sister. It's different from what I had. Maybe it's because she is more experienced than when she had me. She's raised the other three and learned from her mistakes with me. I resent the way she talks to my sister and certain things she lets her do that I wasn't allowed to do." Tony, fourteen, as the younger one, knows that he's getting the benefits of what went before, and doesn't mind the setup: "My brother had to break the ice for me," he says. "I just followed his movements. My mom practiced on him. She's more relaxed with me."

## Complaints About Teasing

Teasing is cited most often by the younger teenagers and the girls. It is a favorite weapon of the older and stronger who enjoy provoking the younger and weaker. But teasing is not necessarily an indication of annoyance or anger. Many older teenagers feel that it's beneath their dignity to be friendly with a young sibling, and affectionate teasing is their way of establishing contact. Meggen, fourteen, tells us, "My brother used to tease me so bad I was always in tears. I don't think he hated me but just liked to see the reaction he got out of me. He teased me instead of talking to me. I hated it. I always wished I had a younger brother so I could tease him."

## The Favoritism Issue—Unequal Distribution of Privileges and Attention

Is there a parent who has not heard the accusation "It's not fair" from a child who feels deprived of a right or privilege that has been given to a brother or sister? Usually this happens with such regularity that we tend to discount it as domestic rhetoric. Our standard response is that we treat all our children alike; that we have no favorites.

But the inevitable truth is that we all have preferences and different feelings about each child. Because we want to be fair, we are disturbed when we sense a partiality for one particular child. However, by recognizing and admitting that partiality exists, we are in a better position to control it. When we deny its existence, the unfairness operates below the awareness level and can become far more destructive.

### Favoritism Because of Age

Parents cannot help treating their firstborn differently. To brand-new parents, that first birth seems quite miraculous; the child even more so. Understandably, he or she becomes the focus of an enormous amount of attention and excitement. And it's a feeling that's never quite equaled by later births. However, parents learn their trade with the firstborn, and the later-born reap the benefits of that experience.

### The Youngest Child

Siblings particularly resent the favoritism accorded to the youngest member in the family. This feeling is more intense when the children are young, and the age difference is small, but older adolescents are not immune, either. Yvette, seventeen, comments: "I get along horribly with my brother. He's twelve and I'm seventeen. My mother really favors him. All my friends notice. My mother thinks he's such a little angel, but he's really such a brat. She favors him because he's younger and doesn't get into as much trouble as I do. My mother says she doesn't treat us any different. What a joke!"

As kids mature, the benefits often balance out. Nate, fourteen, explains: "I always thought my older brother was favored. I guess because he was older he'd get advantages like staying out later. But now I think I have it better because I'm sure when he was fourteen he didn't get to stay out as late as I do. But times have changed."

"My little sister gets treated best because she's the youngest. She's the one that always gets her picture taken. She's spoiled and it's unfair. But I guess I was spoiled when I was the youngest. There were times when they let me get away with a lot of things. I was sure they were going to yell at me and ground me, and they didn't. Well, I guess it evens out over the years." (Glenda, 13)

### The Oldest Child

However, being the youngest is not always desirable, as one thirteen-year-old points out. She says that her parents trust her older brothers and sisters more than they trust her. "I know when my sisters first started college, I felt like I was really nothing. Because they were older, most of the concentration was on them. They had all the privileges and respect. I had the feeling I was pushed down a lot and it hurt. Oldest children are really lucky. But it's better now."

And a fifteen-year-old agrees that being the oldest definitely has its advantages. "I like being the oldest. I get privileges like getting everything first and getting the clothes I want. I get to stay up later and take the car out every once in a while. I get mad at my younger brother and sister, and they're kind of scared of me. I like it that way."

### The Middle Child

It's obvious that there are definite advantages to being the oldest and the youngest. But what about the ones in the middle? One eighteen-year-old sums it up this way: "I was favored because I was the baby of the family. My middle sister always kind of got left out. The oldest ones get special treatment; your first pride and joy. And then the young one is your current pride and joy. But the middle child is sort of floating."

Birth position has an enormous impact on later development. Because older children dominate younger siblings and bear the brunt of their parents' ambitions, they often become high achievers, comfortable with power, authority, and responsibility. Younger children, on the other hand, may breeze through life optimistically, assuming there will always be protectors around. Or, they may have to struggle against feelings of inadequacy (as do some middle children) in order to achieve real independence.

### Favoritism Because of Sex

It is virtually impossible for parents to treat sons and daughters similarly. In all cultures there are contrasts in childrearing practice, and there are specific lessons and expectations communicated to each sex. Beyond this, many of us have special feelings toward boys or girls as a result of our backgrounds and beliefs. Our kids (particularly girls) pick up these preferences and protest what they see as unfairness. Rosita, from a traditional Hispanic background in the Southwest, spells out the situation as she views it in her family:

"I love my brother very much because he's the only brother I have. I had two sisters, but they both died. But my parents show a lot of favoritism toward my brother because he is a boy. Little brothers get away with everything. He has more liberty than I do. I resent that, but know it has to be that way. It always is. Especially in Spanish families." (Rosita, 17)

And Carrie, thirteen, comments: "Before my little brothers were born, my parents were much better to my little sister. Now they are much more into my brothers than me and my sister. Sometimes I feel bad about it. I wonder if they do care or not. We take care of the brothers and they leave us flat. They really wanted a boy. Now they have two."

Elona, fifteen, believes her mother gives her older brother more attention and really caters to him. She says, "I needed a tutor and really wanted one, but my parents didn't do anything about it. But if my brother needed one, they'd get one for him quick. Also, my mother never asks my brother to do anything. I do it all." And one fifteen-year-old boy states that his older sister was not treated as well "because she was a girl."

### Favoritism Shown to the Child with Special Disabilities

Although teenagers realize that siblings who are handicapped need extra parental attention, excessive partiality may still create resentment. Fifteen-year-old Larry complains: "They always favor Nancy because they think she's got a problem. She has a learning disability so we have to treat her special. She screams her head off so my mom gets her a new pair of shoes or a new dress. She's got three closets and they're stocked with clothes and she doesn't wear any of them. I swear, she knows how to use her problem to get the most attention. She really suckers them."

## Other Annoyances

### Older Siblings Who Try to Boss Younger Ones

One fifteen-year-old speaks of his brother's behaving as if he were the father in the house. "He thinks he's the authority figure. I get into an argument with him, he'll slap me across the table. We don't get along at all."

### Parents Who Compare Brothers or Sisters and Ask, "Why can't you be like him or her?"

This is a sure-fire way to create hostility between siblings. Karl, sixteen, explains: "When I'm really in trouble or just do some stupid thing around the house they'll say, 'Alan doesn't do that,' or 'Why can't you clean up your room like Alan?' I think, 'To hell with Alan.' " And one sixteen-year-old deplores her parents' habit of comparing her younger brother to her. She shows a great deal more sensitivity to his needs than their parents do.

"Sometimes I don't like my little brother but I know he respects me. I just want him to be himself. Like it's hard for him to keep up his grades and it was always easy for me. My mom will say, 'Why can't you be like your sister?' I get so mad. I don't want him to feel he has to be like me. He has to be himself." (Lucy, 16)

### Parents Who Expect Older Kids to Set a Good Example and Take on the Bulk of the Responsibility

Linda, eighteen, resents being held up as the role model and blamed for all the conflicts because the older one is "supposed to have more sense." She says, "I'm the example for everyone else, so my mom tells me that's why I have to do good in school. So what I do is keep order so that they don't catch on to anything I'm doing. I really have too much responsibility." And Carl, fourteen, expresses his discontent because of the frequent babysitting responsibility he has, sans the authority. He tells us, "My sister runs wild and I can't do anything about it. At times I get so mad I feel like slugging her. Sometimes I think little sisters are put there just to bug you."

## When Absence Creates Closeness

Relationships generally improve when older children leave home and some distance is put between siblings. With maturity comes greater tolerance and understanding, and brothers and sisters often become reacquainted and closer in their later adolescent years. Sue, eighteen, comments: "When my brother and I were little we fought. But now he's going to college, so we can talk. And he's introduced me to a lot of his friends and he even includes me in things that he does." When older siblings stop beating up younger ones, they may look back with some regret at having been too punitive or too hard. And the younger ones are delighted to be friends with brothers or sisters they looked up to, but had problems with.

Philip, though only in tenth grade, is playing on the varsity football team, but remembers when he was smaller than his brother and couldn't fight back:

"My brother and I never got along until he went to college. I have a short temper with him and he teases a lot. I couldn't ignore his teasing and would end up in fits of crying, 'Mother, where are you?' Now we weigh the same and I'm bigger than he is. The minute he left for college things got better. We write regularly and when he comes home we do things together." (Philip, 16)

For Harry, sibling problems are a thing of the past, and he revels in his new relationship with his sister. "My sister is great. We have a good relationship and now that she's out of the house (she's nineteen), our relationship gets better each year. We had the common fights and problems when we were younger, but we always got along. My sister is something special. She's very open and you can't help but like her. I'm lucky. I'm also glad I'm not an only child."

## The Only Child

Despite all their difficulties with brothers and sisters, most teenagers would not want to be an only child, although some wish they had had the chance to try it. Those who are only children express a combination of positive and negative feelings. Many are quite happy about their status, but some wish they had an older sibling. Girls in particular would like an older brother since he brings boys into the house. Many only girls assume that older brothers get lots of dates for their younger sisters. Almost none speak of wanting younger siblings.

### The Disadvantages

#### Lack of Companionship

Even though there may be squabbles, it's less lonely with brothers or sisters around. A couple of our teenagers explain that fighting with brothers and sisters is a favorite activity that fills time:

"I never thought about being an only child. There's somebody around all the time when you have a brother. Even if you don't like him, he's still somebody around to pick on and talk to. When you're an only child, if you're sick you stay home, there's nothing to do. I don't think I'd like to be an only child." (Jason, 16)

"I would like to know what it feels like to be an only child. It would be nice because you'd have a lot of privacy, I guess. But it could be lonely. I'm even lonely when my brother's not around." (Babette, 14)

"Most of the time I'm content to be an only child. Sometimes when I'm bored and alone, it would be nice to have a brother or sister." (Albert, 17)

#### Too Much Parental Attention

Since parents worry about their kids, many would prefer having that worry spread out over several, rather than focused on one. Bert, who is fifteen, feels, "It would be nice to get all the attention (I have ten brothers and sisters) but your parents would always have their eyes on you all the time. That would be hard to take." And Lizzy, fourteen, has similar thoughts: "Once or twice I really deeply wished I was an only child, but then I'm kind of glad I'm not. This way, not everything is depending on me. I just have to live up to the expectations."

### No Help Socially from Brothers or Sisters

Siblings can be useful in finding dates or making other social contacts among their friends. Many kids have that advantage, and those without it, like Sue Ann, sometimes envy them.

"I hate it. I hate it. Because when you got brothers and sisters you got connections. When you're alone, you got no connections. You have to fend for yourself. It's tough to get dates. You have to go out with your girlfriend's best friend's boyfriend, or whatever. You get stuck with all the rottens. Brothers is what I wish I had. Older brothers." (Sue Ann, 16)

## The Advantages

### No Intrusions from Brothers or Sisters
### Not Having to Share
### Guaranteed Privacy and Attention from Parents

These are the definite advantages of being an only child as stated by our interviewees.

"I love being an only child. I look at all my friends who have such bratty brothers and sisters and they all hate each other and fight all the time. What a hassle. Nobody goes into my things and I don't have people nagging me like all my friends' brothers do. They always tell me how lucky I am." (Al, 14)

"My sisters were both out of the house by the time I was ten. It's kind of like being an only child now. It's nice 'cause I don't have to share clothes, the car or anything. I like it." (Jay, 17)

"A lot of times I wish I was the only one. In big families the smallest kid is the special one. I'd like to be special." (Anna, 13)

"I sometimes think I would like to have been an only child. More privacy, more freedom." (Abby, 15)

If parents can incorporate some of the concentration of individual treatment usually given to the only child with the companionship and sense of sharing usually associated with a larger family, parents will be giving their children the best of both worlds.

## Guidelines for Parents

Sibling relationships will never be completely free of conflicts, but parents can help ease the tensions.

1. *Treat each child as an individual.* This is particularly important when children are close in age. Twins are especially vocal about this issue because parents and other adults have a tendency to refer to them collectively as "the twins" or "the kids."

2. *Spend some one-on-one time with each child, no matter how many there are.* One family with eight children told us that each child has a special time alone during the day with either the mother or father. And on birthdays, only the birthday child and one friend are taken out to dinner.

3. *Don't compare children.* They want to be appreciated on their own merits, not in relation to another sibling. They resent being *held up* as an example, or having to *live up* to one. Both are unrealistic and unfair.

4. *Set ground rules and stick to them.* Let your children know that you will not tolerate constant teasing and physical abuse. (These rules are more easily adhered to if they have been established when siblings are very young.) After setting the rules, encourage your children to work out their own disagreements. Remove yourself from the scene of action, if possible. Siblings must have the opportunity to settle their own disputes.

5. *Don't give excessive responsibility to the oldest child.* They are still children, and although they can help with child care, it should certainly not be their major responsibility.

6. *Make an effort to show equal love and attention to all your children, even though they may not be equally easy to love.*

7. *Encourage companionship for an only child by letting him or her know that friends are always welcome in your home.* This holds true for children in larger families, as well, but it is exceptionally important for children in a small family.

# 9

# Teenagers on Home Rules and Responsibilities

---

- More than 8 out of 10 say that keeping their room neat is a chore they should do (although they don't necessarily do it)
- 66% believe they should make their own bed (but that doesn't mean they do it)
- There is still a sexist division of chores, although less pronounced than in the past
- Teenagers equate punishment with caring—if the methods used are fair and not excessive

---

## Why Families Establish Rules and Responsibilities

Teenagers often consider rules the bane of their existence, yet rules are necessary if a child is to learn how to share and interact with others. Because most of us lead such busy lives, we tend to make demands on our kids and delegate chores simply because we cannot do all the work ourselves. But this should not be the only reason for giving children responsibility in the home. As parents, it is our job to set the direction and emotional tone of the household. Our expectations for our children and the way we parcel out responsibilities has an enormous impact on our kids' future development. The child whose parents impose no rules or responsibilities receives a thoroughly artificial illusion about his place in the world and what will be expected of him. He is headed for trouble when he connects with people other than parents and family. Similarly, the child who is overburdened with responsibilities and rules may become too passive and compliant to cope with adult problems in later life.

Parents who don't recognize the specific importance of rules and responsibilities may use them arbitrarily as weapons for enforcing control. Or, they may relax certain rules as a reward for good behavior. Jesse, fourteen, tells us, "My parents don't make me do the dishes when I get an A in math, but if I do something wrong, I have to wash them all week." However, both of these practices miss the point because our kids aren't learning anything.

Household responsibilities should be part of every child's life. The toddler can put away toys; the five-year-old can get dressed in time for kindergarten. The sixteen-year-old can adhere to a reasonable curfew if one is set. Bed making, dish clearing, dog walking, calling home, are all responsibilities that, if taught early, will help the child learn that he's a contributing member of a family.

There is certainly no one way to handle home rules and responsibilities. What works for one family may not prove successful for another. Some families set no curfews; some give no allowances; others allow their sixteen-year-olds to drink; some don't care if their kid's room is clean; some insist that homework be done right after school; some permit very little telephone use. Who is to say which regulations are right or wrong? We do know that no matter how home rules are established, some guidelines are necessary whenever people interact. Setting and enforcing realistic responsibilities and limits create a sense of security for most children. The game is much easier to play when everyone knows the rules.

## Chores

"Chores are no big deal but my mother is nuts when it comes to trash. It must be a hazard of suburban life or something. Does the trash stay in? Does the trash go out? Who puts it out? We had a trash compactor until our kitten got caught in it. Trash is really a big thing in our house." (A seventeen-year-old commenting on twentieth-century suburban life.)

### At What Age Should Chores Begin?

Encouraging a sense of individual responsibility should begin as early in a child's life as possible. The movement from dependency to autonomy does not have to be forced; it occurs naturally. The cry "I want to do it myself" starts early, but independence can either be fostered or resisted. A mother who is in a hurry to get children off to school or to get to her place of employment may become impatient when her child clears the table or attempts to put his clothes away. She jumps to do it herself in order to save time. But the message that the child receives—"You can't do it properly; I'll do it for you"—is that he or she is incompetent. Such an approach is likely to destroy a child's capacity to cope.

Instilling a sense of competence is a sound means of producing self-reliant teenagers. Even toddlers exult in this feeling. Anthropologist Ruth Benedict writes about an incident in which an Indian grandfather in Arizona gives his three-year-old granddaughter a task that she must complete on her own. The adults wait patiently for her to discover that she has the strength to do it. And they respect her determination to complete the job she has taken on.

> The man of the house turned to his little three-year-old granddaughter and asked her to close the door. The door was heavy and hard to shut. The child tried, but it did not move. Several times the grandfather repeated: "Yes, close the door." No one jumped to the child's assistance. No one took the responsibility away from her. On the other hand there was no impatience, for after all, the child was small. They sat gravely waiting until the child succeeded and her grandfather thanked her. It was assumed that the task would not be asked of her unless she could perform it, and having been asked, the responsibility was hers alone as if she were a grown woman.

If we wait until adolescence before assigning duties, the work habit won't be established and it will be more difficult to encourage a sense of responsibility at that late date. Parents will also find it necessary to do a lot of supervising, which older children resent.

## What Chores Do Teenagers Think They Should Do? Is There a Sexist Division?

| Which chores do you think teenagers should do around the house? | |
| --- | --- |
| Keep their room reasonably neat | 83% |
| Make the bed | 66% |
| Take out the trash or garbage | 56% |
| Wash or dry dishes | 43% |
| Yard work or gardening | 40% |
| Clean the house | 37% |
| Wash the car | 33% |
| Babysit for brothers and sisters | 32% |

The ideal balance, of course, is supervision without domination, which can usually be accomplished if the work habit is firmly planted long before adolescence. As one fourteen-year-old states: "Everyone in the family has been doing jobs as long as I can remember. Even my baby sister, who is three, knows she has to help. We're all used to it."

Hard as it may be to believe, 83% agree that keeping their rooms reasonably neat is definitely their responsibility. Of course, accepting responsibility for a job and actually doing the job are two different things. When we break down their responses by gender, definite sexist trends in the division of responsibilities emerge, although these differences are probably not as pronounced as they were twenty-five years ago.

### Female-Oriented Chores

| | Percentage of teenagers who checked each chore | |
|---|---|---|
| | Girls | Boys |
| Make bed | 76% | 55% |
| Do dishes | 61% | 24% |
| Clean house | 49% | 24% |
| Babysit | 41% | 22% |
| Cook | 36% | 14% |
| Do laundry | 35% | 12% |

### Male-Oriented Chores

| | Percentage of teenagers who checked each chore | |
|---|---|---|
| | Boys | Girls |
| Take out trash | 65% | 48% |
| Yard work | 50% | 31% |
| Wash car | 38% | 30% |
| Paint or make repairs | 34% | 13% |

Although neither sex has exclusive responsibility for any of these jobs, the emphasis is evident. And as teenagers get older, the sexist spread is even greater.

## Girls Do the Housework. Do Boys Get a Free Ride?

Clearly, the feminist movement has not yet turned into a full-fledged revolution. Young females are still much more likely to bear the brunt of housework and child care than are males. And who is assigning these chores? Mother! Accepting her own role as homemaker and baby tender, she seems to mold her daughter in her own ways, but teaches her son that his fate is different. In this manner, traditional roles are passed on from generation to generation. Teenage girls learn their roles by watching and identifying with Mother. And to insure that the lesson hits home, they're also taught that certain household functions are theirs simply because they are females. Not surprisingly, many express bitter resentment.

"My brother sleeps in a bed the same as I do. (I don't mean the same one.) Yet how come my mother feels he should just sleep in it, but I should make it?" (Dora Lee, 14)

"If we go to a park or something, I always have to take care of the babies and I can't enjoy myself. It drives me crazy. She'll be talking to a friend and she leaves the babies with me. When I tell her, she says, 'You're the big older sister and you have to take care of children.' I got mad and told her, 'Maybe my own, but not yours! You had the babies, not us. You should take care of them.'" (Marna, 16)

"I always want to get out of the house and I'm not allowed to because I have to sit home and watch everybody else. It's okay once in a while, but not all the time. I don't think my mom puts enough responsibility on my two brothers. Responsibility falls on me for everything: housework, setting examples, everything. I told my mom how I feel (not my dad because he's really chauvinistic. He always says, 'Girls should do this; girls should do that')." (Anne, 18)

"My brothers don't do a damn thing around the house. My mother treats them like kings, and because I'm a girl I have to do everything. I've never seen them lift a finger to do a dish or anything." (Jennie, 14)

Such protest is not new to the current generation of teenagers. However, today's young female is caught between the forces of female liberation and Mother's insistence that her daughters fulfill female roles in the household. Resolution of this conflict is not easy. Mother's dilemma is no less difficult. She may want her daughter to have the opportunities and freedom of choice that her sons have. But if she neglects what she considers her responsibility—teaching her daughter how to be a good wife, how to run the household and take care of the family—she is failing in her job as a parent. The answer is a more equal distribution of household activities—regardless of gender.

## The Fairness Doctrine

Teenagers tell us that they don't mind doing chores if everyone in the family pulls his or her own weight. Problems occur when jobs are assigned for unfair or predefined reasons such as, "Susan always does that," or "The oldest always does that." Similarly, if one child in the family is constantly being overloaded with work, he or she is bound to feel exploited and resentful.

There is no doubt that job sharing and a nonsexist distribution of chores contribute to a smoothly running household. If we want our sons and daughters to be competent in handling all types of household responsibilities, it is important to encourage each sex to participate in duties that are not traditionally theirs. It will certainly be useful to them in later life if our sons can cook, clean, and care for young children. If they are married, their wives will appreciate their skills and participation; if they are divorced, they will not feel helpless; if they remain bachelors, they will be confident living on their own. Young women will have the same confidence if they are able to make car and house repairs and perform other traditionally male chores.

Seventeen-year-old Jean believes that her parents have found a good solution. "My family has a meeting once a month to reassign chores. Sometimes my sister and I paint, put in the screens, and clean out the garage, and my brothers do the dishes and babysit. My mom and dad think we all should know how to do everything. My dad always teases and says that my brother, Carl, will make a great wife. He's the best cook in the house. Carl is sixteen and when he makes lasagna we're all sure we're home for dinner. When I cook, it's another story."

And Marlene, fifteen, agrees that sharing the workload is only fair. "I know my mom has a lot of work with a little baby to take care of and I understand that she can't be doing everything around the house. So I do the wash and the dishes. And I do clean my room. So do my brothers. I don't feel that I should be paid for those things because she's got too much to do. She's never asked me to watch the baby but if I did babysit I wouldn't think I should be paid."

Like Marlene, most teenagers do not expect to be paid for routine chores. But when a parent gives money for an occasional out-of-the-ordinary job, kids appreciate the chance to earn extra money.

Although they dislike a number of routine chores, there is one job that remains a major point of contention between teenagers and parents.

## The Room-Cleaning and Bed-Making Dilemma

You will remember that 83% of our participants believe that keeping their room neat is their responsibility, and 66% state that they should make their own bed. Parents and adolescents may agree on the validity of these expectations, but they definitely disagree about the methods. Tony, fifteen, sums it up: "We all clean our rooms, but we don't agree with our mom about *how* clean. You should make it decent but I don't think you have to make it ship-shape every day because you're the only one that looks at it. So if *you* don't mind, I don't see what's wrong with it. Just so it doesn't get too dirty. My parents think my wash should be put away every day and my bed should be made. I think it's easier if my wash isn't put away because then it's right on my bureau and I can pick it up. She says, 'Put it away,' so I do it just to keep her happy."

Most parents believe that a neat, clean room is not only important for sanitary reasons, but because it helps the child develop a sense of organization that will prove useful in school and later life. Adults also feel that when objects have their rightful places, they are more easily found. Adolescents counter by pointing out that they like their room sloppy; that they know perfectly well where everything is; that their room should be theirs to maintain as they see fit. After all, isn't their room the one place where they have the right to relax and be comfortable? Isn't their room an extension of their personality?

We parents can either devise some sort of compromise, or have it our own way because we set the rules. If we choose the latter, we have to realize that:

(a) The rule will be broken, not malicously but out of habit.
(b) It will be necessary to invent an effective means of enforcement, something that seems to have eluded the majority of parents.

If a family can arrive at a middle ground somewhere between total dissarray and complete neatness, they have achieved the supreme compromise. We pass along to you one fifteen-year-old girl's solution.

She explains that her mother was upset because her room was always a mess. It was the look of the room that bothered her mother: the unmade bed, the records and books all over the floor. Jennie gave her mother the old familiar "Why-make-the-bed-when-I-have-to-sleep-in-it-tonight-anyway?" routine. Her mother explained that it was very important to both parents to have a neat house, for their own sake and for the sake of company. She told Jennie how embarrassed she would be if guests ever saw Jennie's room. Jennie still didn't agree, but she and her mother compromised. She explains: "My mom got me a comforter that doubles as a bedspread. In the morning I pull it up over the messy covers and it looks great. (As long as nobody looks underneath.) She's ecstatic because my bed looks neat, and I'm happy because I don't have to make my bed." Odds and ends and loose records are pushed under the bed when company comes, but are allowed out when no special visitors are around. Jennie also agreed to vacuum once a week. The room has a reasonably neat but lived-in look, and there is relatively little conflict between Mother and daughter concerning the room's condition. Only an occasional reminder is necessary.

No matter what the chore, teenagers appreciate compliments for a job well done. When we let them know that we are proud of their good work and that their efforts are not taken for granted, we may even find that they volunteer their services when we least expect it.

## Curfew

The curfew issue becomes more important as teenagers get older and want more independence. Most recognize that some time limit is reasonable, whether it is self-imposed, set by parents, or mutually agreed upon. Which method is most advisable? Obviously, it depends a great deal upon a child's level of maturity and sense of responsibility.

### The Self-Imposed or Mutually Agreed-Upon Curfew

If our teenagers come home at a sensible hour based upon the day of the week and the particular occasion, we may not need to prescribe a curfew at all. As long as they let us know where and with whom they will be, why not give them the freedom to use their good judgment?

We have seen how important trust is. Our teenagers want us to trust them and they will usually live up to our expectations. This holds true for the curfew issue as well. Seventeen-year-old Cynthia explains: "My parents allow me to set my own curfew time and they've told me they trust my judgment. I always tell them approximately what time I expect to be home and I keep pretty much to it. If I didn't, they probably wouldn't trust me and set their own curfew for me. This way, I feel independent, but I don't take advantage of their trust." Some even say that when a curfew is lifted, indicating a vote of confidence, they begin to come in earlier because they no longer feel that they have to stay out until the last possible minute.

When teenagers share in the decision-making process, they're more likely to stick to an agreed-upon curfew because they don't feel that parents are imposing a rigid restriction upon them. This method of handling a curfew is usually more productive than dictating an arbitrary time. Trouble occurs when parents appear to monitor all the teenager's free time and demand absolute conformity to a deadline. Wes, seventeen, observes: "The way I see it, a curfew has to be talked about. If a girl has a special dance or something and asks to stay out a little later and the parents say, 'You heard me! I don't want you out past twelve. I don't want to hear anymore and that's it,' the kid gets really pissed. There is nothing she can do except totally blow off all the parents' ideas, just do what she wants for the moment. I've seen it happen a lot. It really turns a kid off when parents have no room to compromise." And Jack, sixteen, agrees: "I wish that I could have a curfew that's reasonable that we could both work out. I think that would be fair. And I also wish she wouldn't check up on me *all* the time."

## Curfew Set by Parents; Sometimes It's a Comfort

Even if a curfew is strict, the teenager will be less resentful if he knows the parent is trying to be fair. As Greg, fifteen, attests; "I don't mind my eleven curfew. I don't drive yet anyway, so eleven is okay. Next year when I start driving, I have to be in by twelve because it's the law. Unless there's a big party or something, what's the sense of staying out late anyhow?" And seventeen-year-old Don explains: "I can't say I like my curfew, but it's negotiable, so that's fair."

When a parent sets a curfew, the decision is often viewed as a demonstration of caring and concern. Kids may complain about it, but underneath they appreciate the sense of security and stability they receive. Quite a few of our female respondents find a curfew helpful, especially if they are not enjoying themselves on a date. It's a perfect way out.

"I always have a curfew. I mean always. But as long as it's reasonable, it doesn't bother me. Sometimes it's a great excuse to come in early if I don't like a guy. I've used it a lot of times for that reason. It doesn't make the guy feel bad; he can blame it on my mother." (Janie, 16)

"I wish I had an earlier curfew. My mother told my date I didn't have to be in until two A.M. and at twelve he said, 'Oh, you've got two more hours.' But I was dying to go home. He would always keep me out until the last minute of that curfew. I don't like that. I like to go out, have fun, then come home. Now my mother knows not to announce what my curfew is. I think she's trying to be too liberal or else she just doesn't know what time most kids have to be in, or else she doesn't care." (Edna, 16)

## Calling Home

Parents can offer leeway on a curfew if they know their teenager has the courtesy and good sense to call home should his or her plans change. This is a procedure most parents favor and usually insist upon. Young people who have always had to let their parents know where they are and when they're going to be late (by phone calls or notes left on kitchen tables) have less trouble following through with the procedure when they are teenagers. They don't usually feel that it is an invasion of their privacy. It becomes a habit, sometimes even a nuisance, but nonetheless important. If children have observed their parents calling home to discuss a change of plans or a delayed dinner, they realize that it is a courteous family policy, not one put into effect exclusively for the young members.

"My mom always lets me know where she is, so I do the same. So does my dad. We have a magnetic board on the refrigerator door and as soon as any of us come in the house, that's the first place we look. My friends all tease me because when they come over they say they can tell all about my family's secrets by just looking on the refrigerator." (Barbara, 15)

"It's a pain in the ass checking in but I know my mother worries, so it doesn't hurt to leave her a note or call her when I know I'll be late. I guess if I have kids I'll worry about them, too." (George, 17)

"One time it was a damn good thing I let my mother know where I was going. My brother got hit by a car out front of the house and my mom was frantic. Her car was on the blink and she called me at my friend's house and I rushed home and we took Scott to the hospital. I don't check in with her every place I go, but she usually knows my plans and where to reach me." (Stephen, 16)

"If I'm going to be out late, I'll call home. If I'm sleeping over, even if it's four A.M., I'll call then. One time the friend I was out with was too drunk to drive home so I slept at his house. It was two A.M., and I decided not to call home but to wait until morning. When I called at eight the next morning, my mother was steaming. She said she nearly called the police, she was so worried. That was one of the only times I was almost punished. When my father got home (she always waits for him to make the decision), there was no punishment but lots of talk. I explained that it was the first time I was ever in that situation and I didn't want to wake them up and that I didn't think I deserved punishment. I call now, no matter what time it is."(Matt, 16)

But not all teenagers are as agreeable about curfews. Many older ones resent being monitored by parents who complain about losing sleep when their teenagers are not home on time. Fred is eighteen and works in a restaurant. Often he is not finished working until after midnight. Like most people, he feels like winding down after work. Usually he meets friends who have been out for the evening, or he will go to a bar for a couple of drinks and some companionship before going home. When his father tried to insist on a one A.M. curfew, Fred blew his stack. "If I can work six hours a night," he said, "I have a right to be out and do what I like afterward. They're crazy, trying to treat me like a fifteen-year-old. I just refuse to do what he says and my father and I are in a real battle about it."

The persistent breaking of curfew should alert us that something is wrong. Our rules may be unrealistically strict, especially in relation to local adolescent customs. (We do not have to adhere to these customs if we feel they are harmful or destructive, but we should at least be aware of them.) Or our teenager may have an emotional problem that we've failed to recognize and may be seeking some resolution through more prolonged contact with friends away from home. In such situations tightening the curfew screws doesn't usually work for very long. Instead, find out why the teenager is so resistant and work out the problem from there.

## Punishment

### Why Punish?

As parents, it is our job to teach our children to behave appropriately and abide by rules, both our own and society's. We try to teach by example, or by using positive reinforcement such as praise or rewards, but when these methods fail, most of us resort to punishment. Because it's so unpleasant, punishment generates more resentment and anger than other training methods, but it is often necessary and effective and most children get used to it at an early age. Indeed, virtually all of our respondents have experienced some form of punishment. They recognize it as a staple of parent/child relationships and a customary way to discourage the breaking of family rules.

Types of punishment vary from family to family. Some parents resort to physical punishment, ranging from a swat on a toddler's behind to actual abuse. Others deny privileges, ground their children, or use psychological tactics, such as withdrawing affection or attempting to instill a sense of guilt or remorse.

When our formerly compliant children become teenagers who insist on making their own decisions, the issue of punishment may take on greater significance. The new pressures teenagers face become far more important to them than their parents' original guidelines. This clash of values and needs leads to arguments, evasions, or direct refusals to obey rules that were never questioned before. A young woman eager to be with her boyfriend finds it difficult to leave him in order to arrive home at the hour her parents have specified. If two couples decide to go to a late movie, and the driver has a twelve A.M. curfew, he may not honor it because he feels he is preventing the others from having a good time. He also may not want to admit that he has to be home by twelve.

## Types of Parental Controls

Most teenagers realize that parents must exercise some discipline and set reasonable limits, and many even acknowledge their parents' right to punish. But at the same time, they may take exception to the method used. The following chart lists the most commonly used punishments—in order of least favored to most favored.

---

1. Grounding
2. Physical punishment (hitting)
3. Deprivation (of privileges or allowance)
4. Constructive or "creative" punishment
5. Self-imposed punishment

---

### *Grounding*

This popular method may mean confinement to the house except for school or important appointments. Restriction of contacts with others means telephone communication with friends is usually cut off or limited. Teenagers label this kind of isolation as the most distasteful of all possible punishments, emphasizing once again their strong need for relationships and functions in the world outside of family and home. Selby, seventeen, lives on a farm and for her the telephone is her one link to the outside world. "They don't let me talk on the phone, and around here there's hardly any houses or people, so the way I communicate with my friends is only the phone. So that's a bad punishment but I guess it's as fair as any. But I hate it!"

"I'd much rather be hit than grounded. At least with hitting it's over quick. Grounding lasts forever and I hate not being with my friends. I could almost do without my parents, but not my friends." (Cheryl, 16)

Knowing how teenagers feel about grounding, it is important for parents to use the control carefully. Overuse reduces its effectiveness and may actually lead to further rule breaking. Arch, sixteen, explains: "My parents ground me so often, I don't pay any attention. I climb out the window in my room for a few hours and they never know it. Whenever they don't know what else to do, they ground me." Constant use of any one particular punishment is rarely effective. As in Arch's case, teenagers can usually find ways to get around it.

### Physical Punishment

Most teenagers are no longer hit, although some would prefer it to grounding because it is a short-term dislocation. Others resent being hit. Still others are so accustomed to physical punishment that they do not consider it abuse, particularly when they feel it is deserved. Larry definitely thinks there is a difference between "whipping to hurt" (which is abusive) and "whipping to help you recognize your mistakes."

"We would get punished when we'd fight. We were sent to our rooms or else we got a good whipping. Sometimes if we would antagonize each other or if practical jokes backfired, we got whipped. Next time I thought twice about what I had done because they were solid whippings with a leather strap. Mother or Father did it. It would make me mad and upset, but I think whipping is important. It makes you respect authority, if parents don't go overboard. My parents never whipped to hurt. They whipped to kind of make you see your mistakes. There was a lot of guilt, too, because we didn't want to make them feel bad. They were really understanding. Whipping was just like we fucked up. It hurt my pride because I always want my mother and father to look up to me." (Larry, 16)

And one thirteen-year-old tells us, "Children should be hurt only on the surface, but not inside." In her view, "inside hurts" include guilt feelings, unkind words, being ignored or distrusted, all of which leave deeper scars.

### Deprivation of Privileges or Allowance

Many parents punish by restricting television viewing, partygoing, and participation in general activities. Often, refusal to give money or the car to a teenager becomes the dominant means of control as he or she gets older. And there is no question that many parents feel it is the *only* method of control they still have. However, the allowance issue is a tricky one. If the main purpose of an allowance is to help kids learn how to manage funds and to give them a feeling of financial independence, holding back the allowance defeats the purpose. Of course, it does limit the teenager's spending power and if the punishable act is money-related it is a valid and effective method of control. Punishment is always more meaningful when it's related to the "crime."

The parents of a sixteen-year-old who had run up a $25 phone bill talking to his girlfriend held back $5 of his allowance each week until the bill was paid. He thought it was a perfectly fair arrangement. "Now" he says, "I keep an eggtimer in my room and set it for five minutes. Then I have her call me back. I always make sure to tell her my time is up right in the middle of when she's telling me something. That way I know she'll call me back because she wants to finish what she's saying. That solves my problem, although her parents are probably having a fit."

Similarly, withdrawing car privileges can be an effective punishment when it "fits the crime." Val, eighteen, explains her belief that this type of discipline is fair: "A couple of years ago I was at the stage when you're really irrational and you want to do what your friends do, and I would always think the punishment I got was unfair. They never grounded me. But when I kept the car out late they'd say, 'You can't use the car tonight.' I deserved it in all cases. I can see that now."

However, other parents rely on this method of control because it's the only one at their disposal. Seventeen-year-old Larry explains: "My mother knows I'm too big to swat anymore and yelling never works with me. She also knows I break grounding, so what's left? The car. I can't afford one, although I'm working on it, so she zaps me by not letting me have the car. It works pretty good because I really want the car, so I've been okay. She threatened to not let me drive if I got one single ticket, so I've been creeping. She also found some stuff in my drawers and I cleaned it out quick. I gotta get a car next summer, but until then she's got me."

### Constructive or "Creative" Punishment

If punishment can be constructive in some way, so much the better. Creative discipline makes more of an impression than a routine grounding or some other conventional punishment. In addition, it often has long-range benefits, as thirteen-year-old Tim attests: "A few months ago, I left the garage door and the back door open. My mom is really paranoid about burglars. When she came home she thought the house had been robbed because the back door was unlocked and the garage door was up. When I got home, she was furious! She yelled, 'Don't you know anyone could have walked right in and taken everything we had?' I'm always running out and forgetting to lock up so I guess she thought she had to do something drastic. She made me put all new locks on the doors (I don't think we even needed them), and then paint the doors afterward. It took forever, but I usually remember to lock up now."

Some parents even manage to turn a punishment into an educational experience for their kids. Fourteen-year-old Nancy told us that she had lied to her father about cheating in school. When he discovered her lie, they talked about it and he decided that for one month she would be required to read the newspaper, including the Sunday edition. (He knew she never read the paper, and hoped that she would continue the habit even after the punishment expired.) Nancy notes: "I hated it, but I guess it did me some good. At least I could answer questions in current events for that month. Too bad it didn't last. I still hate to read the paper." And fourteen-year-old Murray's parents had a similar idea. "The last time I was punished, I got home late because I was down at the creek and it froze over. We were messing around down there and forgot about the time. I got home and it was dark and my parents were worried because they didn't know where I was. They made me do the *Reader's Digest* 'Word Power.' I had to look up all the words and take a test in ten books. But I guess that was a fair punishment. Better than making me stay in."

Devising constructive punishment requires time and ingenuity, but the results are usually worth the effort.

### Self-Imposed Punishment

Perhaps the least resented and most effective punishments are those chosen by teenagers themselves. In fact, they may even penalize themselves more severely than their parents would. Fifteen-year-old Harris and a friend were playing with a BB gun and couldn't resist the temptation of using a neighbor's outdoor lamp as their target. The neighbor complained to police and as Harris tells it, "That evening a policeman came to the door and asked to see me. I nearly died! He asked if I owned a BB gun and when I said I did, he told me to get it. I was sure he was going to haul me off to jail." The policeman questioned Harris about the broken lamp and he confessed that he had more than a passing knowledge of the incident. At that point, "The cop took the gun away and told me it wouldn't be returned (which probably pleased my mother no end because she always hated it). I was so upset because I loved that gun. But I have to admit what I did was pretty stupid."

It is interesting that the consequences of an act are often punishment enough. In this case, the confiscation of the prized gun and the awesome confrontation with "The Law" were devastating to

Harris. However, the lamp still had to be paid for. He continues, "I was sure my parents would kill me, but they were pretty cool. They surprised me. My father asked me what I intended to do about the problem. I told him I would apologize to the neighbor (which I dreaded) and would offer to pay for the light by doing jobs around her house or whatever she wanted. My parents thought that was a good idea and I ended up working for the lady for three months! I felt like a criminal sentencing myself." Because the penalty was self-imposed, it had additional meaning. It also allowed Harris to save face by demonstrating to his family and neighbor his ability to make amends in a mature and responsible way.

### Miscellaneous Disciplines

Some parents discipline by playing on a child's guilt feelings, by bringing up past mistakes, and by making idle threats. But our interviewees feel that these tactics serve no particular purpose other than to relieve parental tensions.

"Now my dad just talks to me, but he used to whip me. He tries to make me feel guilty, so I go along with his little game. I let him think I feel guilty. I'll say, 'I know I shouldn't have done it, Dad.' Then the talk is over and I go about my business like it never happened. If I let him know how I really felt about it, that I didn't care, he'd probably jump all over me." (Dori, 17)

"What they do is constantly bring up the bad things I've done, like when I was supposed to be in at twelve and came in at five after. I'll hear about it for the next twenty years. The next time I come in at five after twelve, I'll hear it again. One time I was grounded for coming home at five after six instead of six on a weekday. Then the next day my father who usually is home by six-fifteen didn't get home until nine. He didn't call either, so that made it better for me. I told my mom if Dad can do it, so can I, and I was ungrounded." (Dick, 17)

"My mother never gives punishments she can keep. She just threatens. My brother and I can always get around her. My father's not as easy but you can get around him, too. One time my mother told my baby sister that if she didn't keep quiet she wouldn't get a birthday present. Of course one week later it was her birthday and she got the same presents, as always." (Susan, 14)

We parents would do well to consider Susan's comment carefully. When our threats are so unrealistic that our kids know they can't be enforced, we lose our credibility and, often, their respect.

## Following Through

"My parents are big ones for making threats. Their threats aren't fair, but they never carry them out so it doesn't matter. Like they'll say I can't have the car for the rest of the year, and you know they don't mean it." (Ron, 17)

"My parents always threaten to take away my stereo as a punishment. I just come back and tell them I'll disconnect theirs, because I'm the only one who knows how to work their stereo. So the only real punishment I get is not being able to go out on a date. That they can control." (Stan, 15)

Teenagers, as well as younger children, want to know that we mean what we say. When they can count on consistency and fairness, they feel secure. Marcie, age seventeen, looks back and tells us what this has meant to her. "Whatever my mother says she's going to do, she does. Even when we were little, we knew she meant what she said. One time my brother was acting up in the car and my mom said if he didn't behave she would put him out. He kept on being a pain, and at the next block my mom stopped the car and made him get out. He was never so scared in his life. She drove around the block and picked him back up, but you better believe he was an angel all the way home. I think she's done a great job disciplining the kids!"

# Guidelines for Parents

## Determining What Is Fair When Setting Rules and Disciplining

1. *The rule itself must be realistic.* Many of us would not hesitate to break a twenty-five-mile-an-hour speed limit if it were imposed on a freeway; the rule would be unrealistic. We must be careful not to impose the same kind of unrealistic regulations upon our teenagers. If they are going to a senior prom, we cannot in all good conscience expect them to return home by twelve. The rule must also be realistic in terms of the child's age. A fifteen-year-old should not have the same bedtime, chores, or curfew that a twelve-year-old has. If parents insist upon one rule for all their children, however convenient that may be, the rule is asking to be broken. And if punishment follows, there is good reason for discontent and rebellion.

2. *Warn about the consequences of an action before punishing.* Mae, sixteen, believes that punishment is unfair if a child doesn't

know that a particular act is unacceptable. "I was grounded once for taking too long on the phone. I think I should have been warned first. I think all kids should get the benefit of a warning before being punished."

3. *Listen to explanations.* If a rule is broken, there may be a good reason, especially if it's a first-time offense. One sixteen-year-old told us that he felt he was punished very unfairly because of an "act of God" over which he had no control. He had gone out on a snowy school night and had promised to be home by nine, which he fully intended to do. The jeep in which he and a friend had traveled got stuck in a ditch and it took the boys nearly three hours to shovel and push their way out. Of course, Jim's parents were frantic, but when he returned home at midnight, they refused to listen to his explanation. They grounded him for two months, and to this day he is bitter about that experience and the unfair treatment he received. Our kids deserve a chance to explain.

In many cases, a frank discussion may reveal a problem about which parents are unaware. Fourteen-year-old Sonnie was not handing in her homework and after two weeks the teacher sent her parents a note. When they asked Sonnie why, she began to cry and explained that one of the boys in her class took the completed assignment from her each morning and handed it in as his. She couldn't tell the teacher because the boy had threatened to attack her if she told anyone. She was much more willing to suffer the "no homework" consequences than to reveal her plight. If Sonnie and her parents hadn't discussed the situation, the entire problem might never have surfaced.

## The Most Distressing Unfairness

### When the Punishment Exceeds the Crime

When a method of punishment far outweighs the offense, it is not only unfair but unwise. There's no reason to ground for a month if a teenager comes home ten minutes later than expected. Eugene, sixteen, explains the principle and the resentment such tactics create: "This is the major part of why we don't get along. I put a nick in the car and my mom grounded me for two weeks. I didn't do it on purpose. I felt bad enough just doing it. I got 'inside' grounding. Sometimes they'll ground me for a month at a time and won't let me have friends over if I do one thing wrong. So I just stopped listening to them. After a while I just go out, and that's why we started not getting along very well."

"They punish me for dumb little things. If I come in late, really late, I deserve to be punished. But if I come in just a little late (even five minutes), I'm not allowed to hang around out front, walk up the street to get a friend, or sit up at the corner. They make me a prisoner. They don't trust me. I don't think many parents trust their kids. The kids that have parents who trust them are really lucky." (Annie, 15)

"If I did something and I deserve to be punished, that's okay. But when I get punished because my mother is in a bad mood, that's really unfair. It stinks." (Lucy, 17)

Teenagers are perceptive enough to know when punishment has more to do with their parents' mood than with an actual wrongdoing on their part. This type of discipline only serves to intensify conflict between parent and child. Kids begin to question their parents' judgment and maturity. They know such punishment is nothing more than an exploitation of a dominant power position. And it is totally ineffectual as a training method. Geraldine, eighteen, explains: "I never really got punished; I just got hit. Punishment is when you're given something like grounding to make you remember what you've done. My mother just hit me a lot. She may have got her anger out, but she did it like a ten-year-old. She never knew how to talk. She always just lost her temper. If a parent really cares, they'll have talks with you. Sometimes my parents would punish me if they didn't believe me when I told them the truth. That's the most unfair kind of punishment. If you're nice and try to be understanding, a kid wants to be good and please you. Otherwise, there's a lot of hate."

## When Punishment Becomes a Mask for Child Abuse

The majority of parents do not abuse their children, but some of our respondents have lived with abusive parents and you will experience their feelings of frustration, hate, pain, and fear as you read their words.

There is no specific rule to determine when the line between punishment and abuse is crossed. But if a child is physically harmed, the evidence is undeniable. One thirteen-year-old's experience provides a perfect example of the crossover. "Sometimes my mother doesn't let me watch TV or listen to the radio or go to parties. I don't like it, but I can understand it. But what I think is unfair is when she keeps me locked in the furnace room and won't let me out even if it's boiling. I passed out once." In this instance, the parents can no longer justify their rationale that punishment is a form of training. The child has become a victim of parental rage. This situation is vividly illustrated by the accounts of some of our other teenagers.

"When I was smaller, my father used to make me kneel for around three hours. He was always hitting me. Now that I'm growing up, it's been a long time since he hit me but they both still treat me like a baby. My mom, of course, still hits me. I mean she really smacks me. One time my mother had to go out and we stayed with the babysitter. Before she left, my mother called my father a really bad name because of something he did. I was afraid the neighbors heard and would tell my father the name. (My mother called him the name when he wasn't home. She was really screaming.) I didn't want him to hear it from somebody else, so I told him when he came home. Then he wrote a message to my mother that he was going out and wrote a P.S. 'Thank you for calling me that certain name.' (I won't say it.) When my mother got home and read the note, she said, 'Claire, get the belt. I mean the leather one.' She hit me so much that she marked me up all over. My father had to come in and take me away from her for a whole day. It was so hot outside but my father told me to wear a jacket to cover up the marks. She tells me sometimes, 'If you don't behave like I want you to, you're going to get it like you did that other time—only harder.' Right now my mom and I don't get along. We argue all the time. I wouldn't talk back because I'd get hit. When she hits me, I want to leave the house and run away. Once I almost did. I told her, 'I have to calm down. Please don't mind if I walk out of the house; walk around the block to cool off. I'll come back.' She said, 'If you leave the house without permission, I'll lock the door. I don't care what happens to you if you leave the house.' I was just trying to tell her that it would be a little walk to calm me down and that I'd come home unless she beat me. If she beat me I'd have to go somewhere else. I told her she could send me to my aunt's or grandmother's to clear the problem. Some girls run away and get into drugs. I don't go for that. I just wanted a walk around the block. When my mother said, 'I don't care what happens to you,' that made me feel bad." (Claire, 14)

"My adopted mother, who died when I was twelve, was a church woman who believed that discipline is the hand on the stick, so I never wanted to be close to her. If I did something wrong, she'd hit me with the first thing she got her hand on. I was really scared. Now, I guess, I'd be called an abused child, but back then, people didn't look into that. I've been through the whole thing: going to school with black eyes, bloody noses, my hand broken. Whenever her husband came home he tried to get her to stop hitting, but she managed to do it when he wasn't there. So I ran away and ended up in different foster homes. You might say that I raised myself." (Toby, 18)

"Parents can hit but I don't think they should punch. That's what my stepfather does, punches and kicks me. I just take it but I don't cry. It gets me very, very mad and I begin to hate him. I ran away three times. Sometimes if he hits me, I go to my friend Jimmy's house. My father started hitting me when he found out I was gay. He says he wants me to be a man. I was around fifteen when my mother told him, 'Gary is gay and you can't do anything about it.' He started shouting and beating me up. He threw my clothes and everything out the window, so I just left. I went to Jimmy's house. He understands. He's not my lover, but we're close friends." (Gary, 16)

"Both my parents hate me and whenever they get mad they beat me. My father does the beating but my mother never stops him. Last time I got a broken nose and two broken ribs. I'd run if I could, but where to?" (Anthony, 18)

"I used to be hit a lot when I was little. I don't understand it. When I have kids I'm going to talk to them. Talk, not hit. One time after I was beaten, I was so mad that I totally went nuts. I had four lamps in my room and I got all the light bulbs and stomped on every single one. Then I punched my fist through a window screen. My mother started to hit me and I hit her back. It was awful. And it didn't solve anything." (Bobbie, 17)

Unfortunately, statistics indicate that abused children very often go on to become abusive parents. So Bobbie, who hopes to talk to her children instead of hitting them, may reverse the trend, but it is unlikely. And an eighteen-year-old who was abused tells us he will never have children because he hates them and knows he would beat them: "My mother always hated children and instilled that hate in me. She always said they were dirty, ugly, and too much trouble."

A swat on the behind when a three-year-old runs into the street or plays with matches reinforces the danger of the situation at the exact moment the action occurs, and will often have more impact than words. But the constant use of physical force merely displays a parent's lack of control and inability to solve a problem maturely and with understanding. If a parent is fortunate to recognize that he or she is losing control, there is still time to seek professional help.

When a parent sets realistic rules, listens to explanations, and relates the punishment to the wrongdoing, teenagers are less likely to resist parental controls. In fact, they may agree that such punishment is deserved. Peter, fifteen, believes, "When kids are little they always think punishment is unfair. But if you do something wrong, a kid should be punished or else he'll keep on doing it."

In view of Peter's comment, which is echoed by many others, how do teenagers feel when parents neglect to carry out their role as teacher?

### Never Punish—Never Care

Some teenagers feel cheated when they are not reprimanded, and they equate lack of discipline with total disinterest and laziness. Fourteen-year-old Dolores says, "I can do anything I want and my parents never punish me. If you want to know the truth, I don't think they give a shit. My father's always working and my mother is too tied up with organization work. Do you know when I was three, I bit a light bulb in half to get some attention!" Others see the issue with comparable clarity.

"My parents give me almost too much freedom. They travel a lot and they went away for a weekend a while ago, and told me, 'No parties while we are away.' What I did was have four or five of my closest friends over. By the end of the night we had racked up about twenty-five glasses in the dishwasher, and I forgot to put them away. My parents came home and found all the glasses. I couldn't believe it; they barely said anything. They're going away again this weekend and all they said was, 'Remember, no friends, no booze.' This time I'll be more careful." (Thomas, 16)

"I hate not being punished. I think a kid should get punished if they do something wrong. My mom will send me to my room for five minutes and then say, 'Oh, go out and have some fun.' I don't like that because I think she's bringing me up wrong. I mean, how many kids have you heard who want to be punished? But I do. I think it's wrong and lazy not to punish kids. Other kids get grounded. I'll show you what I mean. I went to a dance and this kid who took me had to pick up and take home all these people. Well, we didn't get home until four in the morning. My mom didn't like that because she gave me a curfew of three-thirty. The guy slept over at my house and my mom didn't like that much either. He slept in my bed, too. For punishment, my mom should have grounded me for a week or something. I don't like to get away with things. She just lets me go. I don't think she cares." (Jeanette, 16)

Dave, who is eighteen years old, describes what can happen when a family has no central authority. Although he has enjoyed his freedom, he also believes it has made him too self-centered. His comment confirms the importance of imposing rules at an early age. "We're not really a family unit. There's no authority, which is weird. We treat each other like we're living in a commune. If there's something I want to do and somebody tells me it's wrong, if I don't see the wrongness in it, I'll end up doing it. In this house, we're all on the same mental level. I don't think of myself as her kid; I don't think of her as my mother. We treat each other almost as equal. If you're going to have authority over someone, you have to start early. Now that I'm eighteen, it's too late. If you're not used to authority, you don't know how to act. If I had kids, I'd probably be *too* authoritative. I like things to go my way. I know it's wrong but I'm sure it has to do with the fact that I wasn't brought up with any authority. I just do what's best for me."

Of course, the "never punish, never care" philosophy is not a hard-and-fast rule. In many families there is little need for punishment because parents and children share identical values, and if there are conflicts, they are easily worked out. As Jeannie, sixteen, says, "Usually what they think is wrong, I do, too, and I don't do it. If I would crash the car or have an accident (God forbid!) I would pay for it or at least put in as much money as I could. I would think of those things myself. So we don't really have any problems."

## When to Call for Help

When we see our children becoming involved with the life-threatening behavior of drug or alcohol abuse, or with antisocial or self-destructive actions such as chronic truancy, sexual promiscuity, vandalism, or stealing, we have seen that punishment is not always the answer. Outside assistance may be necessary. Deciding when and where to seek such help depends on the severity and duration of the problems. Begin by asking a school counselor, friend, member of the clergy, or physician for referral to a qualified professional. Or look directly in the phone book for family counseling services, mental health agencies, drug and alcohol abuse centers, psychologists, psychiatrists, or social workers. Many communities have hot lines for individuals with drug or drinking problems, suicidal feelings, or for teenagers who are runaways or homeless. Sometimes adolescents monitor hot lines to help each other. Young homosexuals may call "gay switchboards" to gain support when they need understanding.

Don't be afraid to go for help. It takes more strength to face up to and try to solve a problem than it does to ignore it. Remember, you are in charge. You take the most important step when you look squarely at the problem and determine whether it can be handled within the family or whether it requires outside help.

# 10

# Teenagers on Vandalism; Shoplifting; Other Teenagers' Behavior

---

• Almost half (47%) believe that adolescents are too involved with drinking and drugs
• One out of 3 thinks that teenage vandalism could be curbed if parents paid more attention to their children, and if teenagers weren't so bored
• Most teenagers believe nothing will stop the shoplifter except getting caught and facing the consequences. Very few will tell on a shoplifting friend

---

## Teenagers' Opinions of Teenagers

Pot parties! Vandalism! Petty thievery! If we were to judge by newspaper headlines and magazine articles, our teenagers' activities are shocking. The excesses of the minority have colored our image of the majority, and we adults often believe that teenagers have nothing but contempt for our values and standards. When we lecture them on the virtues of hard work, moderation, and responsibility, they favor us with blank-eyed stares. Are we really raising a generation of hedonistic, disrespectful rebels? Have they turned their backs on the work ethic? To find out, we asked teenagers how they felt about their peers.

Their responses reflect the normal conflicts of growing up. On the one hand, they are constantly exploring and experimenting; participating in activities that seem dangerous or foolhardy. On the other side, they are cautious members of a larger world, deploring the excesses, the self-indulgence, and the egocentricity of their society. Their disapproval (when it occurs) represents a form of self-control; it's their way of checking behavior that frightens them. Moreover, it foreshadows the attitudes that they are likely to develop as they become adults and fit into the more conventional and conservative ways of the adult world. Indeed, when our teenagers become parents, they will probably disapprove of their adolescents' outrageous actions. They will probably find it difficult to talk to their own children. But in the meantime, they are enjoying their freedom, although many worry where it will lead.

The table below could easily express the views of concerned parents. But it does not. These are the judgments of teenagers themselves.

---

Do you think that most teenagers:

| | |
|---|---|
| Are into drugs and drinking too much? | 47% |
| Don't seem to care about anything? | 32% |
| Don't respect adults? | 28% |
| Are generally okay? | 29% |
| (Some checked more than one response) | |

---

You may remember that in an earlier chapter nearly 7 out of 10 said that they felt good about themselves. Clearly, teenagers have a much higher opinion of themselves than they do of their peers.

### Nearly 5 Out of 10 Say Teenagers Drink and Use Drugs Too Much

Some, like Fernando, a sixteen-year-old in a Northwestern city, deplore the excessive use of drugs and alcohol. And his fears about the future of the world certainly reflect a measure of personal fear as well. "There is much too much drugs and alcohol. When you look into the future, we are supposed to be the ones leading the way. So many kids are smoking (including me), popping pills and getting rowdy. They're getting into things they can't handle like running away and pregnancies. They think that they can get away with anything they want, mess up the world as much as they want. What they don't realize is when they grow up, it'll be their world that they have to fix up. Sad story sometimes, you know?"

## 32% Say Teenagers Don't Care About Anything

"I don't like most teenagers. I like people older than myself. Ones I can talk to and relate to better. I don't like the stuff most kids my age are into. They don't take things seriously and don't care about much." (Claire, 15)

Others go a step further and accuse teenagers of caring only about themselves. Many blame this problem on the fact that kids get too many things without having to work for them. Toby, seventeen, explains: "I don't think most teenagers realize what life is all about. They never have had any real responsibility, just schoolwork and play. A lot of my friends have a job but they still get money from their parents. If they had to go out on their own and try to support themselves, they probably wouldn't bitch so much about their life at home, or be so self-centered."

However, teenagers do worry about the direction of their lives. They care more than adults think they do. The young person who does poorly in school, and who eases his anxiety by cutting classes and pretending he doesn't care, carries an internal burden of depression or apprehension. The tension may be skillfully disguised, as Bill's was, but it's there to be seen if we are willing to acknowledge it.

Bill had ambled through elementary school quite comfortably. He was bright. Schoolwork was not too demanding. He was an excellent athlete who was bored by the mechanics of grammar and arithmetic. Instead of concentrating, he spent his time in classes fantasizing about scoring the winning touchdown or hitting the home run that won the series. In junior high school his grades started to slip. C's and an occasional D replaced the A's and B's to which he was accustomed. More homework was given; term papers and book reports were required. But these heavier assignments did nothing to encourage his interest in academics. By the time he entered high school, cutting classes was routine. Playing on school teams was the only thing he cared about, and his natural skill made him a first- or second-stringer most of the time. He continually struggled to keep the number of failing grades below the maximum allowable for remaining on the teams. He began to worry about the future in his junior year, when friends started discussing colleges and their plans to leave home.

But Bill had no idea how to change his life. Because he had let his work slip for so long, he believed it was impossible to catch up. He began to think of himself as the boy who would make it through high school and end up working at the local gas station. He would be stuck at home while his friends went to college. Although he cared a great deal about his situation, he was ill-equipped to cope with his problems. He had spent too many years pretending that school was unimportant; conning his parents and teachers into accepting his academic failures, relieving his own anxieties by joking, laughing, and fantasizing.

Bill did precisely what he feared for two years. He had a succession of depressing dead-end jobs, and he began to drink heavily. However, his last boss was someone to whom he could talk. He believed in Bill and encouraged him to think about college. With this support and his own awareness of the handicaps he'd face without higher education, Bill summoned up the courage for another try. He is now in the second year of a two-year college, doing well and planning to transfer to a university.

## Nearly 3 Out of 10 Say Their Peers Lack Respect for Adults

Ever since the family unit became the foundation of human society, adults have complained that teenagers have no respect for authority.

Is this true? Yes and no, depending on one's definition of respect. For those adults who equate respect with obedience, the complaint certainly has validity. But would we really want total obedience, particularly if it interfered with a teenager's development of self-reliance and independence? Pleasing as this prospect may seem at times, most of us would probably say no. If, on the other hand, respect means recognizing the validity of adult experience, and listening, rather than automatically rejecting our knowledge and wisdom, most of us definitely would want this kind of respect. Are we getting it? Not entirely, according to 28% of our respondents. Melody, seventeen, concurs, but believes there's room for improvement on both sides: "Teenagers do a lot of dumb things. Today's kids are hardheaded. I know, because I am. They don't listen to their parents, they just do what their friends do. They don't respect the law, either. But I don't think that parents or cops make it much better when they start calling kids idiots and assholes. After a while that kid is gonna believe it. That's when the dope and robbery comes in, and the hustling. Kids become no good because they believe they're no good. Respect has to be two-way."

Many, like Fred, sixteen, have mixed emotions. He explains: "I think every teenager needs more of an authority figure, someone to help him out but not run his life."

Fred's comment pinpoints the difference between the two definitions of respect. Our kids want us to listen and offer help and advice but they also want us to respect and support their efforts to be self-reliant. And if we can provide that kind of respect, they're more likely to return it. Benita, who is eighteen, has come to the conclusion that respect for authority (and parents in particular) increases as teenagers approach adulthood. She says, "You want to do what your friends are doing, and you don't think your parents or any other adult knows anything. And yet you need someone older to talk to who can understand where you're coming from, who can put themselves in your shoes. As you get older, you begin to realize that some of the things your parents told you were right."

## Peers Are Confused and Searching

Teenagers are just as tough when it comes to criticizing their peers' attitudes and character. They talk about the peer pressures to get high; the wildness of the times in which "girls want to be men and guys want to be girls." They describe the world as a mixed-up, crazy place, filled with crazy people. Some reject their peers altogether. However, alienation from adolescent society does not permit them to resolve their anxieties, only to avoid them. There will be adults who favor judgments such as Lucy's, but we question what she is missing in her own development as a result of her withdrawal from her peers. She says, "I try to keep away from most kids as much as possible. I live in a separate world from them. We have nothing in common except age. I think most of them are very confused and totally out of it. The fact that a lot of them can't be their own person and don't know enough about themselves makes them follow a crowd. It's depressing to see people fall into pits like that."

There are those who interpret adolescent confusion as a "search for some special quality of life." Alyson, a very articulate eighteen-year-old, makes the following observation: "One thing that characterizes today's teenagers is that they all, in one way or another, are looking for something. I believe that's why they are into drugs, alcohol, and even cults. I think people turn to these to try to delay coming to terms with real problems. Society today stresses the individual over the group more than ever before, and teenagers seem overwhelmed with this. I think the 'something' they are looking for is a kind of inner peace. They are rookies at this because previous generations haven't prepared them for it. But when they reach what they're striving for, I think that they are going to be a strong group of adults that will do a lot for this world."

### 29% Say Teenagers Are All Right

Those who are optimistic about today's adolescents feel that they are more aware, perceptive, and worldly than previous generations have been. Jeffrey, sixteen, comments: "They're growing up faster than the older people used to, and they're living real-life experiences a lot sooner. They do get into drugs a little too heavily; it's a major part of teenagers' lives right now. But although there are always going to be a couple of bad eggs, I think the majority of us are all right and I wish adults wouldn't give us such a bad name."

For the most part, teenagers are willing to accept responsibility for their own behavior. They are neither crybabies nor blame-placers. Alyson has aptly derscribed them as "rookies" when it comes to solving life problems. Some are failing, some are withdrawing. But most of them are learning and trying to establish some sense of personal certainty in a threateningly unstable world.

Robert, who at eighteen has had some opportunity to observe, reminds us that all teenagers cannot be judged en masse. He offers a precise sociological summary. "There isn't such a thing as a typical teenager. The kids who are on their way to college are obsessed with getting good grades and 'making it.' There are some kids who don't care about anything but drinking and getting high. And I guess ghetto kids are worried about just surviving."

## Vandalism

Teenage vandalism has always been considered an expression of disrespect for and hostility toward adults and their standards. Destructive vandalism in schools, in homes, and on our streets worries not only adults but teenagers themselves. Not one of our respondents defended or justified vandalism, not even those who have engaged in it. They call the vandals "smart ass," and accuse them of wanting to "wreck it" for other people. Those who have been victims are enraged by this blatantly antisocial act. Ralph, thirteen, says, "I think people who vandalize should be shot. Some kids broke all our car windows and stole our tires. They'll never get caught."

## Can Teenage Vandalism Be Stopped?

---

What do you think would help stop teenage vandalism?

| | |
|---|---|
| If parents paid more attention to their children | 34% |
| If teenagers had more to do so they weren't bored | 33% |
| If teenagers had to repair or pay for the damage they did | 27% |
| If teenagers had better jobs to earn more money | 24% |
| If the police and judges cracked down on the vandals and gave stiffer punishment | 23% |
| Nothing can stop it | 10% |

---

### More Parental Attention

Our kids feel that prevention begins at home. They believe parents have to control their children, and they define such control in terms of supervision and caring. Rachel, seventeen, states: "The trouble begins when parents who are irresponsible don't care what their children are doing, and don't know where they are even at ten in the morning. They let their kids loose, so they end up hanging around with the wrong people and getting into trouble." Although fifteen-year-old Michelle agrees to some extent, she doesn't place all the blame upon parents: "Vandals are trying to get attention, but you can get attention other ways, like telling your parents if you don't feel they're paying enough attention to you. Maybe they don't even know it."

Thoughtful teenagers analyze vandals' motives quite perceptively. They seem to feel that vandals are looking for a response not only from parents but from society as a whole. Ronnie, eighteen, believes, "The only way to stop vandalism would be if everybody was born millionaires and perfectly content. When you spray-paint walls or something, you're doing it to get back at somebody, whether you know it or not. When you break somebody's window you either hate that person, or you're striking out at somebody else, maybe somebody you're jealous of. So there's no such thing as meaningless vandalism. There's no way to stop it. A kid may do it to get recognition. Maybe a struggling artist has no other way of having people see his work. That's why letting kids draw on walls legally is a good idea. But there are just some kids who are always going to destroy what's good in the world. Just as there are some adults who do the same thing."

### Eliminate Boredom

Mark, fourteen, sums up the attitudes of many when he says, "I think people that vandalize don't have anything better to do." This viewpoint also corresponds to the popular belief that if adolescents had jobs, they would have less free time to get into trouble.

### Repair or Pay for the Damage

Quite a few believe that vandals should be forced to make amends for the damage they do. "If kids got caught and were made to clean up their mess and pay for it," says Rudy, fourteen, "they wouldn't be so quick to do it again. But the cops just let it go."

### Stiffer Punishment

Many teenagers condone the use of force and punishment to curb vandalism. They stress that police should "crack down" and "get rid of the law that says you have to be over eighteen to be thrown in jail." The misconception that children below the age of eighteen cannot be imprisoned is sadly belied by the number of preteen youths who are locked in public facilities. Teenagers' solutions are often oversimplified, but their suggestions clearly indicate that the vast majority seek active solutions for the problem. They're not willing to ignore it. As adults, we bear a responsibility toward our own children and teenage population in general to impose rehabilitative and corrective consequences for this kind of antisocial behavior. (See page 257 ff. on shoplifting.)

### Some Believe Nothing Can Be Done

Although some suggest talking to the culprits, they are not very hopeful about this approach. They honestly believe that dialogue with vandals is useless because they "don't have much sense." One sixteen-year-old expresses his pessimism "Unless you can put guards or police on every street corner or on every floor of buildings, I don't see how you can stop it. If they don't do it during school, they're going to do it after. You can't lock bathroom doors, and unless you have twenty-four-hour security, nothing can stop it."

One sixteen-year-old boy from an upper middle-class family recounts his experiences as a preadolescent vandal. He doesn't defend or excuse his actions; he simply explains them. In doing so, he offers a short but expressive course in the torments of growing up and the peer pressure involved. "I think parents have a lot to do with it, the way their life-style is. I don't want to blame it all on the parents though, because you get a bad-apple kid every now and then. It's also the kind of group you're hanging around with. I was vandalizing, really heavy. I was following a twelve-year-old kid around, and him, me and my brother got a little vandal group going. We totally ransacked the school, you know. Broke hundreds of dollars' worth of windows, and broke inside. Just because it was something to do. I didn't really know right from wrong. I couldn't have been more than seven years old and the other kid I was following was so much older. I guess the best thing for parents to do is explain how wrong it is to their kids, like my parents did. Plus plenty of, ah, good hitting. There's an awful lot of vandalism in sixth and seventh grades. Kids feel they have to destruct things. It gets out all their aggressions, that's for sure. There's so much pressure from school and parents. You're too old to do certain things, and too young to be free. It's a hell of a period of time. But still that's no excuse."

Our teenagers do offer some constructive solutions: parents should be aware of their kids' activities and make an effort to spend time with their children; kids should be given oportunities for employment and positive self-expression; when they vandalize, police or other authorities should respond quickly and enforce punishment, counseling or reparative actions.

## Shoplifting

Shoplifting is far more prevalent than most of us care to realize. From time to time public corporations and retail businesses announce that as thievery increases, the consumer pays in higher prices. Our survey confirms that some young people find it an attractive although frightening activity.

Almost all of our respondents admit having taken something without paying for it at one time or another, whether it was a piece of gum or more expensive items such as radios or makeup. Although the great majority of adolescents feel that shoplifting is morally wrong, very few, only 6%, would tell on a friend if she or he were shoplifting. In a previous survey of 636,823 children, conducted in association with Xerox Education Publications, we discovered that even the younger children don't feel it is important to "tell" when shoplifting is involved. Only 19% of children, grades 4 through 9, say they will report shoplifting incidents to an outside source.

## Why Shoplift?

A number of adolescents engage in shoplifting as a lark, something to do, a game of lawbreaking to see if they can get away with it. Others do it because they want or need the article, and don't have enough money to buy it. And a small percentage of our respondents feel that teenagers shoplift because they want attention. What they do not mention are the deeper causes that may underlie this behavior. Sometimes shoplifting is an unconscious means of satisfying a need for parental affection. It may also be an expression of anger at a world that doesn't seem to care.

Eliza Ann is fifteen years old, the second of four children, and the daughter of a well-to-do banker. She is an angry child, who feels that she's been neglected and overlooked by her parents. She and a friend were stopped by a store detective while leaving a crowded discount department store. She was carrying an album by her favorite rock group and two jars of makeup. She had no receipts. Following the frightening experience of an arrest and a warning not to enter the store again, Eliza Ann was sent home with her parents. Her mother and father were disturbed by her apparent lack of remorse. She blamed the store personnel for being nasty in their attitude toward her and said she would do it again if she weren't so frightened of being caught. Her parents were solid, law-abiding people who had preached honesty and respect both in words and example, and they couldn't understand their daughter's confusing behavior. They sought help from a skilled therapist who encouraged them to examine their own actions and feelings. They began to recognize that they had always concentrated on teaching their children to do the "right thing"; so much so, that they had neglected to try to understand how their children were feeling. After months of family counseling sessions, Eliza Ann was able to tell her parents that she felt overlooked and unloved. This revelation, coupled with her parents' greater understanding of her needs, paved the way for genuine change.

### Something to Do

For some, shoplifting is "a sort of social thing that's neat or cool or exciting." Sixteen-year-old Mary Jane found herself playing that game. "Yes, I have shoplifted and it was really weird, because I don't know why I did it. My parents give me money for everything. I didn't need anything. It wasn't even because I wanted to see if I could get caught. Afterward I thought I should take everything back. I was with a friend and we took dumb things like nail polish and makeup. Here we were in sixth grade and I didn't even wear it. We both just sat there and wondered why we did it. Neither of us thought it was neat because we got by with it. It was just something to do. We never did it again." Teenagers who come from upper-income families, and who don't need the merchandise they take, are the ones who usually shoplift "for fun." One fifteen-year-old describes the Saturday afternoons that she and three friends (all wealthy) devoted to shoplifting excursions. She explains: "We couldn't wait for the weekends so we could go from store to store and see how much we could take. I look back now (we did it two years ago) and know how dumb we were."

### Wanting the Article

Often, shoplifting is an impulsive activity, confined to articles that are quickly consumed, such as candy or gum. These thefts are rarely premeditated; the availability of the item is such that it can be taken quickly and easily, and then forgotten about. And most of the time, kids have little guilt or remorse. Deirdre, fourteen, is an exception: "Once I took a piece of bubble gum, but after I took it I laid a penny on the counter. I knew my dad wouldn't let me have the bubble gum and yet I wanted it. He's a dentist. Another time I stuck my hands in my pocket and I felt something. I was with a girl (one my mother didn't like), and I pulled out a bag of M&M's and said, 'Where did these come from?' My friend said, 'Oh, come on. Just forget about it. They'll never know.' I was scared half to death. The girl wouldn't take them back, so I did. It took me about fifteen minutes, I was so scared."

### Needing the Article

When teenagers don't have enough money for necessities, stealing becomes a means of support, as Lexie, eighteen, explains: "I've shoplifted, only I guess you'd call it more stealing. But I only stole food because I was on the streets and I was in a tough situation. I would go to the back of a Kentucky Fried Chicken place and kick open the door and take some chicken. But that's all. I only did it because I was hungry."

"I know a lot of kids shoplift just for the hell of it, but not me. I was in this group home and they didn't want to give us money for hygiene supplies. So me and Pat went to the supermarket and we stole a bunch of ladies' shavers, baby powder, baby lotion, cold cream. We got caught, though. A man was standing there and said, 'Can I check your bags, please?' So he took us in the back, took down our names and said he never wanted to see us again in that store. I know it's not right, but sometimes there's nothing else you can do." (Carolyn, 17)

"When I was twelve, thirteen, fourteen, I did it a lot. When I was fourteen, I got caught, and I never did it again, and I never will. I was so scared! I was grounded for a year. I did it because I was broke. I didn't take stuff just to take something. It wasn't just a kick. If I needed socks, I would take socks. I had no money and I didn't see anything wrong with it. I guess I was pretty stupid; but now I think it's morally wrong. You just don't do that. At least, I don't." (Betsy, 17)

## Why Some Don't Consider Shoplifting a Serious Offense

When the theft is considered slight, or the harm to the store owner insignificant, the teenager may feel that no serious wrong-doing has been committed.

"Yeah, I've done quite a bit. For the last year I don't think I have, though. Little, unimportant things; sort of a spur-of-the-moment type thing. If I wanted something and wasn't willing to pay for it because I didn't think it was worth it, I just took it. But I don't consider that serious shoplifting." (Harry, 17)

"Everybody takes stuff, especially when they were little. It's not right and most of them don't continue to do it. But even when they do it, it doesn't hurt anybody. The big stores don't even know the stuff is gone and they won't miss it. They're rich anyway. But something like vandalism hurts everybody. That's really destructive." (Donald, 16)

Adolescents as well as adults often measure the significance of illegal acts in terms of their effect upon the individual. Shoplifting, often a crime against a "big guy," such as a department store, isn't considered in the same category as vandalizing (often a devastating personal tragedy if it is perpetrated against one's home, as contrasted to a school or office building). Many adults get away with petty larceny and feel no guilt if they are able to cheat the "big guys" such as Internal Revenue, the telephone company, or the public transportation services. Riding on a bus without paying the fare is often considered a triumph of ingenuity, the rationalization being, "The fare is too high." Fifteen-year-old Joseph's comment indicates that he has adopted the same kind of attitude he often sees in the adult culture: "I shoplifted a couple of times but I felt bad doing it, so I returned the stuff one time. The second time I figured the store ripped me off and charged too much, so what the heck."

## Getting Caught

The one fact on which all kids agree is that the most effective way to prevent shoplifting, their's or someone else's, is to get caught. Both casual and repeated shoplifters confirm what Eddie, thirteen years old, tells us, "If kids get caught and punished, they wouldn't be so quick to do it again. I know I'd be so afraid I'd get caught and go to detention school or jail. A friend once told me he got arrested and they took him to a room in the police station and asked him all sorts of questions and took his picture. He was so scared what they was gonna do to him. But they let him go. They shouldn't have."

Many agree that the police treat habitual shoplifters too easily; that letting them off with only a warning encourages them to continue stealing. Fourteen-year-old Katherine, who comes from a comfortable middle-class family, elaborates: "I've taken pens, pencils, books, clothing, jewelry. I've even tried to take a pair of shoes—clogs. But that's when we got snagged. Actually, it wasn't me that got caught. I'm very careful. But my friend got caught, and some of my stuff was in her bag. The cop took us to the police station and booked us overnight. But her parents came and took us home. We had to pay a little fine that was initiated to us in front of a judge. I didn't think it was that big a deal. It doesn't go down on our record unless we do it again and get caught. Then it goes as a misdemeanor. It didn't even scare me that much, but enough so I may not do it again for a while because of my record. If I hadn't gotten caught, I would have continued. The main reason was money. I didn't have much at the time and it was just easier to take the things than to go out and get money, which is hard to do nowadays. Besides, the shops have all this merchandise and it wouldn't kill them. Also, it was exciting. Sort of a challenge. I won't do it again unless I really need to, unless I get into a deep financial problem. If that happens, I'll probably start off small and build up."

Prosecution and stiff punishment are often recommended. Despite the fact that criminological research has demonstrated that harsh punishment alone is not an effective deterrent, many, like Susan, sixteen, continue to believe in the punitive method. She says, "I think kids should be prosecuted if they shoplift. If one kid could set an example for all the others, if they would put one kid in jail for a couple of years, that would be a hell of an example. Heck, if they kill somebody, *they* should be killed. They should be put to death. The same for vandalism—not killed, but prosecute those kids! What's wrong is wrong."

When shoplifting becomes a ritual act of teenager daring or an easy way of gratifying a desire, the clear enforcement of limits is necessary. Often, the most effective cure is the fear that follows getting caught. Usually this action in itself, combined with direct confrontation with police, is enough of a shock to prevent further theft. Such dishonesty cannot be overlooked. It must be confronted, and the possible consequences must be made clear.

## When Getting Caught Is Not Enough

If shoplifting or vandalism is a habitual activity, counseling or therapy for the individual and the family may be advisable. Community clinics offer these services as well as group sessions in which kids are encouraged to help one another. If this approach proves ineffective, it may be necessary to remove the child from his home and place him in a special school that offers both education and round-the-clock supervision and guidance. In the best places, therapists, teachers, coaches, nurses, house-parents, and even the cooks meet regularly to discuss each child and to formulate approaches that will be helpful to him. As the process of rehabilitation continues, the teenager is gradually reintroduced to life "on the outside," and his ability to live with his family is tested before he's released.

Unfortunately, such facilities are not always available, particularly to families without money. And when children are remanded to detention centers rather than treatment centers, they usually learn more about how to continue crime than how to stop it. Confinement for a *short* period, however, may be the best deterrent against continued antisocial activities. A good scare can accomplish a great deal. But appropriate confinement must include adequate protection for the incarcerated teenager against beatings, rape, and violation. Neither society nor the children who have committed the wrongdoings are helped by punishment that is so harsh that it destroys the individual's will to change.

## What To Do If a Friend Is Shoplifting

A large proportion of teenagers take a firm ethical stance against shoplifting. Not only do they avoid such behavior, but some of them do their best to convince good friends to stop shoplifting.

---

What would you do if you knew your best friend was shoplifting?

| | | | |
|---|---|---|---|
| Tell no one | Don't tell anyone; just let the friend get caught. (That's the only way the friend will stop.) | 41% | |
| | Try to talk the friend into stopping | 28% | 81% |
| | Do nothing. You would never tell on a friend | 12% | |
| Tell some- one | Tell your friend's parents | 11% | 19% |
| | Tell the police | 8% | |

---

Parents are often shocked or dismayed that their own children would allow behavior such as shoplifting to take place. They assume that unless their children do or say something about it, they are condoning it. These parents must recognize that their youngsters are caught in a moral bind. They don't approve of shoplifting, but they value loyalty to a friend. It's not easy for anyone to confront a friend about a moral issue. However, some do make this effort.

"If a friend I knew was shoplifting, I'd probably give her money so she wouldn't have to do it again. I'd try to talk to her and explain that everything's out there, and if you work for it you can get it just like everybody else." (Angie, 16)

"If a friend of mine was shoplifting, I'd probably break all his fingers. If I talked to him and he said, 'It's none of your business,' then I'd probably tell his parents for his own good. I'd probably lose him as a friend, though." (Jon, 16)

Angie and Jon, however, are in the minority. Donna, fourteen, expresses the majority view quite convincingly. "Let 'em get caught and hopefully it will scare the shit out of them. If it was a really good friend of mine, I'd try to talk to her but talking only goes so far. If she's made up her mind to take something, she'll do it no matter what. Let the cops catch her. That's the only thing that will work."

# 11

# Teenagers on Religion and Country

---

- One-half state that they plan to follow their parents' religion
- 76% would fight for their country
- 90% think the United States is the best country in the world

---

R eligion and patriotism; the bedrock of our society, and two concepts that have been subjected to much criticism in recent years. What are our teenagers' views on God and country? In general, they subscribe to our traditional adult beliefs, but they move into periods of uncertainty that stimulate their own thinking and judgment. Some grip tightly to what they have learned and resist doubt and exploration. Others try to bolster their independence by automatically defying whatever is orthodox. Still others listen to all sides, then come to their own conclusions.

## Religion

The teenagers with whom we spoke were raised as Jews, Catholics, Baptists, Protestants, Seventh-Day Adventists, Mennonites, Lutherans, Quakers, Methodists, Presbyterians, Jehovah's Witnesses, and agnostics. They have strong convictions about the existence of some kind of supreme force, but they are far less certain about the necessity of organized religion. Most of them show little enthusiasm for attending church or synagogue on any regular basis. As thirteen-year-old Meg sees it, "I don't think you have to go to church to find God. My parents try and make me go by saying God wants you to go. I think it's just the same praying at home as praying in church. He doesn't care where you do it. I don't think I'll be as strong for religion as my parents, but I still feel towards God as they do."

## How Many Plan to Follow Their Parents' Religion?

| Do you plan to follow your parents' religion when you are older? | |
| --- | --- |
| Yes | 53% |
| No | 15% |
| You're not sure | 24% |
| Your parents don't have any religion | 8% |

Of the 53% who say yes, some report that they may not necessarily accept all of the traditional beliefs and customs. Vicky, thirteen, a Mennonite, says, "I believe in the religion, but I don't believe in all their ways. Like their rules and regulations. I'll stay a Mennonite, but I probably will not go along with everything they teach." The same sentiment is voiced by sixteen-year-old Malcolm, who is Jewish. He says, "I used to go to the synagogue and do all the prayers. I had my bar mitzvah. I'll probably celebrate the holidays but not as religiously as my parents. Oh, I hope God's not listening right now!" And a sixteen-year-old Catholic has similar doubts even as she confirms her belief in God.

"I wouldn't change my religion but I think women should be priests and I think the Catholic view about some TV shows is ridiculous. No church should tell you what you can or can't watch. I'm very anti on some of the things the church teaches, and I only go to mass to please my mother. I don't go to confession. Like I don't think telling a priest things is going to make anything better. Just tell God you're sorry. The church doesn't like it and they say you shouldn't argue. But it's there to question, and I question my religion!" (Sue Ann, 16)

Even those adolescents with fervent religious beliefs are not sure that they will practice their family's religion, although the history of prior generations suggests that they will.

"I definitely believe in God. I'm not a religious fanatic or anything, but He's a big part of my life. It's not like I just pray once a month when things are really going bad. I depend on Him. I know I'll follow some Christian religion, but it might not be Episcopal." (Rona, 18)

Our teenagers' doubts and questions need not be a cause for parental worry. It is a healthy expression of their desire to make their own decision, a process that will, in the long run, strengthen their ultimate convictions.

### Determining Their Own Religious Beliefs

Adolescents who examine their religious teachings do so in two steps. First they question the absolute truth of those teachings. Then they try to reason out a meaningful spiritual philosophy that is consistent with their other values and ideas. This process is common in adolescence, and it's not related to any specific set of religious ideas.

"Sometimes I get these religious streaks and start reading the Bible. And sometimes I just don't believe in anything. I might stay a Presbyterian, but maybe I won't. I have my own ideas about religion. It's not really set. With all the scientific things I know now, it's tough to believe what you read in the Bible." (Evan, 14)

"My mother is very religious and believes everything the church tells her. Some things are very true but other things I have to find out for myself. I have to learn. I don't believe in the straight biblical concepts. I guess that's why I have trouble when I go to church. I don't have blind faith." (Janie, 18)

One fifteen-year-old believes in the Bible, but interprets its words in a manner that complements his own sense of self. He explains: "The Bible says, 'Thou shalt not put any other God before me!' What I want to know is, 'Who is me?' I think it's you, yourself. Whoever is reading the Bible."

The vast percentage who affirm belief in God insures the continuation of some form of religion in our society, be it organized or personal. In fact, many of them intend to raise their children with some kind of religious faith, because, as one seventeen-year-old says, "It's good for kids to believe in something. To think there's a God to protect and help you." And Loretta, eighteen, comments: "I'd send my kids to Hebrew school and then let them make their own decision."

## Belief in God

Their belief in a deity is influenced by their own spiritual needs as well as by religious teachings.

"God made the world and made people come down here to do a

mission. They have to leave their mark before they leave the earth. It's up to us to deal with everything and bring the world up. He's looking over us and protecting those who need help and all that shit. He, She, a Spirit. Who knows? He wasn't black. Saw a picture in a book. He was white. I don't care what color He is, He's doin' his job." (Glenn, 16)

Sixteen-year-old Eve admits that she prays for favors. She believes that God is a protector and a moral example. She says, "He's always going to be there for me, but I'm not always going to be there for Him. I try to be more perfect, but it's very hard. Sometimes I only pray when I really want something."

Vince, sixteen, is the son of an ex-minister. His mother and brother changed their religious affiliation, and Vince has struggled to reach his own definition of God and religion. "After a lot of thinking," he says, "I came to the conclusion that the God I respect does not need people worshiping Him, doesn't need to preach damnation. The Christian religion has some holes in it, because no one is going to burn in hell."

Some who question the existence of God do so because there is no physical evidence. As one boy puts it, "I don't believe in anything I can't see." Others express a doubt that many adults share: how can a supreme being allow evil to flourish while virtue often goes unnoticed? Corinne, fifteen, explains: "I do and I don't believe in God. That's one of the things I'm confused about. I always wonder how God could let terrible things like birth defects, rapes, murders take place. I can't understand how bad things happen to so many good and honest people, and evil people get away with so much."

Almost none of our teenagers (believers or not) want to accept the notion that God or any other spirit could be a punishing force rather than a benevolent one.

"I've never really been brought up on any religion in particular so I'm not a follower of anything and never have been. Sometimes I could believe that there is a God or some kind of high power over everyone that watches over and helps you in times of need. But then at other times when He doesn't help you out, I don't know. I don't want to think of my God as a person who punishes people because if He's supposed to be higher than everyone else, I wouldn't think He'd do evil things that He doesn't want people to do to each other. I just don't have any strong beliefs." (Clarissa, 15)

One fourteen-year-old calls herself an atheist, but plans in a year or so to visit churches and synagogues and listen to everybody's opinion. Even the avowed disbelievers often hedge their bets. Although they question God's existence, they want to keep their options open, just in case.

In determining their religious beliefs, teenagers are influenced by a combination of tradition and iconoclasm. These forces have equal impact in shaping their views on patriotism and loyalty to country.

## Country

### Will They Fight for Their Country? 76% Say Yes

| | | |
|---|---|---|
| Yes, if it went to war for any reason | 21% | |
| Yes, if it went to defend another country | 7% | 76% |
| Yes, if it were attacked | 48% | |
| No, never | | 24% |

These statistics may surprise some adults who believe that the antiwar movement has spawned a generation of young people totally opposed to war on any grounds. But more than 7 out of 10 would be willing to fight if the government declared war. Their views are powerful and realistic. Unlike previous generations, they see no glory in battle. They know that death and suffering are the inevitable byproducts of war. They don't want to fight, but they would if they were called. They believe they would have no other choice. Juan, thirteen, defines his patriotism and his fears. He speaks for many when he says, "Sometimes I have these thoughts about being drafted. I wonder what I'd do if they sent me a letter. It's good that you go fighting for your country, doing the right things for your country. But I think, 'Oh, oh. I might be dead on the floor. Shot.' I'd go though."

Many appreciate the liberties they have and believe it's their duty to protect those freedoms. Sherrie, sixteen, explains: "I'd fight because America's a good country. You have your freedom. In other countries like Russia you have one kind of school, one religion, one everything. No choices." Seventeen-year-old Merle concurs. "I would definitely give my life for the United States. It is the best country. No way I'd let some assholes from outside come and mess up this country."

Almost half (48%) would fight to protect their country if the nation were attacked, but they would not necessarily go to war for any other reason. One fourteen-year-old sums up the feelings of the majority of our teenagers when he states: "Of course I'd fight to save the country, but I sure as hell wouldn't want to." We adults can take comfort in the fact that our adolescents will not desert their responsibilities as long as they recognize that war is necessary for survival.

Since America's survival is so important to them, we wondered how they felt about their country in general. Do they retain any vestiges of the anti-American sentiment that was prevalent in the late 1960s? We asked:

---

Do you think the United States is:

| | | |
|---|---|---|
| The best country in the world, even though it's not perfect | 52% | 90% |
| Okay | 38% | |
| Not as good as some others | 10% | |

---

Nine out of 10 have positive feelings about this country, although they realize it's not perfect. And that figure is consistent, regardless of age or gender. Why, then, are one-quarter of our teenagers reluctant to fight if called upon to do so?

### The 24% Resisters

Under the actual threat of war, the number who vow they would not fight under any circumstances would probably diminish. But there are strong feelings among the 24% of the adolescent population who state that at this time they would not participate in a war.

Some teenagers recognize their dilemma. They don't want America to be taken over by a foreign power. Yet they find war an unacceptable method for settling differences. Michael, seventeen, explains: "I would evade the draft as much as I could. I might assist in some way. Maybe medically or to help the damaged areas. But I wouldn't help to continue the war. I know your country has to be protected, but sooner or later if young people wouldn't fight, governments would have to find some other way to settle their problems."

Many others are simply unwilling to endanger themselves, and they're not ashamed to express their fears. One boy says it directly: "I'd try to get out of fighting because who the hell wants to get killed?" To many, a prison term seems more desirable than facing the risk of death. Alice, seventeen, would make that choice, and she admits that she doesn't blame men who don't want to fight. Yet she also recognizes the problems that would be created by not fighting. "We're all scared. But if everybody thought like I do, we'd lose. We wouldn't have anybody to fight for us. Somebody's got to go."

For some, fear is secondary to their disillusionment, which stems from the Vietnam experience and loss of faith in governmental leaders. These kids would examine the reasons for fighting, and then decide whether to flee the country, go to jail, join as a noncombatant, or take up arms. Some are so adamantly against war that they have already made their decisions.

"War worries me now because I see my world finally coming together and the draft bugs the heck out of me. I'm not afraid of leaving home. I think it's more that I've seen what military training does to a person mentally. This friend's brother came back from the marines and he's very nervous now. He used to be cool. He carries a gun all the time. I would do anything to get out of a situation like that. Probably go to Canada. The army makes a robot out of you. You can't even think for yourself. My mom always said to me, 'If the army wants you, they're going to come and take you. You have no choice in the matter.' And I told her when I was fourteen, I would go to Canada. I know it was more out of fright, but now it's the training and what it can do to you mentally. God, you lose your mind. Forget it." (Gilbert, 18)

## The Fruits of Vietnam

Most teenagers see a great difference between fighting to defend a foreign country and fighting to defend their own. They have seen the consequences of an unpopular war and they are bitter. Charles's comment is typical:

"I'd never fight. My brother came back from Vietnam and who thanked him? There's no guarantee for me. If I get a leg blown off, is the government gonna take care of me? They'll just send us out somewhere to be killed, and for what? I'd run to Canada as fast as I could go." (Charles, 18)

Pete, a young man of seventeen who lives in a university town, would not fight for another country, but expresses strong feelings for his own. "We're the best country in the world but we still have a lot of problems. If we were attacked, I'd feel an obligation to do something, not necessarily fighting. We help out every other country and they couldn't care less. They just take advantage of us. So why lose our lives to defend them, when if another country came along and made it worth their while, they'd probably turn on us. They spit on the nice guys. We're too damn good to them all. It's us we should be watching out for."

Blind patriotic obedience appears to be another casualty of the Vietnam era. The image of the U.S. as an exploiter of other countries is a troubling one for some teenagers. Fifteen-year-old Eloise sees it as one of America's major social problems: "I wouldn't fight. I feel that the U.S. is a really fucked-up place and they always find a way to get their noses into everything. From studying history courses I've found they always want to be so liberal and get out there always helping and putting their noses in everybody's business. I'm not proud of this country. I feel Americans have always exploited people to get what they want, especially black people and that's part of me, so I just don't like this country. I don't even pledge to the flag 'cause I'm not going to be a hypocrite. I think it's going to take people of color to rise up and get their shit together, throughout the world."

But fifteen-year-old John, another black youth, disagrees. "I like this country. It's been hard on me and yet I like it. I'd go to war if I was needed. If they'd take me, I'd join them."

Finally, some adolescents are not willing to fight because they feel that traditional combat is useless; that nuclear holocaust is inevitable. One sixteen-year-old from an Eastern private school explains:

"The next war will be nuclear because if it's not, it would be like a chess game without using your queen. Since we'll die anyway, why go to fight the make-believe war before the real one?" (Danny, 17)

Our teenagers have important decisions to make. They have no pat answers and they do not accept ours without questioning, analyzing, and even disputing. Like each generation before them, they have to find their own way of putting their convictions into practice.

# 12

## Teenagers on Race and Prejudice

- 64% say they have friends of another race
- 25% say they would date someone of another race
- More whites (47%) than blacks (26%) would refuse to date interracially
- More boys than girls (30% vs. 20%) say they would date across racial lines
- 34% believe that police do not treat teenagers of any race very well
- Another 26% believe that police treat white teenagers better than nonwhite teenagers

### The Background of Race Relationships

Today's teenagers are the first generation to have come of age in the aftermath of the civil rights movement. Older white generations knew about segregation, unbreakable white-only employment restrictions, and other discriminatory practices. Yet they continued to believe that blacks and other minorities were treated well and were generally satisfied. There was little awareness or concern among whites that television shows and commercials, print advertising, movies, and other mass communication processes were populated virtually only by whites except for specialized roles. It was believed natural that white and black children would attend separate schools. Most whites were content with the "separate but equal" custom. Black parents, however, were angry and distressed about the barriers they and their children faced in seeking employment, in obtaining advanced education, in gaining decent housing. The fight against discrimination as well as the emergence of black power and creativity that has surged through our society since the sixties, has been a reality in the lives of today's teenagers. Consequently, they have grown up in a climate markedly different from that of their parents. How have these changes affected our teenagers' attitudes and beliefs?

## Social Relationships Among Teens

|  | Yes |
|---|---|
| Do you have friends of another race? | 64% |
| Would you date someone of another race? | 25% |

This chart tells the story of race relations among American teenagers. Friendships that cross racial lines are fine, but dating is quite another matter.

Teenagers' attitudes about race relationships both reflect their parents' views and stem from their own experiences. Unlike past generations, the vast majority of young people disapprove of discrimination or prejudice. Most of them find it unfair and unjustified. Yet we know that race riots occur in high schools and that violence breaks out frequently in metropolitan centers where the two races attend classes together and share other facilities. At the same time, there is far more interracial social contact and dating than there has been in the past. Which of these phenomena represents the real state of race relations among adolescents today? The answer is both. White and nonwhite teenagers agree that they do not want to be prejudiced. But they are wary and often distrustful of each other. They are also aware that friends and parents may be hostile if they develop close contacts across racial lines. Although almost two-thirds say that they have friends of another race, blacks report a larger percentage of interracial friendships than do whites.

### Interracial Friendships

Do you have friends of another race?

|  | Blacks | Whites |
|---|---|---|
| Yes | 74% | 62% |
| No | 26% | 38% |

The term friendship covers a wide spectrum. A few adolescents report having good friends or many friends of another race. The largest number, however, include in this category school friends who are not really considered "best friends." Many teenagers struggle with the paradox of living in a society that practices racial separation but preaches racial equality. The more reflective ones strive to make sense of these inconsistencies and to understand the reasons for racial conflicts. "Sometimes I'll hear about what a group of blacks have done and it angers me," comments Molly, fourteen. "But I feel they do things sometimes because they're pushed into a corner. If it was whites and the other way around, we'd be the same way."

Some enthusiastically endorse crossing racial lines. June, fifteen, says, "I'm really color blind. I have quite a few black friends and love them as well as my white friends." And thirteen-year-old Ross tells us, "I'm prejudiced with nobody. I don't mind if they are white, black, Puerto Rican, Chinese, whatever; as long as they are good people."

But more frequently their comments reveal mixed emotions; they deny being prejudiced while at the same time they hang on to old stereotypes. "They're all right," states one fifteen-year-old, "if they're not out to get you." He is using a popular adult method for resolving the internal conflict between feeling prejudiced yet believing that prejudice is morally wrong. Mike, fourteen, illustrates the "They're okay, but ..." principle: "I don't go out with black kids. Actually, there was one at my old school and we were pretty close. But I would never invite him over to my house and go out with him because I feel kind of embarrassed or something. But we talk to each other on the phone."

Some, however, are not hesitant about admitting negative attitudes toward blacks. Frank, seventeen, comments: "If I gave my money to somebody to hold, I'd give it to a white person. I don't like the way they talk sometimes. You can't understand them and I guess you'd have to say I'm prejudiced." One sixteen-year-old's words include a shot of anti-Semitism mixed in with her obvious prejudice against blacks:

"I know a couple of Jewish people and they're very smart. Very intelligent. I really envy them a lot, but I don't like the way they talk. They are highly educated but they hide that by talking like scum. That is really disgusting and it annoys me. They talk like that so they'll appear like the scummy other kids. They're 'out' and they want to be 'in.' It's ridiculous. I'm not prejudiced against them, though. I'm prejudiced against blacks. The whole of them. I don't like them at all. I don't trust them; they're sneaky; they're very sly. They do things behind your back. They're the main cause of the playground problems. I think they should ship them out of there and into their own playground. They should stay in their own territory." (Kathy, 16)

And fifteen-year-old Andrew tells us, "I don't mind whites in small doses, like one-on-one. But I don't go for big groups of them."

Instruction in racial separation is part of our American heritage. While growing up, our children notice that the races usually live in separate areas of the city or community. They are aware that heads of government, mayors, school principals, teachers, judges, landlords, doctors, and those with money are—with some notable expectations—not usually black. Children of all races are often warned by parents not to mix with children of another race. Separation breeds distrust, and distrust is fertile soil for the development of prejudices. Some of the negative attitudes teenagers develop are the result of neighborhood and other peer influences. These attitudes often surface following a run-in with members of another race. All are powerful influences, but none is as potent as parental prejudice.

## Parental Influence on Cross-Racial Friendships

Infants are not born with prejudgments about individuals who differ from them in skin color, religious preference, or any other characteristic. They learn from parents to give meaning to these differences. If they are encouraged to see people as individuals and to avoid generalizing (favorably or unfavorably) about groups, teenagers are unlikely to develop rigid prejudices. But that means avoiding the pattern of characterizing and stereotyping *any* group—"the Jews," "the Catholics," "the blacks," "the whites," "the teenagers," "the rich kids," "the poor kids," "all women," "all men." And such an effort is not easy for anyone. In some communities, religious or citizens' groups sponsor interracial workshops for families who wish to improve their understanding of each other's racial background. When parents try to free themselves of prejudice, their children usually adopt a similar attitude, although that doesn't always happen. Bette, sixteen, remarks: "My mom likes blacks but I hate them." However, most of the teenagers who say they have no prejudices come from families who share that view. Some have parents who were active in the civil rights movement, or who work with people of another race and are comfortable in their associations.

"I have many black friends. They're just as good as whites. My parents don't have any prejudices, either. My dad teaches high school and he's a football and track coach. Most of his best athletes are black, and he gets along well with them. That's probably why I grew up without any prejudices." (Rich, 15)

"My father was in the movement back in the sixties so our whole family believes in civil rights. Every kind of color." (Curtis, 16)

In families where racism is overt, young people sometimes criticize parents who are hypocritical or who demean members of another race by name-calling. Deirdre, fifteen, tells us, "My mother has got me so confused. One minute she says, 'Accept people how they are,' and the next minute she is saying, 'All these whites are trying to keep you down.'" And Alma, seventeen, says, "Even though my parents are prejudiced, I still have a lot of black friends. I refuse to go by their bigotry. My grandparents even said to me that if I married someone black, they'd know I didn't love them."

### Reacting to Economic Differences

For some teenagers, racism is linked to the economic status of minorities. Many of these kids hear their parents speak disparagingly about our "welfare state", about "giving the poor a free ride." They are particularly vulnerable to such views because they have been taught to equate hard work and economic achievement. Sixteen-year-old Carl expresses just such an attitude: "I know some black kids but they're not really friends. The only prejudice I have is against anybody who's on welfare, and usually that's blacks. They should try to get out and work like everybody else. My dad makes remarks about blacks a lot and I guess maybe I agree with him."

Parents who are concerned about preventing the development of racism should make an effort to avoid this "blaming the victim" approach. Instead, they might explain to their youngsters how discrimination hampers minorities' opportunities.

Prejudice based on economic status is not one-sided. Minority teenagers often resent the affluence that they see in some white families. Jack, fourteen, says, "They got everything. The power and the money. I don't like hanging around with them."

## The Black Perspective

Black youths who have firsthand experience with prejudice talk about their need to be careful and self-protective in their dealings with whites. Arthur, sixteen, won't go to a white friend's house even when invited by the friend's mother, because if anything were missing, he would be blamed. He continues, "That's why my mother always told me to stay out of other people's houses. Then they can't blame you for anything."

There is no doubt that young people adopt some of our prejudices and develop some on their own. But when a valid friendship is established, most of them will hold to it with tenacity, regardless of what parents tell them.

## Two Sides of Racial Fears

Our adolescents do not have the solution to racial problems. They are as trapped as we are by the history and the myths of interracial relationships. Two comments from boys—one white, one black—describe the wall of fear and suspicion that often separates the races.

"I have some black friends, although I've developed some kind of nonintellectual reaction toward them. A kind of emotional thing. I've been mugged by blacks and never mugged by whites, so I feel more fright if I see five black kids walking toward me." (Mark, 17)

"What really upsets me is when I'm walkin' down the street and a white person crosses over to the other side because they're afraid of me." (Willard, 16)

They see it as it happens and wish it were different.

## Interracial Dating

When it comes to dating someone of another race, the difficulties increase.

Whites are generally taught by their parents not to consider non-whites as dating or marriage partners. Although blacks and other nonwhite minorities learn a comparable prejudice, it is evidently

Would you date someone of another race?

| | Whites | Nonwhites |
|---|---|---|
| Yes | 21% | 42% |
| No | 47% | 26% |
| Don't know | 32% | 32% |

less restricting. Frequently, parents stress racial guidelines simply because they want to spare their children unnecessary pain and hardship. Regardless of how unprejudiced they may wish to be, they are aware that interracial couples and their children encounter many additional problems in our society. Their protectiveness is understandable.

## Sex Differences in Dating Attitudes

Boys and girls differ on the issue of interracial dating, but the trends are quite similar. It is far more "No" than "Yes."

Would you date someone of another race?

| | Total | Boys | Girls |
|---|---|---|---|
| Yes | 25% | 30% | 20% |
| No | 43% | 40% | 46% |
| Don't know | 32% | 30% | 34% |

One out of 4 would be willing to date someone of another race. This decision depends upon the interplay of three prime factors: their own feelings, their parents' views, and the judgments of the larger society (including peers). And the strength of these factors determines their attitudes about interracial dating.

## Attitudes of Boys

### Self-Determination
Boys who respond affirmatively are less likely to be influenced by parents or society than are the girls. They are conscious of their

parents' attitudes, but they cope either by hiding the facts or avoiding direct confrontation.

"Yeah, I'd date a black girl. Color doesn't matter. I've seen many intelligent black people and many dumb white people, and vice versa. I know a lot of black girls and if I really liked one of them, I'd date her no matter what my parents said." (Ken, 15)

"I would never tell my parents if I were dating a black girl. I'd just say I'm taking someone out. They'd never know." (Dennis, 15)

"I'm not prejudiced, but my mother is. I'd date a white girl, but my mother, she says, 'Don't bring any white girl in my house.' " (J.D., 17)

### Influence of Parents

Although many boys will not abide by their parents' wishes concerning interracial dating, there are those who certainly do give parental views serious consideration. They often do so in order to avoid major hassles. Raymond, sixteen, explains: "No, I don't really think I'd date a black girl. Well, maybe there's one I would. But it wouldn't work out too well, especially with the parents' situation. That's ridiculous. I'm a Jewish boy. My mom would kill me. But if I really liked the girl, then I think I would probably see her."

It's a difficult decision for many adolescents because they're pulled in two directions: on the one hand, they're attracted to the particular boy or girl; on the other hand, they have to wrestle with obvious parental objections. The older the teenager, the more likely he or she will be to make an independent decision regardless of parental influence. Girls may react similarly, but they definitely feel more pressure from parents and society.

## Attitudes of Girls

There is no doubt that young women's activities are much more sharply scrutinized than are boys'. Once again, the sexist trend. Many parents are more protective of their daughters because they're afraid the girls will be exploited by boys. Parents also anticipate social disapproval from friends, and their daughters share this apprehension. Yet many of the girls fight for their right to date without parental interference.

### Self-Determination

One white thirteen-year-old hits the core of the issue—two people and how they feel about each other—as she says, "I'd date a black boy if I liked him a whole bunch. I wouldn't date a white boy if I didn't like him a whole bunch."

### Influence of Parents and Society

Many girls are just as anxious as boys to avoid confrontations with parents that might result in long-term divisiveness. Rachel, eighteen, explains, "I wouldn't care, but I think dating a black guy would probably hurt my parents too much and I wouldn't want to start with that. It's not worth it, really. A different religion would bother them, too. I would hope that the person I end up marrying is my religion and race." And sixteen-year-old Kitty feels that family conflict would be inevitable: "I'd date a black guy. Why not? But my father would probably murder me and my mom would say 'Oh, no! Not my daughter! What would the neighbors think?' It would be mass confusion in the house. My mother would worry how it would look socially. She's hung up about that."

Most young women are well aware of society's attitudes about interracial dating, and they are very perceptive about the difficulties involved. Carolyn, fifteen, speaks from experience when she says, "People just don't accept people as people. They're afraid of things that they don't know enough about. It's kept minorities down for so long. If I were to like a white guy, I could never even mention it. 'What do you mean, you like a white guy?' To most people white and black are not normal. It's not what you feel inside, it's what society goes by. A white guy may want to kiss you but he'll think, 'I couldn't.' They'll be close to you to a certain extent, and you know they might like you. But being the way things are we could never make it. The whole thing would be behind closed doors. People just wouldn't accept it. When you get grown you can go into a more populated area where different ideas are accepted. Like in New York City it's not going to be such a big thing when you see a black guy and a white girl, or vice versa."

Sumi, eighteen, recognizes that each race has fostered its own concepts of attractiveness. She observes, "Friends and dating are a little different. Probably yes, I would date a black. I've never met anyone, but I think so. I don't think my parents would object. My father wouldn't care that much but my mother might question it a little. For her, she wouldn't see the attraction because you don't just develop those kinds of attractions. You were never taught what is handsome in a black man. I think she would have a hard time understanding."

Both blacks and whites make a definite distinction between friendship, dating, and becoming really serious about someone of another race. Many of them agree that a relationship which could lead to marriage simply creates too many problems, particularly for possible offspring. They know they are likely to feel isolated when they spend time with each other's families and long-time friends. They will have to depend primarily on each other for support. If they decide to marry, they will have to be helpful and understanding when their children are rejected by children of the nonintegrated majority. Therefore, most adolescents plan to keep interracial relationships on a strictly friendly basis.

## Teenagers and the Police

When it comes to the issue of police treatment, two distinct themes emerge: how adolescents rate the general attitude of the police toward teenagers, and how they see the situation in relation to race. We want our young people to become committed participants in our society; to believe in its regulations and methods of enforcement. If they do not feel that the law is on their side or enforced fairly, we will be raising a generation of kids who find it necessary to resist and evade the law rather than support it.

### How Fair Are the Police?

One-third believes that all racial groups receive the same treatment. Another third agree, but specify that *all* teenagers are treated poorly. And the final group believes that discriminatory practices are a reality. Of these, one-quarter believes that blacks are the pri-

---

Do you think that:

| | | |
|---|---|---|
| The police treat white teenagers better than non-white teenagers? | 26% | ⎫ |
| The police treat nonwhite teenagers better than white teenagers? | 6% | ⎬ 32% |
| They both get treated the same? | | 35% |
| Neither gets treated very well? | | 34% |
| (Some checked more than one response) | | |

---

mary victims. This is a serious assertion by a large group of American teenagers. And when we break this down according to race, we find that blacks are more likely to perceive discrimination than are whites.

|  | Whites | Blacks |
| --- | --- | --- |
| Whites treated better than nonwhites | 24% | 37% |
| Nonwhites treated better than whites | 6% | 3% |
| Both treated the same | 37% | 29% |
| Neither treated very well | 35% | 31% |

### Whites' Observations of How the Law Treats Minorities

Some of our interviewees (both white and black) base their opinions on hearsay or what they have read or seen on television. Others speak from experience. Georgie, a fifteen-year-old New Yorker, says, "When I got arrested, my friend got treated worse than me because he was black. He got treated bad, but they didn't treat me bad. They hit him and pushed him, but not me. They put handcuffs on him, but not me. White cops get black people arrested and beat them and everything. I see it at the train station. In some parts of the country they're really friendly, though. Black and white. If you do something wrong or try to hurt them, the cops will hurt you. Otherwise, they leave you alone." And Angie, fourteen, from a Philadelphia suburb, comments: "I was in town last week and there was a black and white man fighting. This particular policeman treated the black one a lot rougher than the white one, and it was the white one's fault. I didn't think that was at all fair."

Many white teenagers believe that this kind of discrimination stems from police distrust of nonwhite adolescents. "They don't trust them as much because they've heard so many things about them like they're no good. It shouldn't be that way, but it is," states one thirteen-year-old. Another thirteen-year-old observes that blacks in so-called good neighborhoods are treated better than those in bad neighborhoods.

Although only a small percentage feel that minority groups receive favorable treatment, two teenagers tell of their experiences in this regard. May, sixteen, recounts: "I saw a raid down by where I live and there were a couple of black kids and a couple of my friends. They treated the blacks so neat and they were clubbing my friends. They were white cops. They were being so gentle with the blacks. I don't think they want lawsuits because blacks are the minority groups." And a seventeen-year-old tells about her day in court: "I didn't get a fair shake from the law. I went to court yesterday. We had a black robber that came into my room and I identified him in court. He pleaded guilty. I don't care if he pleaded guilty; he stole my stuff and we won't get any of it back. They let him off easy because he hadn't stolen much before. Well, they'll put him out on the street again and give him a chance to see how much he can get next time. Sometimes the law is too tough, and other times they are not tough enough." (June, 17)

### Nonwhites' Observations of How the Law Treats Minorities

"One day I was waitin' on my white friend. He snatched a pocketbook and after they caught him he was out the next day. It was done and over with. He didn't have to go back to court or nothin'. One of my black friends snatched a pocketbook and he wasn't out for a week. And still had to go back to court. The white lady pressed charges against my white friend, and he still got out with a clean rope. And my black friend, the lady didn't even press charges and the D.A. tried to hold him. Tried to send him up, and that was his first offense." (Jimmy, 15)

"Since my mother died and I've been out in this wilderness, I don't think I ran into too many people that are prejudiced. But with the law, it's different. If a white cop will bust a Hispanic or a black, they don't give them the break they'll give the white person. I've seen this happen myself. One day these white guys got busted for some smoke so the cops took them in the car and then let 'em go. A little while later I seen 'em comin' over laughin' and goofin'. The cops kept their smoke, but they let the kids go. If it was us, they would have took us in, Hispanic or black. But one time I got a break from this black cop. I was takin' my brother to the bus terminal and the black cop came by and seen me smoke. I didn't have enough time to throw them out. Two joints fell out of my pack. He seen them. I said, 'Oh, shit! How did that happen?' And he said, 'Now go pick them up.' Then he said, 'Lean over that rail and dust the joints on the tracks. I don't want you to think I would keep them.' There's cops that *do* keep them. Anyway, he gave me a break. Let me go." (Santo, 17)

"They always go after the black kids. So when we used to steal in supermarkets, the guard never said nothin' when he saw Vince, my white friend. But when me and my black friend walked in, the guard started followin' us all over the place. So what we did was we had Vince do the stealin' and we walked around." (Sparky, 15)

### Teenagers' Observations of How the Law
### Treats Adolescents (Regardless of Race)
#### Positive Views:

Most adolescents are not blindly antiauthority. They recognize both the difficulties of police work and the decency with which many law enforcers treat young people. They particularly appreciate second chances that may be given, and even wonder sometimes if too much leniency is shown. And when teenagers believe that a crime has been committed, they often agree that punishment by the law is well deserved. One eighteen-year-old comments; "If black or white kids do bad things, they should get it. If they're old enough to do the crime, they're old enough to pay the time."

#### Negative Views:

Thirty-four percent of our interviewees feel that courts judge even more on the basis of age than of color. Anne, fourteen, says, "If somebody is seventeen and they got in a car accident, the judge thinks, 'Oh, he's just a hot rod.' It may not be the kid's fault at all, but he's the one who'll get the short end just because he's a teenager. It's not right." And Walter, fourteen, agrees. "I don't think it matters, black or whites. They just don't like teenagers or have much respect for them."

Their opinions may not always reflect what's actually happening, but the important fact is that they *feel* they are discriminated against. If our young people are to have respect for the law, it is crucial for them to have evidence that the law is fair to everyone, regardless of sex, race, or age.

## Chances of Succeeding in Life—The Influence of Race

Many of our kids have come to the conclusion that equal opportunity does not exist. And it's a viewpoint that transcends racial lines. However, some dispute this position, citing minority groups that have made it up the ladder.

## If You Work for It You Can Get It

Many believe that although blacks may have to work harder, the opportunities are there for them. As one young man attests: "I don't think color gets in the way. If you're really good, you'll make it." Those who espouse the "anyone can make it" philosophy are telling us that the work ethic is the important factor for success. Josh, sixteen, states: "Other minorities have been able to pull themselves up, so blacks can do it, too, if they try. Jews have done it all their lives and never expected help." Rosalie, fourteen, agrees. "If a person is smart enough and has the ability to do things, they'll go to the top." Miguel, who is Hispanic, sees both whites and blacks receiving some preference over his group, but he is optimistic about the changes he sees:

"Anyone who wants something badly enough will get it. I'm from Puerto Rico, but if it's tougher it just means that you have to work harder. There was a time when it was tougher, but now it's becoming less and less. There's more chance now. For example, blacks couldn't get jobs as easy as whites. Now it seems that people are hiring them *because* they are black. That hasn't happened to us Hispanics yet. But I believe if you want something badly enough, you can get it." (Miguel, 17)

A small number echo Miguel's belief that minorities (particularly blacks) receive additional opportunities because of their color. They speak of colleges looking for blacks, and the job market seeking blacks who may even be less qualified than whites. As one sixteen-year-old girl sees it, "Nowadays it's minorities first." The predominant opinion, however, is that racial discrimination hampers the opportunities of minorities.

## Less Chance For Nonwhites

Many teenagers across all racial lines believe that members of minority groups are going to have a tougher time competing and achieving.

### Opinions of Whites

Fred, sixteen, learned about discrimination firsthand when a man who was part-Mexican, part-black, applied for a job on a fishing boat as a shrimper. "I saw the prejudice right there, I was really disgusted. This guy got turned down for a job. The boss simply said, 'We don't need nobody.' This was a pretty good guy named Norm. He was qualified. He shrimped. He didn't have a license, but he was a shrimper. Went up to get a job when they were hiring and they wouldn't take him. I noticed they had all white crews. They don't carry blacks or Mexicans. The Mexicans they put on river boats way out in the middle of nowhere, which is really disgusting because Mexicans have ambitions too, you know."

### Opinions of Blacks

Some believe whites are just born lucky, while blacks have to struggle; that white kids have money and black kids don't. Vernon, fifteen, explains: "The way the world is fixed, white people are the higher level and the black people are the lower level. Like if you was my age and you and me went to get a job, the first thing they'd think is the white boy isn't gonna steal, but the black dude might rob me blind." And a variation on the same theme comes from another fifteen-year-old who believes that if a black boy from Harvard and a white boy from a mediocre college were competing for a job, the white boy would have a better chance of getting it just because he's white.

Interestingly, some black teenagers believe that blacks are not willing to help each other; that instead, they tend to be jealous of each other's success. Anna, eighteen, says, "One black man who is a millionaire can live down the street from another black who is poor. Instead of one black helping the other black (like white people do), the black brother sits there and condemns the other one because he's poor. And the other one condemns the rich one because he's made money. He says, 'That dude doesn't deserve a Mercedes.' The problem is that he's envious and resents the other guy's success." And she believes: "Kids, more than adults, just accept people as people."

We are still living with the consequences of centuries of racial (and religious) discrimination, but as one fourteen-year-old comments optimistically: "Things are getting better with time, thank goodness." A statement of hope—but not necessarily a reality.

# 13

# Teenagers on the Future

• 92% think they will achieve what they want in life. **77%** say they will get there through hard work
• What they want most is to be loved, to be healthy, and to do the kind of work they really like
• 7 out of 10 think girls need to prepare for a career as much as boys

## What They Want Out of Life

"I only want two things in my future.
Love and a damn good job." (Shelly, 16)

Statistically, here's how it looks:

| What do you want most in life?<br>(Check one or two) | |
| --- | --- |
| To be loved | 41% |
| To be healthy | 38% |
| To do the kind of work you really like | 29% |
| To be successful in your work | 25% |
| To be rich | 22% |
| To be married | 13% |
| To do something worthwhile for the world | 9% |

The teenagers of the eighties differ in many ways from the flower children of the sixties. Sixties' teenagers exalted love and peace, and tried to change the Establishment. Today's adolescents also want love and peace, but they are not dropping out and trying to create a new and purer world. Nor do they have to expend their energy fighting against an unpopular war. Instead, they are focusing on themselves and the good life they want. They see a clear connection between hard work and success, although their definition of "good" and "successful" is not necessarily based on financial rewards. Our young people believe that they can pursue and achieve their goals without making too many compromises. They recognize the possibility that they may have to work in an environment that is limiting and depressing, but they plan to do whatever they can to avoid that trap. They do not want to be forced to stay in an unfulfilling job as many of their parents have done. They want to be happy in their work. Money is secondary for many of them. Some of us may find this attitude naïve and believe that they will become more cynical (or realistic) as they mature. But their conviction and dream is one we can support, especially since some of us regret our failure to reach it ourselves.

When they discuss the future, our teenagers mention ambitions and goals we all have had. They want happiness, health, stability, and security. Andy, a teenager from a New York ghetto, explains, "I just want a decent place to live, a decent wife. I want to live where it's peaceful, quiet, where you don't have to worry about your kids being around a shoot-out. I want a nice backyard and I don't want to be in debt." Quite a few of our respondents speak about their desire to remain debt-free. Obviously, their parents' debt-building habit is one they hope to avoid in their own lives.

## How Will They Get What They Want?

We asked:

---

Do you think you will achieve what you want in your life?

| | | |
|---|---|---|
| Yes, because you'll work for it | 77% | |
| Yes, because you're lucky | 8% | 92% |
| Yes, because you can talk people into doing what you want and believing what you say | 7% | |
| No, because you're unlucky | | 5% |
| No, because you won't work hard enough | | 3% |

---

The alarm-sounders have been proclaiming that our young people no longer believe in the work ethic. Yet our evidence is very much to the contrary. Nine out of 10 of our teenagers expect to achieve what they want in life, and nearly 8 out of 10 believe they will get there through hard work. These expectations are consistent across all age groups. Most of our young people do not expect or want to get something for nothing. Nan expresses the feelings of many adolescents when she says, "I want to be somebody. I want to prove to myself that I'm not just wasting my school time. I don't want to be rich, but I sure don't want to be poor. Rich enough to give my kids a good education." Of course, not everyone who announces a belief in the value of hard work is going to follow through. Luck and the con job are given some credit, but they are gambler's methods, and few teenagers fit into that category insofar as their lifework is concerned.

But exactly what type of careers do our teenagers want to pursue? Have the choices changed very much since our own decision-making days?

## Career Decisions

Definite decisions are still in the future for the majority of adolescents. At age fourteen or even at age eighteen there is no need to determine how one's entire life will be spent. Many parents worry about their children's lifework, but how many of us knew what we wanted to do when we were eighteen? (And how many of us still wonder what we'd really like to do?) However, they have specific ideas and leanings, which stem from the experiences they have had, parental examples pro and con, and adult and peer encouragement. Their dreams and plans reflect diversity and, at the same time, affirm the ambitions and energy of youth. They think about becoming teachers, businessmen, doctors, psychologists, forest rangers, lawyers, journalists. Occasionally, as a result of technological advances, a new career surfaces, but in general, the old standbys prevail.

"Either a teacher or on a newspaper staff. There's not much else I can see myself doing. If my father had been a carpenter, I could see myself doing that. But he's a teacher so I can see myself being one too." (Henry, 15)

"People tell me I could make a living selling things. I want to be the best in one big company. Then have my own. I've had an offer to go into business with my stepmother. I sort of passed up the offer. I didn't really feel like working under somebody. I'm going to have my own business and be on the top." (Randy, 15)

A small number respond to the idea of living and working in the wilderness, or at least far away from an urban environment. Part of their fantasy is avoiding the pressures and competitiveness of modern civilization by seeking their own paradise. Sixteen-year-old Andrew seeks freedom from the judgments and controls of other people, and he believes he can achieve this goal by isolating himself in the primitive and unaffected world he loves. "I do see myself with a nice, comfortable cabin with a garden, hogs, just simple things," he says. "I'm working now to get that cabin in the woods. Any self-sufficient type thing where I don't have to rely on other people. Don't have to talk to them, don't have to even look at them if I don't want to. People always tell you what you're doing's no good. They just get in the way. You need some people but the others are just a pain, for the most part." Frank, fifteen, has similar thoughts. "I just want to go up to the mountains and work in the forest. I don't want to be here in civilization at all. I love the wilderness. I hunt, fish, canoe, and camp. I hate civilization. Too noisy, too much trouble here."

As they get older and their knowledge of the world increases, many of them will discover areas of interest they are not aware of yet. But no matter what career they decide upon, there is strong affirmation that the choice is theirs alone.

## The Role of Parent in Career Choice

Although they value their parents' counsel concerning career choice, almost all of them plan to move in the direction that pleases them, regardless of parental admonitions or objections. As Loretta, thirteen, indicates: "I wanted to be a doctor, but my mother told me I wasn't smart enough. My father thinks I can do it, though. So who knows? I'll follow whatever career I want no matter what my parents say. It's my life. I have to do what I want to do." And although Alan's goals are different, he shares the same conviction. "All I know is that I want to work with my hands, even though my parents probably wouldn't want me to. I'll do it anyway, though."

Any individual deserves the right to follow a dream even though doing so may prove to be a minor mistake or a complete disaster. At least the child will never resent the parent for standing in the way, or look back with regret in later life bemoaning "the career that never was" because the chance was never taken. One father with whom we spoke had always wanted to be a musician. He had talent and drive, as well as a very domineering father who forbade his son to enter such an "insecure" profession. He never had the opportunity to fail or, more important, to have the success he believed was possible. He told us that no matter what his own son or daughter decided to do, he would support that decision because "life is too short to be trapped in a career that someone talked you into." We agree that parents cannot live their children's lives for them. Offer whatever good advice seems pertinent but, thereafter, step back and allow your children to succeed or fail in the career of *their* choice.

Sixteen-year-old Adam believes that his parents have discovered the right approach, and his appreciation is a testimonial to their wisdom. "My parents' favorite expression was, 'Use your better judgment.' They didn't dampen any of our spirits at all. Not like most kids. I'm sure their parents have ideas for them and want them to be molded in a certain way. But my father always told us to follow our dreams. If we had a dream, for damn sure do it! Even if you live on pennies a day, as long as it's what you like to do. Don't let anybody intimidate you. My mom agrees, but she says we've got to pay for our dream and go about it the right way. You can't just go out and be happy like a hippie. You got to have some kind of back-up financially. You have to be responsible."

## Careers—As Important for Girls as for Boys

|  | All | Boys | Girls |
| --- | --- | --- | --- |
| Yes | 69% | 57% | 80% |
| No, they won't need it | 17% | 23% | 11% |
| No, they would rather get married and have children | 14% | 20% | 9% |

Boys are not the only ones with dreams and ambitions. Eighty percent of the girls also want a career. They know how important it is to be self-sufficient. And there are some males, like fourteen-year-old Jeffrey, who believe that it may be even *more* important for girls to be prepared. "Girls need it the most because if a guy divorces her or if he dies and leaves her with a couple of kids, how can she support them unless she has a job?"

We hope there are few parents like thirteen-year-old Loretta's, who believe that she's not smart enough to become a doctor; or Joan's, who state that as long as she's happily married, that's all that counts. Today's young people are leaving those ideas far behind, and so are most parents.

## Fantasies and Realities

Since fantasies often are the foundation for plans and decisions, we asked teenagers to describe what they would most like to be doing now or in the next few years. We tapped into a source of dreams that range from the entrancingly impossible to the eminently practical.

The most frequently stated fantasy involves some form of travel, usually with someone of the opposite sex. In Sid's case, he sees himself with a group of "someones," but he is realistic enough to have a companion plan for something more attainable. He imagines, "An island in the Pacific with a bunch of girls all around. Lots of girls. No troubles. Unfortunately that's impossible. I'd just like to have a nice house and a nice business. Something that's going to be fun, where I can enjoy myself while I'm working. That way, living would not be a hassle. No wife or kids. Just girl friends." Many other teenagers express variations of the island fantasy theme. Some want to travel with friends and return to their island to dwell in solitude and peace at a later time.

It is obvious that their fantasies are not too dissimilar from ours. They relish escape from the daily confrontations and pressures we all experience. Jacqueline, fourteen, has a vision: "I'd probably be one of these people that can turn invisible. Snap my fingers and have magic. I'd own a private island where I could invite anybody I wanted. And then I would just disappear if I wanted to. I could go off and see the world. Be anywhere, do anything. Then I could make myself visible again when I wanted to."

Again and again we see that friends play a predominant role in fantasies, and same-sex friends are particularly important to the younger teenagers. Hearing their comments can help us understand the vital nature of peer contact and acceptance. Bea, thirteen, dreams: "I'd have a big party and invite everyone I knew. I'd throw away all my clothes and get a new wardrobe. Probably stock up on candy bars and get fat from them. I'd learn to drive and take my friends with me everywhere so I wouldn't be lonely. Then I'd go to Paris."

Those who have lost a parent to divorce often fantasize spending time with that parent in a real or idyllic setting. Stacy, fourteen, says, "I'd be in a beautiful place and my father would be with me again and my mom would be happy with us, too. Oh, yes. I'd have a whole bunch of cats. I love them."

Many of their dreams involve achievement in some activity, such as "playing basketball in a championship game and making the final shot which wins the game. That would be a thrill!" Others center on career hopes that are glamorous (owning a music studio where one could play and make records), or practical (working in a dog beauty salon that would be the beginning of an animal grooming empire).

Fantasies and dreams are not meaningless. They kindle the creativity that keeps us searching for more satisfying ways of living. Adolescents share our reluctance to accept final limitations on life. They refuse to settle for the dictates of a society that says, "This is the way it is, accept it." And at times, this attitude may upset our equanimity. The anxieties that we experienced as teenagers may be rearoused as we watch our kids overturn conventional ways of thinking. But we have to allow them their questions and hopes. If we scorn their aspirations for a better world by insisting that their dreams are idealistic or unrealistic, we may merely be revealing our own failures and sense of discouragement. But if our teenagers work toward change, they just might attain it.

Today's teenagers will shape the future. And the freer they are to question and evaluate, the more open they will be to understanding and confronting the persistent problems of our society. It is far better for us to fuel their skepticism and resistance than to force their compliance. As we have seen throughout the report, this generation of teenagers is far more similar to prior generations in its basic beliefs and values than it is different. These teenagers still believe in the American dream, regardless of the changes in customs and ideas.

# Teenagers' Advice to Parents

**B**ookstores are filled with volumes of advice for parents. How to get along with your adolescent. How to tolerate teenagers. How to be a friend to your teenagers. Magazines feature articles by renowned educators and psychologists telling us what to do when Johnny comes home listless and red-eyed; what to do if he wants to quit school, get married, join a cult.

We confer with each other before and after arguments with our kids. Mothers talk to their mothers; fathers seek advice from their friends. We look for suggestions and help from every source available: the family physician, teachers, ministers, rabbis, guidance counselors, Scout leaders, grandmas, aunts, psychiatrists, social workers and psychologists.

But instead of turning to all these third parties, why not go to the source—the ones living through it all? We've heard our teenagers talk about us, school, each other, our American society, their impulses, their fears, and their problems. *Their* advice would probably have the most meaning. We're not introducing them as great sages who have answers to all the problems. But we've learned enough to know that they do want to get along well with their families. They may run away, drop out of school, get drunk, get stoned, and even get pregnant. They may steal and vandalize. They may work and study and sacrifice for others, but what they want in the long run is to be able to come home and be accepted, loved, trusted, and listened to. They want to be respected. They want the same things that we want.

Here's how they think we can all get there; how we can survive together and strengthen our relationships. Most of their suggestions make a lot of sense, maybe even more than those of grandmas, experts, and friends.

The question we asked was this:

What advice would you give to parents to improve the relationship between them and their teenagers?

And here's the advice they offer:

### Listen and Understand

"Have patience with your kids. There are a lot of teenagers that keep problems within themselves because they have a fear of what their parents will say if they find out. So try and relate to them and understand what they're going through." (Michele, 18)

"Whatever they have to say, let them talk; then give your views. Don't jump to conclusions. I feel that half the kids aren't ever listened to. They don't have any say in matters after a while; they don't even talk anymore. Ya gotta have a more open relationship with your parents, but parents have to help." (Les, 15)

"I really think it's hard to be a good parent and I'm sure most parents do the best they can. I guess if parents listen to their kids and give them credit for having some brains, that's about the best they can do." (Joan, 17)

### Be Upfront and Honest

"My parents and I are pretty close because we're honest and open with each other. No bullshit." (Don, 17)

"Talk things out. Everything should be open, that's the way I see it. Don't hold back anything, especially anything really big that could be bothering you. Let your kid use his own common sense and praise him if what he's done is smart." (Wes, 16)

### Don't Cop Out When Tough Subjects Come Up

"Parents should talk to their kids about sex, drugs, and alcohol. If their kids are into drugs and alcohol, they should try and get their kids to explain to them why they're doing it. Not everything is addicting. They can't be chicken when talking to their kids." (Mabel, 15)

## Trust Us and Let Us Learn From Our Own Mistakes

"You learn things by making mistakes. My mother drives me crazy telling me to take my gloves, remember my key. If I forget it, it's my hands that'll be cold and my fault if I can't get in our house." (Jeff, 15)

"Trust the kid more, and he'll probably go in the right direction and hang around with the right kids. Ask him if he's doing drugs and pot. If he is, just try and talk him out of it. That's the only real advice I'd ever give anybody. Parents can't live their kids' lives for them." (Jeb, 15)

## Don't Live in the Past

"Parents should stop living in their time because this isn't their time. This is a different world, a different place. What worked for you is not gonna work for them. You gotta move with the world." (Marcy, 18)

"Parents have to relate to what's going on today. Not think about how things were in their day when it was old-fashioned. But they should try to put themselves in thier kids' shoes and remember how it was to be a kid—but relate it to today's problems." (Josie, 18)

## Discipline, but Don't Dominate

"Parents either want to be your pals or they want to be Hitler. The best parents know when to lie back and let life take its course, or when to intervene. When to control or not control. With me, I've never had anybody step in. I've always done things my way, and I'm not so sure that's good. (Andrew, 17)

"Before you punish a child, there has to be a good reason. Don't just punish them at the moment; think about it first. Take about an hour or so and think what their feelings might be, and talk it out with them. Usually, I think that kids can give their own punishments because they will feel guilty enough. I can suggest things to my mother almost inside my head. But everything depends on trust." (Judy, 13)

"You have to have certain rules to go by, and you can't be bending them all the time. A lot of parents are afraid to lose their kids, so they bend too much and give them too much. There are times when you have to be hard because that's the only way to get through to them. My parents were hard on me. I couldn't go out all the time and do whatever I wanted. When you think about it though, you're going to be a better person." (Ramon, 17)

## Compromise

"A lot of compromises helps. I know when my mom and I compromise, it turns out a lot better because I don't feel like I've lost anything, and I hope she doesn't feel like she's lost anything. You have times when you feel down, and when parents get on your back you really blow up. They don't understand that. They've been through it, but I guess they just forget. I guess my big words of wisdom are compromise, understanding, and loving. It's all you can do. If that doesn't work, I guess nothing will." (Alyson, 16)

## Show That You Love, Care, and Will Be There

"I don't think it's right for parents to yell at their kids all the time. They have to work out problems. The parents might care, but they don't let their kids know that they care. Tell them how much they do care, and then it's all right to yell sometimes because it's hard being a parent." (Glenn, 14)

"I would tell the parents to try and show love to their teenagers, and to stand by them. But not act overprotective. Just stand by them when they are having a problem, and always be there when they need someone to talk to." (Dana, 13)

The adolescents who volunteered their time to tell us what it's like to be a teenager did so because they want parents to know their true feelings. If we can hear them and speak to them with similar openness and caring, that legendary gap between their world and ours may narrow. In the words of a fifteen-year-old Midwestern girl, "Parents should probably read this book when it comes out because then they'll know what we think about things. They'll know all the views of the teenagers across the country, and they'll know how to communicate with their own kids. It was fun talking about it."

# Index